The WISC-III® Companion

The WISC-III® Companion

A Guide to Interpretation and Educational Intervention

Steve Truch

pro·ed
8700 Shoal Creek Boulevard
Austin, Texas 78757

© 1989, 1993 by PRO-ED, Inc.
8700 Shoal Creek Boulevard
Austin, Texas 78757-6897

Library of Congress Cataloging-in-Publication Data

Truch, Stephen.
    The WISC-III companion / Steve Truch.
        p.   cm.
    Includes bibliographical reference and index.
    ISBN 0-89079-585-1
    1. Wechsler Intelligence Scale for Children. I. Title.
BF432.5.W42T77 1993
    155.4′13933—dc20   92-40400
                                       CIP

Publisher's Note. The WISC-III® acronym is a registered trademark of
The Psychological Corporation and any use of its name does not imply
endorsement by The Psychological Corporation.

Production Manager: Alan Grimes
Production Coordinator: Adrienne Booth
Art Director: Lori Kopp
Reprints Buyer: Alicia Woods
Editor: Debra Berman
Editorial Assistant: Claudette Landry

Printed in the United States of America

3   4   5   6   7   8   9   10   97 96 95

Contents

List of Figures and Tables

Figures

Tables

Preface

This book is intended primarily for practicing school psychologists and those who are training for this field. Clinical and counseling psychologists who use the *Wechsler Intelligence Scale for Children–Third Edition* (WISC-III®) (Wechsler, 1991) should also find this book of value. It will also be of interest to reading specialists, special educators, and those involved in the more general educational enterprise, such as regular class teachers, principals, supervisors, and other administrators—all of whom must deal with the particular needs of the special child (i.e., the child with some type of learning deficit).

This book is an aid to hypothesis generation concerning a particular child's learning patterns. Those educators who read this book, but who have not taken the specific training courses in psychology normally required for individualized test administration, *cannot* and *should not* use this book as a substitute for interpretation of the WISC-III by a qualified psychologist. Readers without proper training cannot assume that they are in a position to interpret WISC-III profiles simply because they have read this book.

By the same token, school psychologists are not reading specialists. They cannot presume to prescribe reading programs or strategies based exclusively on WISC-III patterns. School psychologists need to have a deeper understanding of the reading process. They must understand sound teaching philosophies and reading methods, and be able to go considerably beyond using a reading test merely for screening and placement purposes. This book will only scratch the surface of that area.

Because the average school psychologist needs to know more than he or she does about reading and the average reading specialist needs to know more than he or she does about intelligence testing and other psychological interventions, the two professionals can best serve students with disabilities by working together using a team approach. Based on my experience, when all the parties who are involved with a student, including parents, work in concert, they generate a most sound academic and behavioral set of strategies on behalf of that student.

Throughout this book, when I use phrases such as "suggested by the WISC-III," I mean that *only suggestions* can be derived from the test results. The person in the best position to determine what does or does not apply in each child's case is the qualified examiner. Usually, this person is the school psychologist who, in turn, must act as a team member, rather than an ultimate authority. The school psychologist must interpret hypotheses in light of teacher and parent observations about the student, as well as his or her own. Before suggestions become written recommendations, the school psychologist must consult with many of the significant others involved with the student.

I have been a consultant to several school districts for nearly two decades. During that time, I have seen thousands of students on an individual basis, and have consulted with as many teachers on a variety of psychological and learning problems. Questions of cognitive ability and individual strengths and weaknesses frequently arise, particularly in the case of students with learning disabilities or other handicapping conditions. Like many of my colleagues, I use the WISC-III frequently to help answer pertinent questions. Despite the development of new intelligence tests, such as the *Kaufman Assessment Battery for Children* (K-ABC) (Kaufman & Kaufman, 1983), the WISC-III is still the most widely used intelligence test; in my opinion, it is likely to remain so for some time to come.

I am always impressed by what the WISC-III does and does not tell me. Being a practical person, I am also always on the lookout for teaching implications that can legitimately be teased out of WISC-III profiles on individual students, especially in terms of remedial reading. I am well aware, however, of the dangers of extrapolating directly from WISC-III profiles to individual reading programs. This book does not do that. It is merely an attempt to help bridge the gap that does exist. The WISC-III is neither a reading test nor a complete test. It does not tell us everything about a child. No test possibly could. To ignore what does lie in the WISC-III profile in terms of the various academic implications it suggests, however, is to ignore a wealth of potentially invaluable information. Nevertheless, the WISC-III is only part of a battery of formal and informal tests and observations about a student. That fact should not be forgotten.

The danger always exists that psychologists who read this book will go directly to scores and numbers and ignore the individual student. This is not a cookbook. The student's behaviors, intentions, and feelings that come across during testing are vital, and are as much a part of the student as any score. It is a great disservice to ignore such behaviors. They are, in fact, part of the diagnostic process. All score interpretations must be complemented by what the psychologist knows and observes about the student in a variety of environments across

time. Thus, input from teachers, parents, and other professionals is extremely valuable. It has taken me over 15 years to accumulate the background knowledge and professional experience just to attempt this project. In those 15 years, I have never stopped my professional reading. Yet I still feel *inadequate* in many ways to interpret WISC-III profiles. I am humbled by the astonishing background needed to interpret the WISC-III. An equally astonishing background is needed to track down all the educational implications suggested by what are seemingly simple scores. This book can only be a beginning, then, for the sensitive psychologist.

The published material available on educational implications of the WISC-II is often offered with no rationale at all, or provides only splintered suggestions for teaching based on individual WISC-III subtests—a conceptually and psychometrically very unsound practice. The suggestions made in this book, particularly in the appendices, are meant primarily for the school psychologist who is looking for something practical to share with a teacher. Exercises are to be modified by the team approach. One cannot, however, ignore the theoretical underpinnings of various teaching strategies and their possible relation to a particular student with a particular WISC-III profile. Without the rationale, psychologists risk reverting to the cookbook or shotgun approach, with their energies scattered in all directions except "on target." Thus, please bear with me as a I provide some of the background information and theory that supports a particular technique that I am advocating. I think you will find it interesting anyway. I think you will also quickly realize that interpreting the WISC-III is something of an artistic endeavor, requiring much skill and ability to synthesize conclusions from the information before you.

I truly hope that those who read this book will find it a useful resource for developing some practical teaching implications and strategies as they arise from using the WISC-III. These are to be then artfully implemented in the remedial programs of those wonderful, special students who need our very best expertise as they grapple with their sometimes overwhelming educational challenges.

Author's Note to This Edition

My book *The WISC-R Companion* was published in 1989. It was based on my extensive experience in the area of learning disabilities. WISC-R profile sheets of actual case examples from my files were used for the book. In this edition, those WISC-R profiles have been adapted onto WISC-III profiles.

Readers should also note that the practice of using factor scores is extremely helpful for the examiner who is looking to develop hypotheses. However, factor scores should not typically be reported.

Questions Frequently Asked About the WISC-III

School psychologists are frequently asked very basic questions about the WISC-III and intelligence testing in general by teachers and parents. Here are 29 of the more common ones. The questions and their answers should provide the reader with a good overview and serve as background information for some of the remaining chapters.

1. *What is the WISC-III? Is it an intelligence test?*

The *Wechsler Intelligence Scale for Children–Third Edition* (WISC-III) (Wechsler, 1991) is one of a class of individual intelligence (or IQ, for intelligence quotient) tests. It is an individual test because it must be administered by a qualified examiner on a one-to-one basis with a student. There are also group IQ tests that can be administered, often by classroom teachers themselves, to a whole class. Scores on the two kinds of tests are related, but the individual test obviously provides more reliable data and more information about how a student responds to a formal, problem-solving situation.

2. *What is the history of the WISC-III? How was the test developed?*

Alfred Binet is considered the father of intelligence tests. The Binet–Simon "1905 Scale" was the first IQ test (Binet & Simon, 1905). It was designed to help the Paris public school system separate students with mental handicaps from those without. The test was first introduced in the United States by Henry Goddard in 1908. Since then, a number of revisions have been made and are still being made to the test, which is currently called the *Stanford–Binet Intelligence Scale: Fourth Edition* (Thorndike, Hagen, & Sattler, 1986).

David Wechsler, an American, conceptualized intelligence as the "overall capacity of an individual to understand and cope with the world around him" (1944, p. 3). He developed the Wechsler–Bellevue test in the 1930s to measure adult intelligence. The *Wechsler Intelligence Scale for Children* (WISC) was developed by Wechsler in 1949 as a downward extension of the *Wechsler–Bellevue Intelligence Scale* (Wechsler, 1939).

Unlike the *Stanford–Binet,* the WISC does not employ the *mental age* concept for measuring IQ. (Using this concept, the IQ score is calculated by taking the student's tested mental age, dividing it by the chronological age, and multiplying by 100.) Rather, it uses a deviation IQ method, which determines how far a student's score deviates (if at all) from the scores of a representative sample of his or her peers. In 1974, the WISC was extensively revised and became the *Wechsler Intelligence Scale for Children–Revised* (WISC-R) (Wechsler, 1974). In 1991, a third revision—the WISC-III—was published. The WISC-III is based on updated norms, improved administration and scoring procedures, and more extensive validity testing than the WISC-R. However, the basic structure of the WISC-R has been maintained and the "third factor" has been enhanced.

All IQ tests occasionally need revision because of the "upward drift" of general intelligence in the population at large. People *are* becoming more "intelligent" as time goes on, so the norms on all IQ tests must be revised to reflect this. Studies have shown a general upward drift of about 3 points every 10 years. (The "drift" is stronger for the WISC Performance Scale than for the Verbal Scale.) Thus, a student who scored 100 on the WISC-R 15 years ago could be expected to score about 97 on the WISC-III today. These sorts of subtleties need to be accounted for by all testmakers. The changes made to the WISC-III from the WISC-R have made a good test even better.

3. Why is an IQ test administered?

An IQ test is administered when one wants information about a student's cognitive profile, that is, how the student thinks and reasons. The WISC-III is often used to obtain such information because it samples both verbal and nonverbal aspects of intelligence. Such information is particularly valuable when a student is experiencing difficulty with school-related work. In the hands of an experienced tester, the WISC-III can help to generate a number of hypotheses (which can lead to further, more precise diagnosis) and lead to recommendations designed to help a student perform or feel better about school.

4. What are some of the pros and cons of IQ testing?

Probably the most serious criticism against IQ tests is that they are culturally biased, particularly against African–Americans. Another criticism is that of the self-fulfilling prophecy (i.e., knowing that a student has a "low IQ" could lead to negative consequences, even a withdrawal of educational services). This kind of thinking is typified by the rhetorical question, "Why bother if the student is really slow?" A more subtle kind of behavior change on the teacher's part also may take place, so that the student receives less attention, less praise, and so on. This leads to less learning, and perpetuates the vicious circle. Other criticisms are that a single IQ score does not do justice to the many aspects of thinking, does not get at the underlying thought processes, and serves only to stereotype students.

An advantage of IQ testing (at least for individual IQ tests) is that a profile of strengths and weaknesses can be obtained. This can lead to improved educational planning. It has also been my experience that, when a teacher discovers that a student has a "low IQ" score, the tendency is to respond to the challenge that score represents, rather than using it as an excuse not to bother. It would be naive, however, to think that "not bothering" never happens. Sometimes, students with undiscovered or unrecognized abilities are "discovered" via IQ testing. This has happened many times in my experience. Furthermore, IQ tests are useful tools to see how students do differ from and compare with each other on a number of standardized tasks. IQ scores are good predictors of academic achievement and successes in other areas, as well.

An IQ test in the right hands is a proper diagnostic tool. It is not, however, a be-all and end-all. An IQ score is only the start for better educational planning and prescription via the team approach. The IQ score should *never* (especially for students from different cultural backgrounds) be interpreted in a rigid fashion, or as being indicative of innate, unchanging genetic ability. IQ tests measure learning across a wide spectrum of tasks. They tell us how students compare with each other in our culture.

5. What is intelligence, anyway?

Much of the next chapter is devoted to answering this question. In my opinion, intelligence is a kind of purposeful "mental energy" that we use to guide our actions in virtually everything we do. It is guided by the self, or ego—the inner, most personal core of our being. Because it is so subtle, we can appreciate only its effects.

6. *How much training do you need to administer the WISC-III?*

The administration and interpretation of individual IQ tests, such as the WISC-III, the Stanford–Binet, the *McCarthy Scales of Children's Abilities* (McCarthy, 1972), and the *Kaufman Assessment Battery for Children* (Kaufman & Kaufman, 1983), are generally taught at the graduate level over a full year's time or more, and are usually part of a program leading to the master's or doctoral degree in psychology or educational psychology. Close supervision is required to ensure that the novice examiner is trained in some of the finer points of administration and interpretation. Considerable practice is required before a person is ready to administer and interpret test results for school purposes. (Some training departments, and even state laws, have added an element of "secretiveness" to the WISC-III, which, I think, only contributes to the unfounded beliefs that people have about intelligence tests.)

The point is that extensive training is required to administer and interpret the WISC-III. In fact, the school psychologist should never stop reading in this area, in order to keep fine-tuning his or her interpretation skills.

7. *Can a classroom teacher administer the WISC-III?*

Because of the extensive training required, the answer is definitely no. Unfortunately, classroom teachers generally do not receive any training in the interpretation of IQ scores. Frequently, teachers are completely misinformed, or not informed at all, or hold a number of unfounded beliefs about IQ testing and what it represents. As a result, they fall victim to the many myths that abound about the IQ and what it may mean for any one student. Thus, school psychologists who inform teachers about the results of an IQ test cannot take anything for granted. Simply telling a teacher a student's IQ score is not good enough. Information needs to be passed on carefully and followed with a written report of the results. Follow-up of educational recommenda-

tions is terribly important. As a member of the educational team, the school psychologist's job is to interpret the WISC-III in terms of the educational implications it has, to consult with the reading specialist about how the hypotheses that are generated can be put into practical reading and other academic strategies, to discuss and help implement these recommendations with the remedial or classroom teacher, and, of course, to convey all this to the parents.

8. *Is the WISC-III highly regarded by psychologists? Do principals know about it? Do reading specialists know about it?*

The WISC-III and the Stanford–Binet are generally highly regarded by psychologists for a number of reasons. These tests provide valid and reliable IQ scores when properly administered. Vast sums of money are spent by the test publishers to ensure that the tests are well standardized (i.e., have representative children from different socioeconomic levels, equal numbers of boys and girls, proportionately the same numbers of urban and rural children as in the population at large, and proportionate numbers of minority groups). The scores have reasonably small measurement error, and the items are rigorously analyzed to see that they discriminate properly.

Because psychologists have a high regard for the WISC-III, this attitude is generally passed on to educators. Again, however, most of this group—principals, resource teachers, reading specialists, other administrators, and supervisors—generally know very little about the WISC-III unless they have received this information in their training or have sought it out themselves.

9. *What ages does the WISC-III cover?*

The WISC-III can be administered to students who have just turned 6, or are as old as 16 years, 11 months. This range covers virtually the entire school-age years.

10. *How subjective is the scoring on the WISC-III?*

Every examiner must remain conscious of the fact that subjectivity can enter into scoring some responses on the WISC-III. The test manual provides guidelines for scoring all the subtests. Those on the Verbal Scale, however, are more likely to have scoring errors, resulting from the wide range of possible responses. Simple errors in addition can also occur, resulting in mistakes on the reported IQ score. Examiners need to double-check their scoring and adding to help minimize such errors.

Despite the element of subjectivity, there is a very high degree of test–retest reliability on the WISC-III (i.e., the IQ score will be very consistent from one testing to the next). Although gross errors can and do occur, their frequency can be minimized.

11. *How does the student's mood on the day of testing affect the test score? For example, does lack of sleep or breakfast affect it? Would a student have better results under more favorable conditions?*

The WISC-III examiner always tries to make sure a student is tested under optimal conditions. If there is evidence that the student has experienced some untoward stress prior to testing, the examiner must determine whether testing should even proceed. Lack of sleep and/or breakfast is common among some students. The examiner has to determine whether such conditions affected the test results to any appreciable degree. Any major or minor stress that the student has recently experienced should be noted in the examiner's report, as well as the examiner's opinion on how it may have affected the results.

12. *If a student is afraid of tests, does this affect his or her performance? Does the student get an explanation of what's happening, and does it affect results? Does self-concept affect results?*

Sometimes, it looks to a teacher as if an examiner takes the student into a room and does something to him or her—"tests" the student. Although the WISC-III is a formal and important test, examiners are trained to first establish rapport with the student, providing some explanation of what is happening and why. Experienced examiners generally find this quite easy to do. Some degree of student fear or anxiety is common, but it is not necessarily a bad thing, as it can actually facilitate test performance. Usually, it disappears quickly as testing proceeds. If it does not, it needs to be noted, or testing needs to be discontinued. Some of the WISC-III subtests are more affected by anxiety than others, particularly the timed ones. In my experience, however, students are rarely so afraid that they cannot be tested.

Self-concept is a very general term. If a student lacks self-confidence and fails to take risks or make guesses on the WISC-III, then the score will be lower than it might otherwise have been. However, proper feedback on the examiner's part can often maximize the student's "risk-taking."

For all of the reasons discussed above, a WISC-III score should never be stated without its *error band*. There is built-in measurement error on every test, because what is being measured cannot be done with the precision that lies in, say, a yardstick or a thermometer. A score, therefore, should be reported as, for example, 100 ± 6. The ± 6 is the *confidence band* of the Full Scale IQ score on the WISC-III. It means that, if the student were tested 100 times, then 95 times out of the 100 (a 95% confidence level), the Full Scale IQ score would fall between 94 and 105. The WISC-III manual makes it easy for the examiner by providing the confidence intervals (at both the 90% and the 95% confidence levels) for all the IQ and factor scores that are obtainable from the WISC-III. These can then be transposed to the front sheet of the WISC-III protocol for easy reference and explanation.

Thus, if a student seemed overly anxious or did not have a full breakfast, the Full Scale IQ score probably lies closer to the upper level of the confidence band. The Full Scale IQ is not a precise score, cast in concrete.

13. *If a student is on medication, how does this affect the test score?*

The effect depends on the medication. A major tranquilizer might have more of an effect than, say,

Ritalin™. Ritalin and Cylert™ are fairly commonly administered to hyperactive students who, in turn, are often referred for individual intellectual testing. In my experience, Ritalin can affect performance on some of the WISC-III subtests, particularly Digit Span, Coding, and Symbol Search, so that the Performance IQ in particular could be elevated by a few points. If an administrator knows that a student is on medication, that fact should be mentioned in the written report and in discussions of the results with educators and parents.

14. *You keep mentioning Full Scale IQ. What is that?*

The WISC-III consists of 13 subtests, six on the *Verbal Scale* and seven on the *Performance Scale.* The raw score the student receives on each subtest is converted to a standard score, called a *scaled score,* by using a set of tables for every 4-month age band from 6 years, 0 months (6-0), to 16 years, 11 months (16-11). The student, therefore, is compared with others his or her age within a very narrow age band. The examiner adds the scaled score totals for the first five Verbal and the first five Performance subtests, and then adds these sums. The total scaled score for these 10 subtests is then converted to a single score, the *Full Scale IQ score,* by using another table in the WISC-III manual.

Both Verbal and Performance IQ scores are calculated. This gives three IQ scores for every WISC-III profile: the Verbal IQ, the Performance IQ, and the Full Scale IQ. It is also possible to calculate *Index Scores* for the four major factors that appear on the WISC-III. Finally, a profile of the subtest scores can be graphed on the face sheet of the WISC-III protocol, which looks like the one shown in Figure 1.1 (all names used in the figures are fictitious).

15. *What does each WISC-III subtest measure?*

Every WISC-III subtest has something in common with one or more of the other subtests. This cannot be forgotten when it comes time for interpretation. In fact, when two or more subtests have

something in common, their results are more reliable than the result of one subtest alone. This interpretive approach is made easier on the WISC-III than it was on the WISC-R. On the WISC-III, separate scores can be calculated for some of the "clusters" or "factors." These are identified as *Index Scores* on the WISC-III. When interpreting WISC-III subtest results, the psychologist should look first at such factors, before making any subtest-specific interpretations.

The following is a list of the WISC-III subtests and the unique abilities each subtest measures:

Verbal Subtests

- Information—general factual knowledge about the world

- Similarities—logical abstract thinking with verbal categories and classifications

- Arithmetic—mental computational skill with basic number concepts and applied problem solving

- Vocabulary—lexical knowledge and language development

- Comprehension—verbalizing practical information; evaluating and using past experience to answer common problems (should not be confused with "reading comprehension")

- Digit Span—auditory short-term memory for random numbers

Performance Subtests

- Picture Completion—visual long-term memory and visual alertness to elements of a picture

- Coding—psychomotor speed using paper-and-pencil output; ability to follow directions

- Picture Arrangement—sequencing and anticipating consequences of social situations

- Block Design—nonverbal reasoning; spatial visualization; analysis of an abstract design into its component parts

Name *Jennifer* Sex ______

School ______ Grade ______

Examiner ______ Handedness ______

WISC-III™

Wechsler Intelligence Scale for Children–Third Edition

Subtests	Raw Scores	Scaled Scores					
Picture Completion	19		10		10		
Information	13	9		9			
Coding	33		7				7
Similarities	16	11		11			
Picture Arrangement	22		8		8		
Arithmetic	15	8				8	
Block Design	42		12		12		
Vocabulary	31	12		12			
Object Assembly	26		10		10		
Comprehension	19	10		10			
(Symbol Search)	16		(7)				7
(Digit Span)	9	(6)				6	
(Mazes)	18		(10)				
Sum of Scaled Scores							
		Verbal	Perfor.	VC	PO	FD	PS
		Full Scale Score		OPTIONAL			

	Year	Month	Day
Date Tested			
Date of Birth			
Age	10	2	15

	Score	IQ/ Index	%ile	95 % Confidence Interval
Verbal	50	100	50	94 - 106
Performance	47	96	39	88 - 104
Full Scale	97	98	45	92 - 104
VC	42	103	58	96 - 110
PO	40	100	50	92 - 108
FD	14	84	14	77 - 95
PS	14	86	18	78 - 98

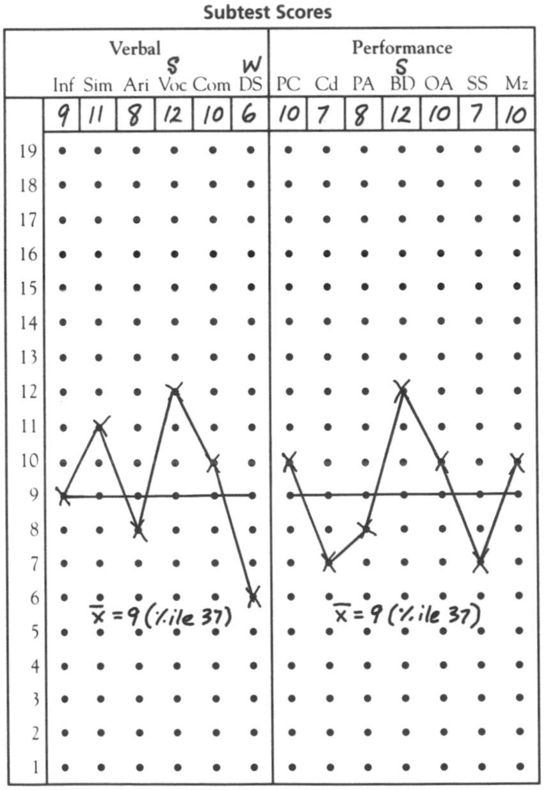
Subtest Scores
Verbal
Performance
Inf Sim Ari Voc Com DS
PC Cd PA BD OA SS Mz
S
W
S
9 11 8 12 10 6
10 7 8 12 10 7 10
19 18 17 16 15 14 13 12 11 10 9 8 7 6 5 4 3 2 1
x̄ = 9 (%ile 37)
x̄ = 9 (%ile 37)

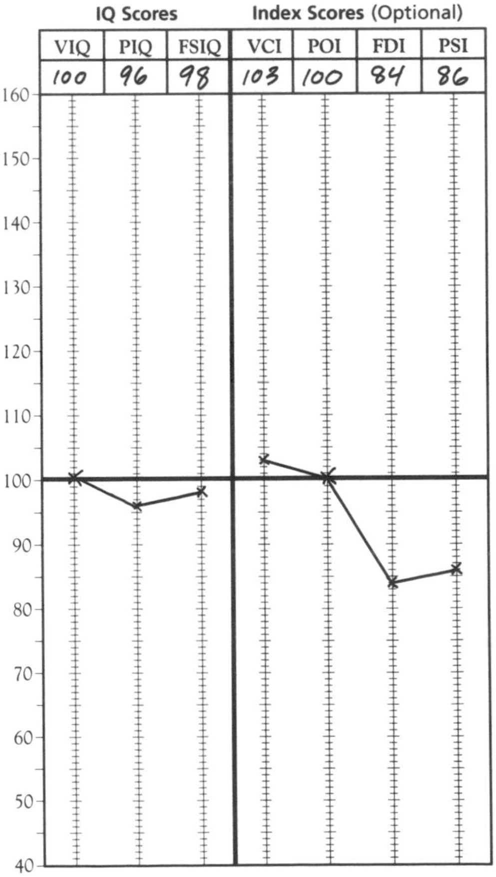
IQ Scores
Index Scores (Optional)
VIQ PIQ FSIQ VCI POI FDI PSI
100 96 98 103 100 84 86
160 150 140 130 120 110 100 90 80 70 60 50 40

THE PSYCHOLOGICAL CORPORATION®
HARCOURT BRACE JOVANOVICH, INC.

7 8 9 10 11 12 A B C D E

09–980004

Figure 1.1. Jennifer's profile.

- Object Assembly—flexibility; anticipating part–whole relationships
- Symbol Search—visual processing speed using paper-and-pencil output
- Mazes—foresight; following a visual pattern using paper-and-pencil output

Everything measured on the WISC-III has been learned, usually incidentally and sometimes by direct teaching, in the course of growing up in our culture. The test, therefore, measures how well students have learned these processes compared with other students.

16. *How much reading is involved in administering the WISC-III?*

On the part of the student, virtually no reading is required. All items can be read by the examiner, with the student responding either verbally or manually. Although the last six items of the Arithmetic subtest are intended to be read by the student, the examiner may read the items if the student has difficulty.

Reading by the examiner is a reason to favor an individually administered test over a group IQ test. In a group test, students must read the questions themselves. If they have reading difficulties, then one cannot obtain a fair sample of their reasoning ability because the issue is confounded by the reading problem.

17. *What are the effects of a handicap such as hearing or vision impairment on intelligence? What about an undiagnosed hearing problem?*

If the student has a known hearing handicap but is wearing a hearing aid that corrects or partly corrects it, the WISC-III can be administered, although the Performance Scale is likely to be more valid than the Verbal Scale in such cases. If the student has a visual handicap, then the Verbal Scale is the more useful measure. There is also a special

adaptation of the Stanford–Binet test, called the Hayes–Binet, that can be used specifically for blind children.

Undiagnosed hearing problems could show up on the WISC-III in the form of a low Verbal–higher Performance IQ split. I do know of some cases where a hearing problem was discovered through WISC-III testing in this way. It is not merely a pattern of scores that indicates the problem, however; keen observation is required on the part of the examiner.

All students, particularly those in special education classes, should have at least a routine audiometric and vision screening. This is frequently done by school or public health nurses, for all school-age children.

As far as these handicaps and their effects on intelligence are concerned, blind children tend to score in the average range as a group, but their distribution of scores is not "normal": Many blind children score in the superior or the inferior range. This distribution is called a bimodal one. Deaf children seem to obtain lower Verbal IQ scores, whereas the results on Performance tests are mixed. Some studies show these children doing worse than students with normal hearing on Performance items, whereas others show them doing as well, or even better.

When testing such handicapped students with the WISC-III, the examiner must be particularly alert as to how the handicap is affecting the responses of each child. The examiner must also be extremely cautious in interpreting the results as being a fair measure of the child's potential.

18. *How much does language affect the WISC-III? Could a foreign student, for example, take it?*

The student's knowledge of his or her own language is an important component of intelligence. Such knowledge constitutes a very important part of the WISC-III—the Verbal Scale (and its derivative indexes). Language is also involved in giving instructions to the student in all the other WISC-III subtests. The only truly culture-fair test, therefore, would be one in which the items came from the child's culture, the items were asked in the child's native tongue by examiners from the same culture, and most importantly, the scores were normed in that culture. Whenever we administer an IQ test such as the WISC-III to a minority-group child, the element of fairness must always be considered.

The examiner, therefore, must be extremely cautious and sensitive to language differences in his or her culture, particularly African–American dialect and Mexican–American language differences. Proportionate numbers of African–Americans and Hispanics were included in the standardization of the WISC-III; however, children were tested *only* if they could speak and understand English.

Minority students may do better on the WISC-III with examiners of their own culture; however, the key to any student's responding is the initial positive rapport and understanding that must be established at the beginning of testing. The examiner must be knowledgeable enough about cultural and language differences that could affect WISC-III performance. Students should not be penalized for use of language that differs from that of the dominant culture, especially where such language is perfectly acceptable in the student's own community. Therefore, the examiner should first become acquainted with any regional differences that might exist in a particular geographic area.

Obviously, then, a student has to have a solid exposure to the English language before the WISC-III can be considered a fair measure of reasoning ability. If a student is bilingual, the examiner should be aware of that fact and remain cautious when interpreting the IQ score.

Students who have recently learned English, or who are currently learning English, cannot be tested with valid results. The only purpose the WISC-III would serve in such cases would be an informal assessment of a student's current language functioning. In no way would it be a measure of intelligence.

Sometimes, useful information can come out of specific subtests. Block Design is considered the most culture-fair of the WISC-III subtests. I recall using the WISC-R Performance Scale only to assess one Vietnamese student who could not speak a word of English. She displayed extraordinary flexibility and reasoning skill on the Block Design subtest; in fact, she obtained the highest possible scaled score. I felt her academic prognosis was excellent, even though it was not possible to calculate a single

WISC-R IQ score. Had that portion of the WISC-R not been administered, her facility in some reasoning areas would not have come to light.

***19.** How does the WISC-III compare with the Stanford–Binet?*

Both tests measure intelligence, but from different perspectives. For Binet and Simon (1905), intelligence was the ability to "judge, comprehend, and reason well" (p. 192). They were very interested in individual differences in ability in such areas as memory, imagination, attention, comprehension, and aesthetic appreciation. Despite their broad interests, their test yielded only one global IQ score, based on the mental-age construct.

For Wechsler, intelligence was the global capacity of the individual to deal effectively with his or her environment. Neither Binet nor Wechsler had particularly well-delineated definitions of intelligence. Despite this, their tests have more than stood the test of time.

The two tests do correlate with each other, however, which indicates that they measure something very similar. Nevertheless, there is enough difference between the tests that the constructs are not identical.

Now in its fourth edition, the Stanford–Binet is still widely used today, although probably not as often as the WISC-III. The Stanford–Binet's strength lies in the fact that it can be administered to children as young as age 2. In addition, the IQ scores go well below and well above the limits of the WISC-III. On the WISC-III, no student can score an IQ below 40 or above 160. Because some students have functional IQ levels below and above these limits, the Stanford–Binet is often a better test to use to assess students who may be profoundly mentally handicapped or exceptionally gifted in intelligence.

***20.** Does the WISC-III take into account cultural differences, environmental deprivation, varying socioeconomic levels, and so on?*

The WISC-III was standardized on a wide cross-section of children from various ethnic groups and socioeconomic backgrounds (Wechsler, 1991). The standardization sample conforms very closely to the 1988 United States census (this poses a slight problem for Canadian children, but a Canadian validation manual is now in preparation). In that sense, the test takes into account such differences insofar as relative group ranking goes. It does not, however, eliminate the advantage that a particular group (e.g., students from highly educated parents) might have on the WISC-III.

The results achieved by each particular child is a different matter. A child who has experienced extreme deprivation, for example, may be functioning very low at one point in time, but could be much brighter and score higher on the WISC-III once he or she is placed in a more intensive, stimulating environment. The question of environmental deprivation is a very interesting one, which I will discuss in more depth in the next chapter. Meanwhile, examiners must be very cautious in interpreting a score as a measure of a student's "potential."

21. *Is creativity measured by the WISC-III? What about special talents?*

Creativity is difficult both to define and to measure. It is not measured by the WISC-III. Neither are any of a class of special talents, such as musical or athletic aptitude, leadership skills, and social skills. Intelligence is only one part of the whole child. Other measures and behavioral observations about a child are needed to provide a better picture of the student as a total person.

22. *Does the WISC-III indicate mental illness or other states of mental instability or emotional disturbance?*

The WISC-III cannot be used to diagnose such conditions. If a child is extremely unstable, however, it is likely that his or her responses, particularly to the more open-ended Verbal subtests, will be bizarre. The examiner needs to determine how unconventional any response or behavior is, and do some further diagnostic work, to help determine to what degree any student is mentally ill or disturbed. If a student is psychotic, for example, his or her behavior will usually be so bizarre that the student is institutionalized long before any referral for intelligence testing is made.

Sometimes, patterns appear on the WISC-III that suggest a child's emotional disturbance; however, such a pattern by itself is not a diagnosis, and should never be interpreted as such. The WISC-III manual contains information on WISC-III results with some special populations, including students who are considered gifted, learning disabled, mentally handicapped, severely conduct disordered, attention deficit/hyperactivity disordered, and hearing impaired.

23. *Does the WISC-III diagnose brain damage?*

Some patterns and responses that a student may make could be associated with organic brain damage. Brain damage can be very localized or very diffuse (i.e., spread over various areas of the brain). No one test or pattern, therefore, could possibly diagnose all types of brain damage. The examiner who suspects neurological difficulties needs to refer the student for a complete neuropsychological battery of tests to help pinpoint any possible damage.

24. *Can students "cheat" on the WISC-III? Can an examiner recognize that? Can a student "fake good" or "fake bad"? Can a student lie?*

Students can try to do all of these things, of course. It is impossible to fake good, but it is certainly possible to fake bad on the test. For example, some students who may want to go to a special education program, such as a vocational school, may not try hard on the test, deliberately trying to get a lower score, which is a prerequisite to entrance into some programs. If a student is particularly clever, he or she may be able to fool an examiner some of the time. Most experienced examiners, however, can quickly recognize how much effort a student is making.

25. *How often would you administer WISC-III to a student?*

The WISC-III, like most tests, is subject to a practice effect. This is especially true for the Performance Scale. The WISC-III should, therefore, be administered infrequently to the same student. Schools wishing to have IQ scores on students should sample ability with a group IQ test three or four times in the course of the 12 years of schooling.

The WISC-III is most often administered to students in special education, or those eligible for special education classes. Intelligence is one factor that should be monitored for such students. IQ scores should be reviewed about every 2 years. If there is reason to believe that the score has changed, then the WISC-III or an alternative test could be administered.

Should the examiner need to readminister a WISC-III on one particular student, then 6 months is the minimum time that should be allowed to elapse between test administrations.

26. *Are kids labeled because of an IQ test score? Is this damaging?*

Such labeling certainly can be damaging. Group IQ scores are generally entered on a student's cumulative record, which follows the student from teacher to teacher throughout the school years. If a teacher puts too much credence in a group IQ score given years before, then that might have a negative effect, depending on what the teacher does with such information. That is why intelligence should periodically be measured for more up-to-date results.

An IQ score, if valid, represents a picture of a student's functioning at a particular point in time. However, that picture can and does change in the course of the student's development.

WISC-III and other individual intelligence test scores are not generally entered on a student's cumulative record. Such scores are confidential. Written parental approval is required to even administer the WISC-III. Furthermore, the results cannot be released to any agency or other professional without the parent's written permission.

27. *Should a student be informed of the results of the WISC-III? How about parents?*

Although there is a widespread belief that providing IQ results could be damaging, little evidence supports that belief. Nevertheless, WISC-III results are normally not given to students. I have frequently discussed results with older students when they are eager for feedback, and have always had good results. Time and care must be taken to explain the results and their meaning. Students' questions usually reveal a number of mistaken beliefs about IQ scores.

Results of the WISC-III are almost always discussed with the student's parents in a face-to-face interview. Sometimes, the examiners give only vague information to parents. Knowing that their child has "average intelligence," for example, tells parents nothing of the child's cognitive strengths and weaknesses. Parents should, when it is appropriate, be given a full explanation of the results. This should include some definition of what intelligence is, how the normal curve works, and what the error of measurement is. The examiner should also stress that the score represents a picture of the student's functioning at the present time, and is not to be construed as forever cast in concrete. The actual scores should be minimized and are probably best explained by using percentiles. Finally, the examiner should explain the importance of the score in terms of the educational strategies that the testing and test results suggest. In other words, parents need to know how the test results directly help their child in school. In this respect, the examiner needs to be aware of the various kinds of "processing problems" that are suggested during WISC-III administration. These observations are particularly helpful for educational purposes.

28. *Does the WISC-III measure dyslexia?*

Dyslexia is a term generally reserved for certain severe cases of reading disability. Some specialists do not like the term at all because it represents a kind of medical term for what they say is essentially an educational problem. In any case, the WISC-III does not diagnose dyslexia or any other kind of reading problem because it is not a reading test.

However, certain WISC-III patterns seem to accompany reading and other academic problems, but the presence of the WISC-III pattern cannot be used to diagnose the problem, because some students who have such patterns do not have any academic problems, and vice versa. The WISC-III is used to give some indication of a student's ability, and is only part of the picture of the whole child. If a student demonstrates a certain pattern on the WISC-III that suggests academic difficulties, these must be confirmed or denied with individual academic testing, teacher observations, other tests, and so forth.

29. What will I, as a classroom or special education teacher, get out of the WISC-III results? Does the test pinpoint problems? Will I understand the student better? Will my expectations change? What recommendations might I expect?

The WISC-III results should be explained by the examiner as carefully to a teacher as to a parent.

The educational implications should be emphasized as much as possible. There is no question that the student will be understood much better and in greater depth as a result of WISC-III testing. Teacher and parent expectations might change, depending on what they were beforehand. One of the most important things to understand is that a student who has "average ability" may not be "average" in all areas. Therefore, expectations may have to be modified for certain skills as a result.

The recommendations that you as a teacher receive will depend on the individual student and the expertise of the examiner. They will also depend on how much time the examiner has to think about the results and draw out all the educational implications possible. Most examiners have time constraints because of long referral lists, but there is hardly any point in administering the WISC-III unless educationally useful information can be drawn from the results. In that respect, this book will hopefully serve a purpose.

Intelligence and the WISC-III: Some Considerations

WHAT IS INTELLIGENCE?

The WISC-III measures intelligence. However, what exactly is intelligence? Many psychologists, from Alfred Binet to modern information-processing theorists, have offered definitions of this elusive word.

For Binet, the original developer of the IQ test, intelligence meant to comprehend, judge, and reason well. For Sir Cyril Burt, intelligence was primarily an innate (inherited) general ability. (Burt was obviously very committed to this view, as it has recently been discovered that he falsified much of his "heritability" data.) David Wechsler defined intelligence as the individual's global capacity to act purposefully, to think rationally, and to deal effectively with the environment. For Jean Piaget, adaptation to the environment via the processes of assimilation and accommodation best reflected intelligence. Piaget's thinking is the basis of much of modern information-processing descriptions of intelligence. Certainly, no one today views intelligence as a fixed, innate ability, but, like Piaget, more as a fluid, everchanging "thing."

C. E. Spearman was the first to propose that intelligence was a kind of mental energy. Although there are conceptual problems with this definition (as with all the definitions), I find it appealing. If we compare mental energy to electricity, for example, we find some similarities. Both are in the real world, although both are very subtle forms of energy. Both can be measured, stored, used in different ways, and transformed. Both depend on "wiring" to carry them. For electricity, this wiring may be copper or aluminum. For intelligence, the "wiring" is the type and complexity of the organism's brain and nervous system. Both also are subject to great fluctuations at any given time. There may be sudden bursts of energy, followed by periodic lows. This ebb and flow of energy continues throughout the life cycle of a person or, indeed, any living thing. Intelligence, then, is certainly not fixed, but continually "more" or "less"—flowing and everchanging in evanescence.

To me, intelligence is expressed and observed as the orderly, purposeful flow of this energy. It is governed by the individual's "will" (if I may use such an old-fashioned term) and the person's decision-making abilities. Information processors call these decision-making abilities *executive functions*—a term, I suppose, that many readers will find more palatable than "will." *Intelligent behavior* is the channeling of this energy for a purposeful act. The act itself may promote the welfare of the person and/or a social group, in which case it could be called life supporting. An example would be the devoting of time and energy—that is, of one's intelligence—to a worthy cause, such as cancer research or making sure the kids get to school on time. Conversely, intelligence can be directed to life-destroying acts of various kinds, such as unwarranted acts of aggression. These are relative terms, however, because in some instances it may be very difficult to determine what is life supporting and what is not.

Intelligence is also very akin to what factor analysts call *g*. Spearman noticed that most tests of ability, such as memory, reasoning, social judgment, and so on, *correlated* with each other. That means that people who did well on one test tended to do well on others. When one performs a complete statistical procedure called *factor analysis* on all these different tasks, then a *common factor* emerges. Spearman called this *g*. It represents what is common to all the tasks. What remains after taking *g* into account, Spearman called *s*, because it was specific to the particular task. Spearman's two-factor theory was too simple to last long, and underwent considerable modifications by Burt and Phillip Vernon.

Figure 2.1 represents a schematic model of *g*. This model is primarily *top–down*. (I will discuss this definition later.) Mental energy, or *g*, "flows" into different tasks from the top, down. It may be transformed, depending on the nature of the task. It follows from this model that we should find evidence of *g* in animals, too, since I do not see any inherent reason why humans should have the exclusive market on "intelligence." Evidence of *g* in higher-order mammals is indeed supported by some experimental evidence (Vernon, 1979).

The reader interested in pursuing these definitions of intelligence in more depth, and learning some of their corresponding educational implications, is invited to consult David Pyle's (1979) book.

Other models and definitions of intelligence include J. P. Guilford's three-dimensional model of human intellect, which posits the existence of at least 120 unique human abilities, each of which (in theory, anyway) can be taught. Many school psychologists are aware of the work done by Mary Meeker (1969) of the SOI Institute, using Guilford's

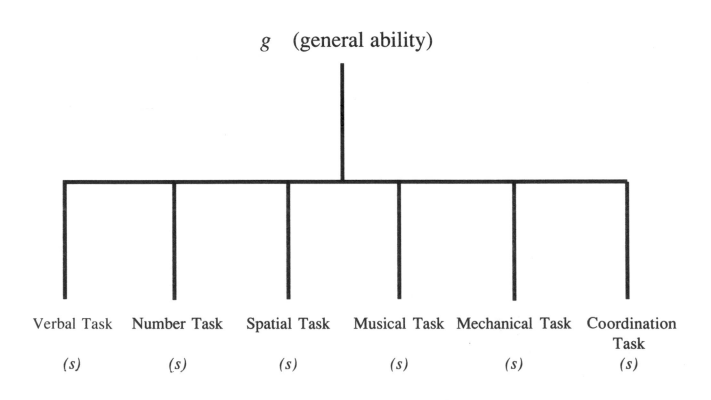

Figure 2.1. Hypothetical representation of general ability (*g*), that which is common to the specific abilities (*s*) of each of the tasks. (The tasks listed are merely examples.)

model as the base. She developed remedial tasks that can be used to help students who have identified weaknesses in many of the 120 abilities. The SOI Institute has developed its own cognitive tests to measure these abilities, together with remedial suggestions of an educational nature. (For more information, contact the SOI Institute, 214 Main St., El Segundo, CA 90245.) I have found some of the material quite useful in certain individual cases. School psychologists and remedial teachers owe it to themselves to read some of the SOI literature and use what they find useful from it. Although I find the approach too "bottom–up" to recommend widespread adoption, it does have its place. Generally, it is far easier to teach s (specific skills) than g (general ability).

Not all the theoretical approaches to intelligence mentioned thus far have accompanying IQ tests. Also, some IQ tests, such as the WISC-III, are developed without benefit of a theoretical framework. Certainly, Wechsler had a strong rationale, but he did not develop the WISC from a theoretical perspective, as such. On the other hand, I do not find newer tests, such as the *Kaufman Assessment Battery for Children* (K-ABC) (Kaufman & Kaufman, 1983), which does have an underlying theoretical basis, nearly as useful as the WISC-III. Perhaps I find the theoretical base too narrow; however, the K-ABC is useful at times.

In any case, as Alan Kaufman (1979) so ably pointed out regarding the WISC-R, the test needs to be understood and interpreted from a number of different theoretical perspectives. This comment also applies to the WISC-III. I will introduce these perspectives as appropriate for a deeper understanding of profile interpretations and ensuing educational recommendations.

The school psychologist should also understand that intelligence is a very broad term, applicable to everything we as humans undertake. Thus, an IQ score will always fall short of measuring how people can do in various tasks and situations. Because of this, it is important not to equate an IQ score with intelligence, even though an IQ score is related to the broad term, intelligence. An IQ test merely samples from a narrow spectrum of possible tasks.

Intelligence, moreover, is not all that is important about being human. Other qualities, such as personality, motivation, creativity, friendliness, and "morality," are all very important in providing an all-around picture of each person. My focus in this book is quite narrow. Although the information I present may be useful and relevant to the school psychologist's needs, it is by no means going to provide the well-rounded perspective that is necessary for day-to-day dealings with students. Only time and frequent interactions with a particular student provide the kind of "feel" necessary to gain a more complete understanding of that student. An IQ score can help that overall understanding, but it cannot replace it.

IS INTELLIGENCE FIXED?

There is a widespread misconception, tenaciously held even nowadays, that intelligence is somehow "fixed" at birth, that we are born with certain equipment that limits how much we can learn or how intelligent we can be. That belief is probably true—within limits. There is an equally tenaciously held misconception that, somehow, a stimulating environment is all that counts, and that the vast individual differences in intelligence that we see and measure are all due to upbringing. That belief is probably also true—within limits.

This *nature/nurture controversy* persists, with staunch advocates presenting arguments for both sides. But an either–or approach should not be used in this complex issue. Both sides are probably right. The evidence for both genetic and environmental influences on intelligence has been eloquently summarized in Vernon's (1979) book, *Intelligence, Heredity, and Environment.* Overall, the evidence at this time suggests that about 60% of what we call intelligence in a population is heritable, about 30% is environmental, and about 10% is an interaction between genes and the environment. However, it is important to stress that the 60% figure applies to populations only, and not to individuals or even subgroups. Furthermore, and very paradoxically,

> Heritability has no absolute value. . . . The heritability of intelligence works out at about 60 percent or more in North America and Britain, largely because members of these cultures do experience fairly similar environments. . . . But if it were pos-

sible to apply common tests and calculate heritabilities in a population ranging all the way from upper middle-class U.S. whites to Australian aboriginals, we can be sure that the effects of different environments would be greatly magnified, and that the heritability percentage would probably fall well below 50 percent. . . . It also follows, conversely, that the greater our success in equalizing environments through social and educational reform, the more will any remaining differences in ability depend on the genes; in other words, heritability will be raised. (Vernon, 1979, p. 204)

Basically, then, intelligence is not a fixed entity. The opposite seems true, which makes sense if intelligence is viewed as mental energy.

It is also important to understand that, simply because something is genetically determined, does not mean that it cannot change. (Some of our physical features, such as eye color, cannot change; however, even so, we could cheat a little and use colored contact lenses.) Height, for example, is about 90% heritable, yet the average height in the population has been rising steadily over the years. A visit to a medieval castle, for example, confirms how short the inhabitants were. Visitors from the 20th century have to duck under the low doors! Why has height in the population risen? Probably for two major reasons: First, a female is unlikely to have a mate who is shorter than she is (a genetic influence), and, second, we have much better nutrition today compared with previous generations (an environmental influence). Likewise, genetics does not "fix" intelligence in the population at large. The same is true for individuals. It is not possible to determine, for any single person, how much of his or her intelligence is heritable and how much is environmental. Even if it were possible to calculate such figures for a person, we know that intelligence is modifiable by environmental conditions, including good teaching. Learning and teaching will always play critical roles in maximizing opportunities for people to use and develop their intelligence.

Partly because of the good efforts of millions of teachers in all countries of the world, it seems that populations and countries, by and large, are becoming more intelligent. Vernon (1979) wrote,

> There is good reason to believe that the average intelligence level of the human race will continue to rise as education improves in underdeveloped

countries; and that, in Western countries, further gains may occur as developments in our knowledge of child psychology and in educational technology increase what Bruner calls human amplifying systems. (p. 207)

Ultimately, even if intelligence were 100% inherited, there simply could not be the same level of it expressed in our culture or in any one person without the stimulation that education and other positive environments provide. A seed may contain all the growth potential and other features of the plant, but it does not grow well, or at all, in an environment where water and sunlight are lacking. The same is true for humans: Each person needs love, nurturing, and stimulation from birth (and maybe even before that).

Intelligence does not fix or determine school achievement, either. There is a correlation between how "smart" a person is and his or her achievement levels in academic skills, but the relationship is by no means perfect. I will discuss the importance of this imperfect relationship shortly, especially in the diagnosis of learning disabilities. In terms of the main idea of this section, however, school achievement has even less heritability than does intelligence. Do not let any parent say that "Susie is just like her mother when it comes to spelling." Certainly, some of Susie's spelling ability may be genetically influenced, and that is always interesting to discover; however, there is a great deal of room for change via teaching. Teaching in the classroom, and what teachers do with students, is very important. As Vernon (1979) wrote,

> Now that the findings of heritability researches and of environmental modifications are beginning to confirm or complement one another, we surely do not need to bother about which is the most important—genes or the environment. Both are essential, and neither can be neglected if we are to plan children's upbringing and education wisely. (p. 240)

"Good" school environments are like "good" home environments. Both nurture the development of intelligence. I do not want to give the impression that developing intelligence is all uphill, however. Just how difficult it is to make lasting changes in IQ scores (and, presumably, in intelligence) will become apparent in the next section.

HOW MUCH CAN INTELLIGENCE SCORES CHANGE?

Intelligence scores can and do change, on their own, from one testing to another merely because of the imprecise nature of the instruments and the underlying dimension of "energy" they measure. This practice effect can be very large on the WISC-III, especially on the Performance Scale. For this reason alone, no student should be reassessed on the WISC-III unless there is a minimum 6-month interval between the first and the second evaluations. There is also the effect of measurement error, which I will discuss later. Aside from these testing considerations, can intelligence levels actually be raised in people? From my own perspective of intelligence as mental energy, I believe the answer is yes. However, there are at least two issues to discuss in answering that question. The first is the issue of *teaching to the test,* which is a common and often desirable educational practice. The second issue is *stimulation:* Can teachers stimulate children and raise their intelligence levels? What does research indicate about that, and what is the latest thinking on this important topic?

In terms of the first issue, IQ tests are not quite like reading or other achievement tests when it comes to remediation. As every teacher knows, the closer the test comes to testing what the teacher has taught, the better that test is in terms of validity. If a teacher knows that a student is weak in reading comprehension, for example, then the student can be assessed using an appropriate test, a remedial program can begin, and the student can be retested. Some of the test items can be close approximations of what the teacher taught. Therefore, teaching to the test is an appropriate educational strategy for academic subjects.

Not so for IQ tests. Teachers could teach to the WISC-III or the Stanford–Binet, and set up Individualized Education Programs (IEPs) with improvement of certain subtests as the objective. They could use materials geared to each WISC-III subtest, for example, and spend a lot of remedial time "teaching" the presumed underlying process. However, the result of that kind of remedial effort would only waste time and not raise "intelligence" as such. Such teaching might raise the IQ score on the WISC-III,

but that score would then be spurious, because intelligence—as opposed to, say, reading—is a much more abstract entity. When measuring a student's IQ, examiners are sampling from a very broad base of learned behaviors; however, the learned behaviors in reading are much more specific. Raising IQ scores cannot be legitimately done in any "canned" way.

As Barbara Holmes (1985) wrote,

> The use of remedial prescriptions (and the *WISC-R Compilation* [Whitworth and Sutton 1978] is a good case in point) tends to result in "teaching to the test." In the *Compilation,* the long-term goal stated for each WISC-R subtest task is to do that particular task itself. All that it does, then, is train "block designers" and "picture completers": that is, WISC-R–competent test takers. Since we have no proof that the academic correlations of the Full Scale IQ will benefit from excellence in block design, the most we can count on is uselessness of the test scores for predictive purposes. (p. 13)

She further stated,

> The arguments presented in this paper are uniformly critical of programmed remediation based on WISC-R profiles. It will be recognized, of course, that the fault is not in the technology but in the erroneous conceptual and theoretical bases underlying the approach. Most damning is the lack of validation for the relationship implied between the test and ability, and ability and academic program. It cannot be overemphasized that, in the absence of empirical support, WISC-R remedial programs can be considered no more than arbitrary exercises, and therefore contrary to ethical practice and professional intent. The real solution to appropriate test usage is to continue to recognize the need for the mediating, interactive role of the artisan professionals, school psychologists and teachers, in maintaining the ideal of individually meaningful educational intervention. (p. 13)

Holmes's comments apply equally to the *WISC-III Compilation* (Whitworth & Sutton, 1993). The approach I advocate in this book is anything but canned and, I believe, is a step toward the ideal that Holmes advanced. I want the reader to know more about reading and intelligence theory. Only then can school psychologists and remedial specialists work together to program appropriate remediation for the individual student. Being knowledgeable makes one more sensitive to what is appropriate for any given student. Although I provide many suggestions, the school psychologist who works with the student must also work with the teacher who knows the student to decide what is ultimately useful and what is not. Those decisions are as much art as they are science.

Despite the fact that the *WISC-R Compilation* has been much maligned, I believe it has a place in the school psychologist's list of useful references. Once the school psychologist has pinpointed some of the student's needs using theoretically sound approaches (many of which are discussed in this book), the psychologist will find some of the very specific suggestions in the *Compilation* to be useful. For example, if there is a need for expressive language development as evidenced by, say, a low score on the Verbal Scale, then some of the suggestions in the Vocabulary section of the *Compilation* could be helpful to the student.

Thus, the first issue—teaching specifically to WISC-III subtests in order to raise intelligence—is both spurious and a waste of precious time. The second issue, that of environmental stimulation, is much deeper. Several kinds of studies bear on this important area of concern.

One common environmental intervention method, usually done at the early childhood level, is to pretest the student with an IQ test, and then introduce some general program of stimulation, designed to enhance some broad areas of cognitive development. A posttest might be administered later, even using the same IQ test (provided that the time interval is adequate), to determine if the intervention had any effect on the student's general and/or specific abilities. Also, the student could be followed up in later years, to see what effect the early intervention had on other variables, such as academic achievement, self-concept, social adjustment, career choices, and time spent in special education classes.

Several studies done at an early intervention or Head Start level have reported very dramatic increases in intelligence test scores. The most widely publicized was the Milwaukee Project (discussed in Vernon, 1979), which claimed to produce increases of about 30 points overall. Unfortunately, these results have never been replicated, and are now known to be suspect. Thus, on the heritability side of the issue, Sir Cyril Burt falsified information, and on the environmental side, the Milwaukee Project is suspect! This shows what can happen when even the most reputable scientists are bent on proving a point, one way or another.

Obviously, the issues are very complex, and the results often are not clear-cut. Nevertheless, I believe that early stimulation can and does produce positive effects on children. Because some problems can be, and are, prevented this way, efforts at early stimulation should be continued vigorously.

Sometimes, however, confusion arises over what to stimulate, and for what purpose. Later, I will discuss what I consider to be a very exciting possibility in the field of early intervention in terms of increasing reading ability and preventing reading problems via the stimulation of phonemic processing.

Gains in IQ scores should not be considered the only measure of success for these programs. Some studies have shown that, although IQ scores drop steadily once intervention ceases, achievement scores do not. Also, fewer students from such stimulated preschool groups are assigned to special education classes later on (Clark, 1984). This important and noteworthy finding has great social significance. Students do seem to function better in the school environment as a result of Head Start–type programs, and there is a resulting positive chain of events—even though not much advantage may be evident in IQ scores alone.

Another line of research has shown that a total and long-term change in environment, such as occurs when children are adopted, can reverse the damage of even extreme early deprivation (Clark, 1984). These changes are manifested in many aspects of the individual's life and are, in my opinion, far more important than changes in IQ scores alone, although these also change for the better. A few studies have shown long-term and lasting positive changes when children are placed in appropriate long-term care (Clark, 1984). Even long-term institutional care is better than a severely deprived environment. This speaks also for the resilience and plasticity of human beings, and demonstrates that long-term care at any age is more important than early experiences or a "head start."

The time, money, and resources available for some projects are not available to the vast majority of school psychologists or teachers. However, at a more practical level, some early childhood mother–child programs, which are far less costly, also have been quite successful (bringing about a 15-point IQ gain over a 2-year period). Although this book is not geared to the early childhood level, I would like to point out some of the essential elements of success in these programs, because many school psychologists do get involved with children in the early years. These programs

1. Aim primarily at showing the mother how to be a better interactor with the child.

2. Aim primarily at developing the mother's and child's language skills both for awareness training and information processing.

3. Teach the mother how to participate in her child's play and speech, and how to accompany this with verbal interactions. Furthermore, the mother needs to be shown how to do this incidentally, while at home, with the child—not only during the tutoring or training sessions. Merely counseling or advising the mother is not enough. Demonstrations must be given.

4. Are carried out for at least 2 years, beginning at about age 2.

The interested reader should consult Levenstein's *Mother–Child Home Program* (cited in Vernon, 1979), which describes a successful program that has been in use since 1965, and that has replicated results.

Direct Teaching of Intelligence: Recent Formulations

Robert Sternberg (1984; Sternberg & Ketron, 1982), a professor of psychology at Yale University, has provided what I consider to be some important distinctions about the teaching of intellectual processes. He named three types of mental processes: (a) metacomponents, (b) performance components, and (c) knowledge-acquisition components. One can intervene and teach at any one or more of these levels.

Metacomponents are higher-order "executive decisions" and processes used by people to plan and monitor what to do when faced with a problem. For example, when given an arithmetic problem, a person has to be aware of and decide what operation(s) to use to solve it. These are the metacomponent decisions and strategies. Sternberg named the Instrumental Enrichment (IE) program of Reuven Feuerstein as an example of a program designed mainly to teach metacomponent strategies. The IE is as content-free as possible and consists of 13 process-type exercises repeated throughout the program (see Feuerstein, 1980, for information on Instrumental Enrichment).

Sternberg commented that IE training can be recommended for a number of cultural and subcultural groups, but that it is limited in the breadth of skills taught and in its potential for generalization. Nevertheless, Sternberg (1984) felt that, overall, "IE is an attractive package in many respects. It is among the best of available programs emphasizing thinking-skill training" (p. 42).

Performance components are processing skills used to actually carry out the task. In the arithmetic example, they are the actual steps used in performing the operations, be they adding, multiplying, or whatever. Sternberg named the Philosophy for Children (PC) program as an example of a largely performance-based program, although metacomponents are also included. The goals of PC are to try to teach 30 thinking skills in children in Grades 5 through 8. The major advantage of PC over IE is that PC maximizes a knowledge-based content, whereas IE minimizes it. Sternberg (1984) wrote, "PC stories are exciting and highly motivating. . . . The thinking skills taught are clearly the right ones to teach for both academic and everyday information processing" (p. 44). "No program I am aware of," he continued, "is more likely to teach durable, transferable thinking skills than PC" (p. 44). Unfortunately for special educators, PC is also heavily reading and reasoning based. Additionally, the story characters are middle and upper middle class in value orientation. Therefore, the application of PC in special education may be somewhat limited. Nevertheless, it is a program worthy of perusal, and could be suitable for some students.

Knowledge-acquisition components are the reasoning components used when first learning new materials, such as multiplication tables. The *Chicago Mastery Learning Reading* (CMLR) program is an example of such a program, as is most of what happens everyday in a classroom, I might add. The CMLR, like the PC, was written for Grades 5 to 8. The program places a strong emphasis on learning to learn. There are two units at each grade level; these consist of comprehension and study skills. To begin with, the units are concrete, simple, literal, and familiar; gradually, they become more abstract, inexplicit, and unfamiliar.

This program seems to have several features suitable for the special educator:

1. The material easily incorporates into any reading program, whereas the PC would best fit into an enrichment or philosophy curriculum (certainly, very few schools have this) and the IE does not easily fit into any curriculum.

2. It emphasizes learning strategies.

3. It can be used with a wide variety of students, including those above and below grade level.

4. It can be used with a wide range of socioeconomic groups.

5. It has immediate applicability to school and life situations.

6. It seems developed for the heart of where many handicapped students have difficulty in the first place—acquiring knowledge.

The weaknesses of the CMLR are the limited range of skills it covers (reading and verbal comprehension only) and its weaker theoretical foundation.

Overall, these programs are exciting developments in education. I would caution against jumping on any bandwagons, however. Remember, the teacher ultimately creates the program. To date, only a few school districts have actually made the direct teaching of thinking skills one of their stated objectives. As more and more districts do so, however, programs such as the IE, PC, and CMLR will gain more attention. Educators need to be in a better position to evaluate such programs, and Sternberg's metacomponent, performance component, and knowledge-acquisition component distinctions should be very useful as a framework for such evaluations. Educators can then choose or develop what is best for their own goals.

These distinctions can also be useful for an informal "process analysis" of many academic and cognitive tasks, including those of the WISC-III. For example, if a student did poorly on one of the Arithmetic subtest questions, was it because he or she (a) did not know what operations and procedures to use in the first place (including a lack of metacomponent awareness), (b) broke down in the performance of the task (perhaps the student subtracted as was called for, but obtained an incorrect answer), or (c) did not acquire the knowledge in the first place (such as the multiplication tables)? Careful observation and error analysis, as well as testing the limits afterwards, can help answer some of these questions and provide a direction and theoretical framework for some remedial strategies.

Top–Down and Bottom–Up Information Processing

Top–down information processing is primarily conceptually driven processing—that is, processing that begins with learning and demands meaning. For example, in the sentence, "The pig was in the _____," several words can "fit" in the empty space. Some likely candidates are "yard" and "barn," or even "garden." Top–down processes or conceptual knowledge allows people to make these guesses, but the guesses or predictions have to fit the context or overall meaning of the sentence.

Bottom–up processing is data driven. What is *predicted* must match what is *written*. The information is sequentially pieced together to form a whole, so meaning is derived from the data. Sounding out a word in isolation is an example of a primarily bottom–up process in reading. The reader is urged to rely primarily on phonics, finally acquiring meaning from the knowledge of what the written word stands for.

The distinction between top–down and bottom–up processing can be applied to reading. Mature readers seem to use a combination of top–down (meaning and syntax cues) and bottom–up (phonics cues) processing when reading. Flesch recognized this, when in 1949, he wrote, "And that's the way we read. We race along, making quick guesses at the meanings of little bunches of words, and quick corrections of these first guesses afterwards" (p. 23).

The business of meaning acquisition in reading is very important (although it takes for granted that decoding is already intact), and should be woven into the remedial activities that special education teachers provide for their students. Appendix 2A contains several practical strategies for emphasizing the act of "predicting" and meaning acquisition in reading, using primarily a *whole language* approach.

Top–down and bottom–up processing can be applied in a number of areas besides reading. For example, John Naisbitt in *Megatrends* (1982) observed that trends always start bottom–up. Trend-setting ideas or products are most often observed locally first, and usually in one of a few states (mainly California, Florida, Washington, Colorado, or Connecticut), before being adopted nationwide. Fads, on the other hand, are always top–down.

Darwin's theory of evolution, as another example, is primarily a bottom–up explanation. However, as Buckminster Fuller once commented, all the evidence is just as consistent with a top–down interpretation as well. In my opinion, the universe is conceptually driven. Orderliness seems to be an inherent part of its makeup. Once started, however, the evolutionary process is both top–down and bottom–up interacting together.

It is important to note that neither top–down nor bottom–up processing is inherently superior or inferior to the other. Because both are frequently needed in concert for the best results, that should be the basic principle in providing instruction to students. Whether a bottom–up or a top–down approach is emphasized with a particular student depends on his or her needs.

Now, I use this distinction to evaluate further the thinking skills packages discussed above. It seems to me that IE is far too top–down. Students engaged in learning in school must work with some sort of basic content. If the content is too far removed from their ordinary experience, as it seems to be in IE, the chance of transfer to everyday tasks is limited. CMLR, on the other hand, uses knowledge acquisition, which is bottom–up, as the basis for training the metacognitive, or top–down skills. PC also uses this combined approach; however, as previously stated, this program has some other drawbacks for special educators.

Special education students, who usually have difficulty acquiring knowledge, need programs that make the transfer as easy as possible. Thus, when the day comes—as it already has in some states and provinces—when remedial teachers must also teach thinking skills, then the CMLR program will have to be looked at carefully. I am using "program" in the broad sense of "that which is designed by the teacher." Again, I do not advocate the canned use of canned programs in the school system. Such programs can be used, but usually need to be modified in light of the teacher's objectives for a particular student or class. They can be part of a teacher's overall program.

The broad goal of special educators, at least until now, has been to improve achievement, not intelligence. Intelligence tests sample from a broader range of life and learning experiences than do achievement tests. The latter tests depend heavily on formal learning, and the skills they measure are far more specific than those measured by intelligence tests. Of course, there is some overlap between the two, and IQ tests can predict achievement scores to some extent. The correlation between the two kinds of tests is around .60 on the average. (A correlation coefficient [r] is a measure of how two variables are related. If A and B are perfectly related inversely [i.e., as A is increased, then B is decreased by the same amount], then the correlation coefficient would be -1.00. If A and B were perfectly related in a positive way, then A and B would increase proportionately, and the calculated r would be $+1.00$. Correlation does not imply causation. If A and B are correlated, then [a] A might be the cause of B, or [b] B might be the cause of A, or [c] A and B could both be related to some other cause that is common to both.)

The correlation between IQ scores and achievement scores is statistically very significant, but in no way perfect. Therefore, when comparing intelligence to achievement and making judgments about where a child should be achieving because of an IQ score, educators and psychologists need to be very cautious indeed. This point will be discussed in greater depth in another section of this chapter.

Educators and psychologists must not hold unrealistic expectations for students or make rash promises to parents. The business of "raising" intelligence is complex and difficult, and it is a life-long process involving many factors outside the control of the school.

Psychologists and educators need always to keep in mind the importance of the child's home background in their efforts to educate the child. I discuss the importance of the home, in terms of cognitive development, in the following section.

IMPORTANCE OF THE HOME

Every teacher, remedial or otherwise, intuitively knows that there is no substitute for a good home. Some home environments are very incompatible with normal cognitive and emotional growth—indeed, are destructive to both. Fortunately, the effects of extreme deprivation in such homes seem to be reversible. Nevertheless, little is known about what stimulates "normal" growth, although a few correlates are known.

The Berkeley Growth Study, for example, found that higher IQ scores in children are associated with (but not necessarily caused by)

1. Higher socioeconomic status of the parents

2. Superior play facilities

3. Parental concern that children get a good education

4. Parental harmony, and

5. Mothers who appear worrisome, tense, highly active and energetic. (cited in Sattler, 1982, p. 52)

McCall, Applebaum, and Hogarty (1973) found that, of a group of children who showed increases or decreases in IQ scores as they grew older, the group showing increases had families that encouraged their children in a clear way by providing structure and enforcement of consequences. This does not mean severe punishment. In fact, severe punishment was clearly associated with the largest decreases in IQ scores. Children who made the biggest gains had parents who adopted a middle-of-the-road discipline policy—neither too severe nor too lax. Being lax, however, was better than being too severe.

Very high correlations were found in another study (cited in Sattler, 1982) between total ratings of the home environment on

1. Quality of language models available to the child

2. Opportunities for enlarging vocabulary

3. Feedback about appropriate language usage

4. Opportunities for language practice

and general intelligence ($r=.69$), as well as academic achievement ($r=.80$). Do these results mean that the child's capacity for learning is already largely fixed before the child enters school? Some eminent authorities, such as Vernon, believe so; however, more recent evidence seems to suggest that the type of schooling the child receives *does* make a difference.

A good portion of this book is devoted to remedial teaching strategies as they are suggested by the WISC-III profiles (and supplemented by additional testing as needed, of course). I firmly believe in the huge difference teachers can make in the lives of their students. However, I would like to temper my enthusiasm by pointing out that everyone needs to enter the educational enterprise with their eyes open. The importance of other factors, such as the home and genetics, should not be underplayed. Admirable goals of improving IQ scores and academic achievement through well-contrived interventions may still fall short, despite the best efforts, because of such factors. The evidence clearly supports the notion that some environmental factors that influence the development of intelligence—such as low birth weight, early poor nutrition, parental harmony, socioeconomic status, certain personality characteristics of the mother, father absence, father nurturing, discipline models in the home, and the child's own temperament—are well beyond the school's control.

Educators and psychologists must do what they can, then, with what they have, to their best ability, every day. All those factors cannot be controlled. However, the kind of school environment the teacher creates has, I believe, a very profound effect on the child—for better or worse. For students who are at risk in terms of their family backgrounds, the quality of the classroom and the teacher's relationship with those students may be all the nurturing that those students have.

INTELLIGENCE—MORE DEFINITIONS

Now is a good time to make more definitional distinctions of the term *intelligence*. Following Vernon (1979), I call them Intelligence A, Intelligence B, and Intelligence C. I find these distinctions very useful in explaining the results of IQ scores to both parents and teachers.

Intelligence A refers to innate genetic potential. It is that portion of intelligence that is heritable for an individual. It is the genotype. There is simply no way of measuring Intelligence A.

Intelligence B refers to the interaction between Intelligence A and the environment. It is affected by culture, home environment, birth weight, birth trauma, malnutrition, and a host of other factors. It is the phenotype.

Intelligence C is the score on an individual test of intelligence. Intelligence C2 is the score on a group test of intelligence. The two Cs are correlated, but by no means identical. The score on an individual test of intelligence is a better indicator of the child's potential, and gives considerable information on individual strengths and weaknesses not available from group tests. Intelligence C is used to infer Intelligence B. Vernon claimed, however, that the Verbal Scale of the Wechsler scales (and the verbal portions of the Stanford–Binet) is a direct measure of Intelligence B in our culture (but, of course, not all aspects of B).

Because of the fluid nature of intelligence, any score from any IQ test, group or individual, should be interpreted only as a snapshot. It gives a picture of a child's cognitive development at a particular point in time. If the film is properly loaded, the camera is held steady, and other conditions are right, then the picture will be clear. Likewise, if an IQ test is administered properly and the child is made to feel comfortable and do his or her best, the IQ score will be a valid and reliable estimate of the child's development at that point in time. However, because the score can change over short or long periods of time, such "snapshots" need to be taken reasonably frequently to get a better long-range picture.

The younger the child, the less reliable the IQ score is of matching that child's IQ score at a later age. Scores obtained on elementary children are much more stable than those of preschool children.

Brighter children show greater changes from one test time to another than do children with lower IQs (Sattler, 1982). This research finding has been confirmed in my own experience with students. One year, a student may qualify for a district's gifted program; 2 years later, the student will score lower and perhaps no longer technically qualify, only to score higher again at a third testing.

Because of such fluctuations in Intelligence C, all scores from all IQ tests must be treated with caution. It is paramount that parents and educators understand this, so that no wild generalizations about a student's potential are made on the basis of an IQ score.

WHAT IS POTENTIAL, ANYWAY?

IQ scores are often interpreted as an estimate of the student's *learning potential*. Although I find this interpretation useful in my day-to-day work as a school psychologist, it must be used very cautiously. The IQ score, if valid and reliable, may be a good indicator of the student's academic potential at that point in time, but it cannot be rigidly adhered to. The IQ score is not necessarily an indication of a fixed potential for more learning. As far as I can tell, that potential is infinite for everyone—within lifetime limits.

To illustrate this point, I like to use the Russian psychologist Vygotsky's concept of the "zone of potential difference." The idea is quite simple. First, one measures a student's performance in a certain area. Then, one sees how well the child performs after certain external prompts, cues, or strategies are added. The improvement noted, which may be small or large, is the zone of potential difference for that child on that particular task. Remember, however, that I am not talking about teaching to a subtest. The zone of potential difference indicates what might be possible with good, general remediation.

Reading specialists employ a similar concept when they want to find out what the reading potential is of a student who has a reading problem. If the student is a poor reader and can function at only, say, the 10th percentile for his or her age group when asked to read a story, but is able to answer questions displaying good comprehension of the story when someone else reads (say, at the 75th percentile for his or her age group), then the student's score on the listening comprehension task is a good indicator of his or her reading potential. The assumption is that, with proper instruction, the student should eventually be able to read independently at the 75th percentile of the age group. The zone of potential difference for this student on this task, then, is a whopping 65 percentile points.

Similar reasoning can be applied to the concept of intelligence. When a child's current performance is being measured, the zone of potential difference is rarely being measured. The result is a measure of current functioning within an error limit. Does this mean that intelligence tests such as the WISC-III should not be used to place students in special programs? My experience indicates that IQ tests are very useful in placement decisions, but the placement decision should not be based on an IQ score alone.

Suppose a student has been having great difficulty with reading and other subjects, despite modifications by the teacher and remedial help. If a WISC-III assessment shows an IQ of, say, 70 ± 6 (percentile 2), then one could say that the child's learning potential was nowhere near average at the time of testing (provided, of course, that the examiner was confident the student did his or her best). That being the case, the student might better be placed in a program geared to his or her current level, such as a class for students with educable mental handicaps. Such situations occur frequently in all school systems. In my experience, schools do a great deal of good for the child by placing him or her in a special class. The so-called labeling is very helpful, provided the label is not seen as something that is forever fixed. If the child is placed in a special class and forgotten, or if teachers and parents do not work to "stretch" the student as far as possible, then the placement will be harmful. However, the alternative of letting the student sink or swim in the "mainstream" is even more unpalatable. A regular classroom teacher can go only so far in trying to meet the needs of handicapped students, even with the help from extra personnel. These students' needs are usually far better met in special programs. Nevertheless, mainstreaming should occur when-

ever and to whatever extent possible. Should a student make enormous gains in the special program, most schools would be only too happy to fully reintegrate the student.

The WISC-III Full Scale IQ score by itself, however, may not be a good predictor of a student's academic potential. Suppose a student's Full Scale score was 100 ± 6 (percentile 50 ± 16). This student's score on the surface can be interpreted as indicating average learning potential.

Because mental energy does not seem to flow evenly between individuals, or within the same individual at times, learning potential might be a misleading term. "Average IQ" implies, to most people, that the student should be at least "average" in all he or she does. This assumption is simply contrary to fact and quite unreasonable. However, educators and psychologists mistakenly make such assumptions all the time in school systems. (I will say much more on this point when I discuss the diagnosis of learning disabilities.)

Questions that really need to be asked include the following: "What *kind* of learning?" "To what type of task will this student respond best?" "When can we expect 'average' performance, and when do we have to modify our expectations?" The WISC-III can help answer these questions.

As I mentioned in Chapter 1, the WISC-III provides several different scores, each having educational implications. The Full Scale IQ is the most stable score, and corresponds to general ability, or *g*. The test also yields a Verbal and a Performance IQ, as well as four Index Scores. The Index Scores are based on a statistical procedure called factor analysis. This procedure determines which subtests are grouped together because they "load" on some underlying common factor. The factor is then given a name. The Wechsler scales have been factor analyzed numerous times. On the WISC-R, three distinct factors typically emerged. These have been enhanced on the WISC-III, and a fourth factor has been added. The factors, their names, and the subtests that load on each factor are listed in Table 2.1.

Factors I and II, Verbal Comprehension and Perceptual Organization, correspond very closely to the Verbal and Performance IQs, respectively. Factor III, Freedom from Distractibility, can be considered primarily auditory processing, whereas Factor IV, Processing Speed, can be thought of as visual processing. Not all children's scores on the

TABLE 2.1. The WISC-III Factors

Factor I (Verbal Comprehension)	Factor II (Perceptual Organization)	Factor III (Freedom from Distractibility)	Factor IV (Processing Speed)
Information	Picture Completion	Arithmetic	Coding
Similarities	Picture Arrangement	Digit Span	Symbol Search
Vocabulary	Block Design		
Comprehension	Object Assembly		
	Mazes[a]		

[a]Although the WISC-III manual does not list the Mazes subtest under any factor, I list it under Perceptual Organization, where it has been listed in previous Wechsler tests. However, Kaufman (1992) suggests that Mazes should not be administered, given its unreliability and its low correlation with g.

WISC-III show this distinct pattern, but many do, and the educational implications must be teased out by the examiner.

An example of a four-way split is shown for Arnold in Figure 2.2. The WISC-III manual provides equivalent IQ scores and percentiles for each factor. The error bands for the 90% and 95% confidence levels are also provided in the manual.

To calculate a scaled score average for each factor, simply total the scaled scores that load on each factor and divide by the number of subtests. Round off the answer to the nearest whole number. When the scaled score average for each factor differs by 3 or more points, then the four-factor split can be legitimately interpreted. (See Kaufman, 1979, for a full treatment of this issue.)

For this student, the very large discrepancy among the four factors becomes apparent in both the IQ scores and the percentiles. Using Kaufman's rule-of-thumb interpretation of a significant difference, one can see that the Factor III average of 7 is significantly lower than the averages on the Factors I and II. The third factor, therefore, can legitimately be interpreted as being significantly weaker than Factors I and II. When a factor average is 3 points (or more) lower than any of the others, then, according to Kaufman, such interpretations are psychometrically valid.

Thus, for this student, the Full Scale IQ is 99 ±6, but look at the difference in factor abilities! Many educators and parents base their expectations of a child's potential on the Full Scale IQ and miss the important implications of the factor splits. In Arnold's case, expectations for all academic tasks based solely on his Full Scale IQ would be a great disservice to the student because his factor abilities are unevenly developed—significantly so. His

verbal and performance abilities are about evenly developed, as is his visual processing speed, but the Freedom from Distractibility Factor is not, and seems to preclude academic success in certain areas at the present time. Thus, some modification of expectations is necessary, and some type of remedial help is suggested.

What are the educational implications for Arnold? There are many; however, the WISC-III scores merely suggest certain hypotheses. Like a good detective, the school psychologist and remedial teacher must track down the clues, do further testing if necessary, and develop a program based on the student's individual needs. To make matters more complicated, the factor splitting of scores by itself cannot be used to diagnose learning problems, because some students show such splits on their WISC-III profiles, but display no academic difficulties.

With these cautions in mind, let me make a few attempts at hypothesizing about Arnold. Because both the Verbal Comprehension and the Perceptual Organization factors are developed to an average extent, this student might be expected to display good skills in many areas of his life, including some aspects of academics. For example, this student might be a good reader. His facility for language is solidly average, and he can show this when asked. Sometimes, however, students with low scores on Factor III have not "cracked the code" in reading, and are not good readers. Therefore, more detective work is necessary to address that hypothesis. If Arnold is not overly shy, he would be expected to express himself verbally, at least to an average extent. Therefore, his answers to oral questions in class would show him as having the ability to do the work. This oral demonstration is very

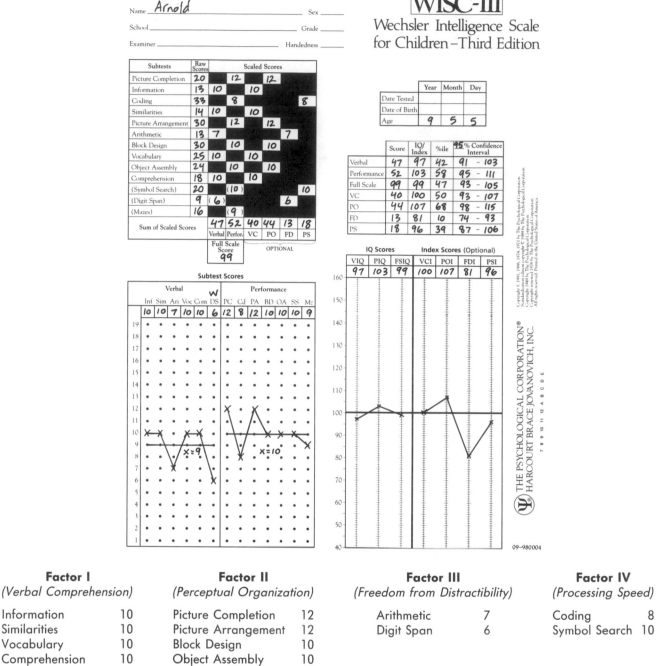

Factor I		Factor II		Factor III		Factor IV	
(Verbal Comprehension)		*(Perceptual Organization)*		*(Freedom from Distractibility)*		*(Processing Speed)*	
Information	10	Picture Completion	12	Arithmetic	7	Coding	8
Similarities	10	Picture Arrangement	12	Digit Span	6	Symbol Search	10
Vocabulary	10	Block Design	10				
Comprehension	10	Object Assembly	10				
		Mazes[a]	9				

Avg. (40) = 10		Avg. (53) = 10.6 = 11		Avg. (13) = 6.5 = 7		Avg. (18) = 9	
(percentile 50)		(percentile 63)		(percentile 16)		(percentile 37)	

Using the WISC-III Manual:
VCI = 100		POI = 107		FDI = 81		PSI = 96	
(percentile 50)		(percentile 68)		(percentile 10)		(percentile 39)	

Note. The discrepancy in percentiles is because of the rounding-off procedure.
[a]Mazes is not included in the Perceptual Organization IQ in the WISC-III manual.

Figure 2.2. Arnold's profile.

important, because most classroom teachers (and, of course, parents) base their academic expectations for a student on how well they see him or her performing in oral situations. Once the expectation is set, then if Arnold is not performing at least to this average extent in all areas, the adults begin to ask themselves why. Then a vicious cycle can begin. Because the teacher expects average work in all areas, he or she may become very upset when Arnold does not produce. Labels such as "lazy" are then applied, and a negative set of expectations is introduced. The teacher might pressure Arnold to perform at the same level as the rest of the class. When Arnold cannot perform to expectations, the teacher may keep him after school until all his work is completed. This extra pressure might cause undue stress for the student, but maybe he does not like to show it, so Arnold bottles up the stress until he gets home, and then lets his parents know how much he hates school or a particular teacher. And so on. This is all speculation based on a few scores, of course, and all of these guesses must be followed up. Interviews with the student's teacher and parents will serve to confirm or deny many of them, and thereby suggest appropriate courses of action. Because some students are lazy, accurate diagnosis becomes more difficult. As a rule of thumb, however, nobody should assume that a student is lazy. Students may feign laziness as a cover-up.

The concept of the zone of potential difference should also be employed. Arnold is functioning at an average level in Factors I, II, and IV. His zone of potential difference in these factors may not be very large (depending on his age and other factors). For Factor III, the zone may also be large or small, depending on the nature of the problem and its severity. The type and frequency of remediation, the attitude of the student and the parents, and so on, are all important considerations when it comes to a prognosis.

Moreover, even though the name for Factor III on the WISC-III is Freedom from Distractibility, distractibility itself may not be the underlying problem. There are many possible reasons why the student scores low on this factor, such as poor facility with numbers, poor auditory short-term memory, difficulties with simultaneous or sequential information processing, difficulties with phonemic manipulation, or a combination of these or other reasons. The educator and school psychologist must seek the causes.

In this case, Arnold actually was a poor reader and a very poor writer, but his facility for numbers was excellent. Much of his academic performance was consistent with results on Factors I and II, but his written output was very weak. Arnold had to make speed–accuracy trade-offs all the time because of his alphabet coding difficulty (note how neither Coding nor Symbol Search detected this problem). If he wrote quickly, he became very sloppy. If he slowed down, he was able to be neat, but his output was low. Indeed, a very vicious cycle had been set up with a very negative home–school interaction, in which each side blamed the other for the boy's problem. In this case, the problem was genuine: The student could not, without modification, match his verbal potential with his written output. I discussed the results of my testing and the educational implications with Arnold's teachers and parents. A short-term remedial program was set up with the goal of increasing his written output. In the meantime, his teachers decreased the amount of written work he had to do, thus easing some of the pressure caused by unrealistic expectations. Within 6 months, the student had made significant gains in written output. This increase was documented, because charts were used to track his gains. He still could not produce as much as his classmates, but he was producing much more than before. Arnold, his parents, and his teachers were much happier.

This example illustrates how important it is to go beyond the scores themselves. The scores are merely suggestive. Diagnoses and solutions require energy and creativity—intelligence in motion on the part of educators concerned about the student.

Because of the frequency of the occurrence of factor splits, I will have much more to say about interpreting them in Chapter 5.

Bannatyne's Recategorizations

Alexander Bannatyne (1974) grouped the WISC subtests in a different way. Because his groupings are based on a logical interpretation, they are not as vigorously supported or researched as the factor-analytic groupings. Bannatyne did his work on the original WISC, but the regroupings apply equally well to the WISC-III. His groupings are as follows:

Conceptual	Spatial
Similarities	Picture Completion
Vocabulary	Block Design
Comprehension	Object Assembly

Sequencing	Acquired Knowledge
Arithmetic	Information
Digit Span	Arithmetic
Coding	Vocabulary

Note that Picture Arrangement, Mazes, and Symbol Search are not listed at all, whereas Vocabulary and Arithmetic are listed under two different headings.

I have found that Vocabulary falls in both the Acquired Knowledge and the Conceptual categories so often as to be a hindrance to interpretation. For example, suppose a student obtains the following scores on the Verbal Scale subtests:

Information	5
Similarities	7
Arithmetic	6
Vocabulary	5
Comprehension	10

Using the regroupings, a significant difference results between the Conceptual (scaled score average = 7, or percentile 16) and Acquired Knowledge (scaled score average = 5, or percentile 5) categories. However, the fact that Vocabulary is a subtest in both categories is puzzling.

Nevertheless, Bannatyne's regroupings are very useful in interpreting some profiles. Students with learning disabilities, for example, often obtain the following pattern of scores on Bannatyne's categories: Spatial > Conceptual > Sequencing > Acquired Knowledge (Sequencing and Acquired Knowledge may be equally low, however). This pattern was found for learning disabled students as a group on WISC-R, so the presence of the pattern in a specific student's profile cannot be used to diagnose a learning disability. The pattern is merely suggestive, and should be followed up by other tests. This pattern also was not found in the WISC-R scores of learning disabled students from minority groups. The pattern in those groups was generally

Spatial > Sequential > Conceptual (Smith, Coleman, Dokecki, & Davis, 1977).

Although the pattern is present on the WISC-R, it has not yet been researched using the WISC-III and was not found to be a predictor of learning difficulties on the *Wechsler Preschool and Primary Scale of Intelligence* (WPPSI) (Wechsler, 1967), the downward extension of the WISC-R (Badian, 1981). Interestingly, no boys who showed this pattern on the WPPSI at age 5 developed reading problems when followed up 3 years later, but about half the girls who had the pattern did.

Also useful is the so-called ACID profile. Frequently, scores on Arithmetic, Coding, Information, and Digit Span (ACID) are significantly lower than scores on other subtests. This profile seems to suggest learning problems. Information and Arithmetic, from Bannatyne's Acquired Knowledge cluster, fall into the ACID group. According to Sternberg's distinctions, it seems that students with good conceptual abilities have internalized the metacomponents, performance components, and learning components required to perform well on verbal–conceptual tasks as tapped by subtests such as Similarities, Vocabulary, and Comprehension, and on the perceptual–performance tasks as tapped by most of the Performance subtests of the WISC-III. However, these students have not acquired or developed the same strategies for the ACID or Freedom from Distractibility group. Sometimes, the metacomponent awareness is present. For example, the student knows what to do on the Arithmetic or the coding subtest, but cannot perform (or performs incorrectly) or has not learned the critical subskills necessary. Thus, the ACID group taps into some areas that appear to be very important for school-based learning. This can be useful information in some ways; however, in and of itself, the profile is not diagnostic, only suggestive.

Bannatyne's Sequencing category is also useful to consider. It is important to remember that sequencing, as such, may not be why the student scores low on the Arithmetic, Digit Span, and Coding cluster of subtests. Sequencing difficulties may be part of the reason, but that hypothesis must now compete with or complement the other possible explanations for the low scores. Interpreting a WISC-III profile is never easy or clear-cut!

Perhaps, the teacher, psychologist, and reading specialist, based on observations, decide that sequencing *is* a difficulty for the student. How can that knowledge be linked to a reading program? Appendix 2B provides some reading strategies that take into account the sequencing problem. If distractibility is also determined to be involved, then some of the behavioral strategies and principles for classroom management found in Chapters 3 and 5, and in Appendix 2C, will be helpful.

INTERPRETING A WISC-III SCORE: SOME INITIAL CONSIDERATIONS

The raw scores on the WISC-III are converted, through the use of tables provided in the WISC-III manual, to a number of standard scores, which are interpretable scores. Raw scores, by themselves, do not tell very much.

Whenever one samples scores on a large number of people, the scores fall into a "normal" distribution. This simply means that some of the scores will be very low, some very high, and a majority clustered around a central point. One can develop a frequency distribution of these scores; when the distribution is graphed, it looks like Figure 2.3. This curve (also known as a bell curve because of its shape) is a mathematical representation of what exists in the real world of scores.

For example, the Information subtest of the WISC-III has 30 items; the subtest can be administered to a child as young as age 6 or as old as 16 years, 11 months. If a student aged 8 years, 2 months, answered 15 of the 30 items correctly, the raw score represents only a 50% correct rate. Does this mean that the student did poorly on this subtest? From the raw score alone, it is not possible to answer that question. Maybe the score is good, and maybe not. The answer depends on how other students in the same age group did. If the student's peers, on the average, answer only 8 of the 30 items correctly, then this student scored much higher than his or her peers. If, on the other hand, the student's peers score correctly on 20 of the 30 items on average, then this student scored below the peers.

To determine the distribution, the test must be normed. To determine how any age group of students does on a test, *representative samples* of students must be selected in that age group. A nor-

mal distribution of scores is determined for each subtest and the test as a whole. From the raw scores, the test developer can calculate standard scores applicable to each age group. These scores are used to see how a student's standard score compares with a representative sample of other students of the same age. As it turns out, in the example I am using, the raw score of 15 for a student who is 8 years, 2 months of age also converts to a scaled score of 15. Now, what does *that* mean?

Every distribution of scores has a midpoint. Any number can be assigned to represent the midpoint. In the case of the IQ score, the midpoint is usually represented by 100. For each WISC-III subtest, the midpoint is represented by the number 10. Thus, if 10 is the midpoint, we know that 50% of the students will score above 10, and 50% at or below 10. In fact, we know exactly what percentage of students will score above and below any given point on the distribution. We can, therefore, convert the standard score of 10 to a percentile, and see where each student stands, compared with his or her peers. In this example, a standard score (called a scaled score on the WISC-III) of 15 is very high, falling at the 95th percentile compared with the student's peers. By contrast, if a 14-year-old student achieved a raw score of 15 on the Information subtest, then the corresponding scaled score is only 7, which is only at the 16th percentile compared with other 14-year-olds. By the use of these standard scores, then, 8-year-olds can be compared with other 8-year-olds, or with any other age group.

Table 2.2 provides some scaled scores and their corresponding percentiles. Study the table carefully to get some feel for how the scores are distributed.

Besides scaled scores and percentiles, the examiner can use the same raw score to calculate other standard scores, such as stanines, grade equivalents, and age equivalents (test ages). On the WISC-III, the standard score itself and perhaps percentiles are most frequently used. These are all manipulations of the same raw score data. For my own purposes, I prefer the use of percentiles to explain results to both teachers and parents. This preference also extends to achievement tests, where I continually see the abuse of "grade-equivalent" scores.

Once the student's raw scores on the WISC-III are transferred to the front page of the test protocol, the process of converting them to scaled scores for each subtest begins. This is quite easy, because the

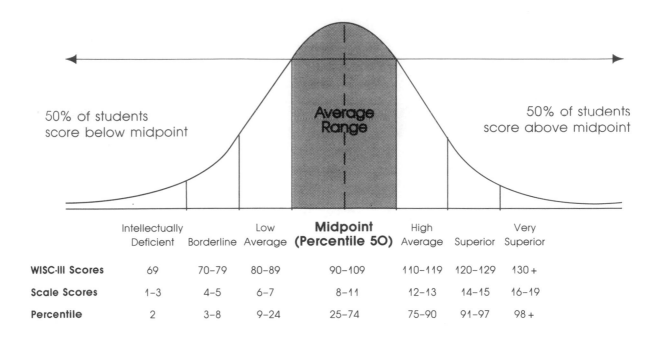

	Intellectually Deficient	Borderline	Low Average	**Midpoint (Percentile 50)**	High Average	Superior	Very Superior
WISC-III Scores	69	70–79	80–89	90–109	110–119	120–129	130 +
Scale Scores	1–3	4–5	6–7	8–11	12–13	14–15	16–19
Percentile	2	3–8	9–24	25–74	75–90	91–97	98 +

Figure 2.3. The "normal" curve for WISC-III scores.

manual provides a table for every 4 months of chronological age. The examiner simply looks up the appropriate age table, and the conversion is there. Because a new table is provided for every 4 months of age, the student is being compared with a very narrow age range, thus increasing the accuracy of the comparison.

The examiner then totals the scaled scores for the five main Verbal and five Performance subtests, and adds the resulting two numbers. By using another table in the manual, the examiner can calculate a Verbal IQ, a Performance IQ, and a Full Scale IQ on the test protocol for that student. Additional tables are provided for the index scores.

Symbol Search, Digit Span, and Mazes are "optional" subtests, which means that they can be used to calculate an IQ if results of one of the main subtests are spoiled for some reason. Although spoiling rarely happens, I always administer the Digit Span subtest because of the additional and very valuable information it provides.

The Digit Span Subtest

The Digit Span subtest consists of a digits-forward and a digits-backward series. The student is presented with random numbers and is asked to repeat them. The student is first presented with 2 digits forward, then 3, 4, and so on, up to 9 digits. There are two trials for each series. When the student fails both trials, then the backward series is introduced.

TABLE 2.2.   Percentiles for Subtest Scaled Scores

Scaled Score	Percentile
19	99.75
18	99.62
17	99
16	98
15	95
14	91
13	84
12	75
11	63
10	50
9	37
8	25
7	16
6	9
5	5
4	2
3	1
2	.38
1	.13

The student is given some practice trials and then asked to repeat 2 digits backward, then 3, 4, and so on, up to 8 digits. If the student fails both trials of a given series, testing is discontinued. Raw scores for the two tasks are then summed, and a single scaled score is determined from the raw score total.

A memory span of 7 ± 2 digits is normal for adults. This span gradually increases between the ages of 2 and 16, presumably because the child gradually acquires mnemonic strategies, such as chunking and rehearsal. Such strategies are very important in many academic subjects, including reading.

Sometimes, students perform markedly differently on the digits-forward and the digits-backward series, but this information is lost when the scores are combined and averaged. As a rule of thumb, if a student's span is greater or lesser by 3 digits on either task, that difference has some diagnostic significance. For example, if a student is able to recall 7 digits in the forward series (even on only one trial), but only 4 digits in the backward series, then the span is significantly different for the two types of tasks. The information-processing requirements for these tasks are quite different, and different explanations are possible. Some authorities (e.g.,

Kaufman, 1979) regard the digits-forward series as a sequential task, because the information is to be remembered in its correct sequence, whereas the digits-backward task is seen as a simultaneous task, because the numbers must be remembered as a group and then broken down into their constituent parts. The distinction between sequential and simultaneous information processing also has a number of educational implications, which will be dealt with in Chapter 6.

Cooper (1982) considered digits-forward a serial task involving mostly auditory sequential memory, and digits-backward as a task involving more complex mental operations. The student may rely primarily on an auditory strategy to begin with, according to Cooper, by subvocalizing the digits, then saying them aloud. If the digits go beyond 3 or 4 in number, however, this strategy is inadequate. The student should be better off trying to visualize the digits mentally, and then "pick them off" from this visual array. The examiner needs to be alert to whether the student is able to switch strategies appropriately.

Brighter students may find digits-forward boring and digits-backward more challenging. The examiner must determine which of many possibilities has the most explanatory power for each student's performance on any one subtest.

Evidence indicates that learning disabled students have difficulty employing mnemonic strategies for many types of memory and academic tasks. The Digit Span subtest of the WISC-III is no exception. A number of studies have shown that students with learning disabilities perform particularly poorly on this subtest (Torgeson & Houch, 1980). However, at this point, this deficiency cannot be generalized to reading or other academic tasks. Furthermore, there is a learning disabled group that does poorly on Digit Span, and another that does not. Nevertheless, by careful observation of the student during this deceptively simple subtest, the alert examiner can glean some hypotheses that may suggest useful remedial strategies. The student who finds it difficult to visualize digits, for example, also may not visualize when reading. However, some evidence indicates that encouraging students to visualize can improve reading ability (Carrier, Joseph, Krey, & LaCroix, 1983). Appendix 2D provides some concrete steps for encouraging visualization in the task of reading.

Finally, because memory span develops with age, it is sometimes useful for the remedial teacher and the WISC-III examiner to have some idea of where the student stands developmentally. The scaled score provides this information only for the combined tasks. Sometimes it is useful to have separate norms for the digits-forward and digits-backward series when there is a discrepancy. Fortunately, Gardner (1981) has developed tables that can be used to obtain separate norms. Also useful are Tables B.6 and B.7 in the WISC-III manual.

By way of summary, here are some recommendations from Mishra, Ferguson, and King (1985), who undertook a review of the Digit Span literature:

> First, in light of the research, the forward and backward components can be analyzed separately. Second, digit span should be considered a measure not only of memory, but of attention span, sequencing ability, symbolic or numerical skills, mnemonic strategies, and speed of item identification. Better interpretations will be made when the psychologist weighs a number of hypotheses before arriving at a conclusion. Third, the psychologist should be well acquainted with the score patterns, of which digit span is a part, that are typical of certain impairments. Finally, even in view of all the research, the practicing psychologist needs to recognize the strengths and limitations of the subtest. Despite a century-long history, indicating the importance of digit span in memory research and in mental ability assessment, it should be noted that the task, at best, provides only a glimpse into the cognitive make-up of the examinee. A sound understanding of the sources of variance accounting for differences in digit span performance is still far from attained. The recent research on the cognitive basis of digit span performance, however, has begun to reveal the nature of the association between memory, learning, and thinking. The presence of such association should help clinicians feel confident that digit span tasks are an integral part of ability assessment procedures. (p. 45)

The relationship between auditory short-term memory, which the Digit Span subtest partly measures, and reading, is important to understand. I will discuss this relationship in more detail in Chapter 5.

Calculating and Interpreting Individual Subtest Strengths and Weaknesses

Once the scaled scores are entered on the front page of the WISC-III protocol, the examiner should calculate a Verbal and Performance scaled score average. The examiner totals the scaled scores of the six Verbal subtests, divides by 6, and rounds the answer to the nearest whole number. The same is done for the Performance Scale. The averages are then graphed on the profile and the corresponding percentiles are determined. From the graph, the student's individual strengths and weaknesses can be determined. The rule of thumb is that any subtest that deviates from the student's own Verbal and Performance average by ±3 points, should be regarded as an individual strength or weakness, depending on the direction of the difference. (Figures 1.1 and 2.2 illustrate this. Note that each subtest that deviates by 3 or more points from its corresponding Verbal or Performance mean is marked with an S for strength or a W for weakness.)

At this juncture, many examiners begin a bottom–up interpretation, giving subtest-specific interpretations to parents and teachers. This is not a psychometrically preferred practice. The subtest-specific interpretation should be used only after other hypotheses are exhausted. This makes sense. Any test with, say, 30 items, will not be as reliable as a test with, say, 60 items. Thus, if one can combine subtests and arrive at a more stable measure of presumed underlying strength or weakness, one has a stronger base for educational intervention.

The Freedom from Distractibility factor is a good case in point. There are many possible reasons why a student scores poorly on this cluster, as already mentioned. It is up to the examiner to track these down. For example, if the student scores poorly on the Digit Span subtest, then many examiners immediately invoke an explanation of poor auditory short-term memory, which is what is specifically measured by this subtest. Although poor auditory short-term memory, as evidenced by a low score on Digit Span, may enter the picture, this hypothesis should be examined first in conjunction with the score on Arithmetic. If auditory short-term memory was an observed factor on the Arithmetic subtest and is also upheld by teacher observations, then that interpretation is far more reliable than one based on the Digit Span subtest alone, and becomes the primary explanation for the low score on Factor III. Again, I urge the reader to look to Kaufman for more information on these subtleties.

The Average Range

Figure 2.4 shows Danny's completed profile on the WISC-III. Danny's Full Scale IQ is 97 ± 6. That score falls at the 42nd percentile. Is this average?

Many people, parents and teachers included, have the mistaken idea that an IQ of 100 is "average." A score of 100 is in the average range, because it is the midpoint of the distribution of scores. However, not all IQ scores are exactly 100, even though 100 is the single most frequently occurring score. In fact, 50% of IQ scores fall below 100. Many people are amazed when I tell them this fact, but it could not be any other way. Have another look at the bell curve illustration (Figure 2.3) to verify this point.

Once a midpoint is set, then half the scores will fall at or below and half above this number. In the case of the IQ, half the IQs of all children in North America will be below 100, and half will be above 100. If the midpoint is 10, as for the individual WISC-III subtests, then half the scores will be below 10 and the other half above 10. If grade-equivalent scores are used, then half the students will score below and the other half above grade level. This does not mean that half the students are "underachieving," however.

Then, what is average? One can see why there could be disagreement over this (and there is), because average has to be a range of scores rather than a single score. Some people like to set the average score as any score falling between 85 and 115 on an IQ test. About 68% of all children score between these two numbers. Because this is a majority, then, so the argument goes, that range should be considered average.

I consider that range too generous, however. A score of 85 falls at the 16th percentile. My experience has been that students whose IQs consistently fall in the 80s have considerable difficulty with mainstream academics, especially in the upper grades. To call such students average is to set an unreasonably high expectation for them, one they most often cannot attain, at least in mainstream academic programs.

The average range I prefer is 90 to 109. This includes 50% of all students, and is—in my experience—a more realistic standard. Even 90 is only at the 25th percentile and is, therefore, a minimum-standard average. By contrast, an IQ score of 109 falls at the 74th percentile.

Different states and provinces may set different criteria and cutoff scores for average and other classifications, thereby affecting who goes into what special classes. This variation can be confusing to parents and professionals alike, but nothing can be done about it from a theoretical perspective. Because average is an arbitrary range, people will argue over it. Many diagnostic problems therefore ensue. To use an uncomplicated example, a student whose IQ falls at 85 and who shows a 2-year lag in reading might be labeled learning disabled in one state or province, and a slow learner in another.

In the elementary grades, these differences may not cause serious placement problems, because resource room teachers frequently serve a heterogeneous group in terms of IQ scores, and are usually more interested in helping any student with difficulty than students with specific diagnostic labels. However, many placement (and, therefore, funding) problems are created by the often arbitrary nature of these classifications. Later on, in junior high school, for example, a prevocational program, rather than a learning disabilities program, might be more suitable for the student. If the law says that the student is average, however, because of an 85 IQ, then the student could be placed in yet another learning disabilities class with more attempts to "catch him up." This unnecessarily frustrating situation is discouraging to the parent, student, and teacher. The student's practical needs are not likely to be met, and the end result could be more frustration and dismal academic progress. Such is the "stuff" of endless educational lawsuits. Thus, it is important to make special placement based more on needs than on scores.

WISC-III™
Wechsler Intelligence Scale for Children – Third Edition

Name _Danny_ Sex _____

School _____ Grade _____

Examiner _____ Handedness _____

Subtests	Raw Scores	Scaled Scores					
Picture Completion	19		11		11		
Information	10	8		8			
Coding	23		5				5
Similarities	15	12		12			
Picture Arrangement	26		11		11		
Arithmetic	12	6			6		
Block Design	26		9		9		
Vocabulary	28	13		13			
Object Assembly	21		9		9		
Comprehension	18	11		11			
(Symbol Search)	14		(7)				7
(Digit Span)	10	(7)			7		
(Mazes)	16		(10)				
Sum of Scaled Scores		50	45	44	40	13	12
		Verbal	Perfor.	VC	PO	FD	PS

Full Scale Score **95**

OPTIONAL

	Year	Month	Day
Date Tested			
Date of Birth			
Age	9	2	20

	Score	IQ/ Index	%ile	95 % Confidence Interval
Verbal	50	100	50	94 – 106
Performance	45	94	34	87 – 103
Full Scale	95	97	42	91 – 103
VC	44	106	66	99 – 112
PO	40	100	50	92 – 108
FD	13	81	10	74 – 93
PS	12	80	9	73 – 93

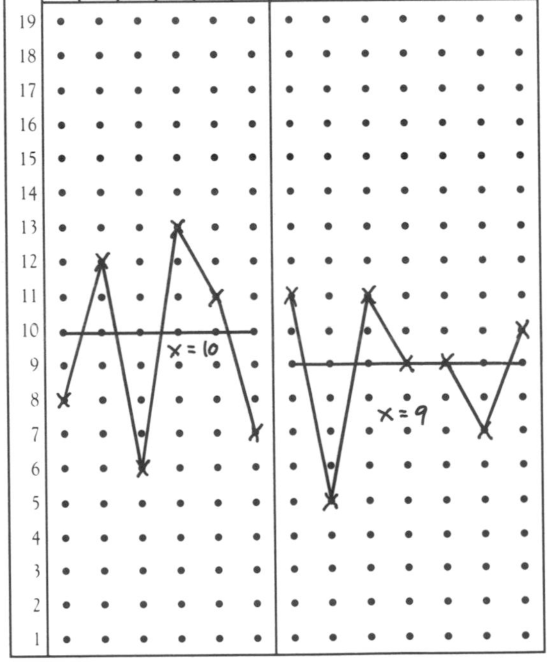

IQ Scores			Index Scores (Optional)			
VIQ	PIQ	FSIQ	VCI	POI	FDI	PSI
100	94	97	106	100	81	80

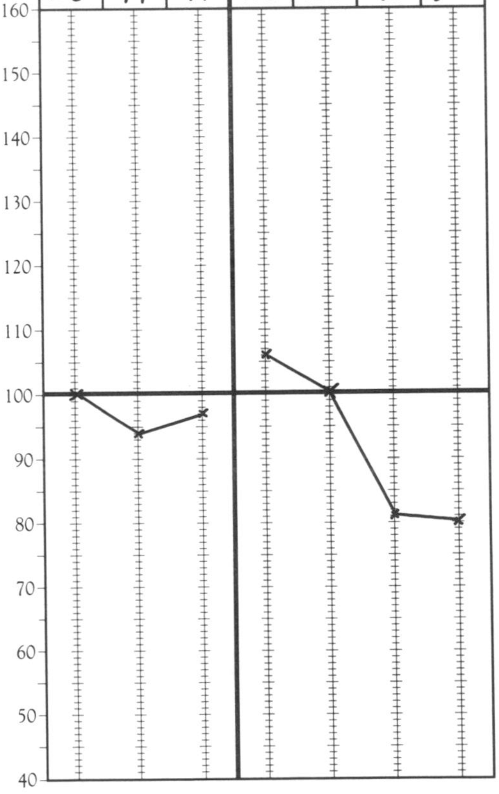

Subtest Scores

	Verbal							Performance						
	Inf	Sim	W Ari	S Voc	Com	W DS		PC	W Cd	PA	BD	OA	SS	Mz
	8	12	6	13	11	7		11	5	11	9	9	7	10

X = 10

X = 9

THE PSYCHOLOGICAL CORPORATION®
HARCOURT BRACE JOVANOVICH, INC.

7 8 9 10 11 12 A B C D E

09–980004

Figure 2.4. Danny's profile.

Standard Error of Measurement

The standard error of measurement is another very complicating factor. I have reported Danny's Full Scale IQ as 97 ± 6. The "± 6" is known as the confidence interval. The confidence interval is based on the standard error of measurement, which in the case of the WISC-III Full Scale IQ is only 3.20. The values of the confidence intervals change depending on the degree of certainty sought (i.e., 90% or 95% confidence). Values for both levels of confidence are provided in the WISC-III manual and technically are based on the standard error of *estimation* (see Wechsler, 1991, p. 169).

This technicality aside, the confidence interval is an acknowledgment that, when we measure intelligence, we are not using a precise instrument. When we measure a table using a tape measure, the error of measurement is very small, because length is measured on an equal-interval scale, which has a zero point and exactly equal portions between the units of measurement. Something that is 4 meters long is exactly twice as long as something that is 2 meters long. Furthermore, we can meaningfully add, subtract, multiply, or divide those measurements.

For IQ scores, however, the error measurement is quite large. In the case of 97 ± 6, what we can say by way of interpretation is, "If I were able to test Danny 100 times today (without his getting tired, or there being a large practice effect), then 95 times out of the 100, his Full Scale IQ score would fall between 91 and 103. This is the range of confidence that can be placed in the obtained score of 97. Notice that the range of confidence is quite large, extending from percentile 27 to 58. However, this score is still clearly within the average range. The WISC-III manual provides the confidence intervals for each of the IQ scores and the indexes. These intervals are based, as mentioned, on the standard error of estimation rather than the standard error of measurement. The examiner can choose either the 90% or the 95% confidence interval and then enter the numbers on the front of the protocol.

Now suppose that the obtained score was 88 ± 6. The range of confidence in this case is 83 to 94 (percentile 12 to 37), or low average to average. Does this student have average ability? At this point, it is a judgment call; the examiner must consider other factors, such as the particular distribution of sub-test scores (remember that if the profile splits into factors, then the Full Scale IQ is regarded as an underestimate) or how well motivated the student seemed to be when taking the test. The examiner might feel that the obtained score was an underestimate for a variety of reasons, or there might be a school or a state policy on the matter. In any case, the judgments are not easy to make at times, and must be done with great care—particularly if placement in a special program is at stake.

An IQ score is not an equal-interval score, as is evident in Table A.4 in the WISC-III manual. An IQ score of 95 is percentile 37, and a score of 100 is percentile 50; this is a difference of 13 percentile points on an IQ difference of 5 points. An IQ score of 125 falls at the 95th percentile, but an IQ score of 130, which is also 5 points higher, falls at the 98th percentile; this is a difference of only 3 percentile points at this upper end of the distribution. At both the higher and the lower ends of the distribution, the percentile differences are much smaller. Thus, one cannot say that a student whose IQ score is 120 is "twice as bright" as someone whose IQ score is 60. In a mathematical sense, a standard score of 100 is twice as great as 50 (and that is why standard scores are used in the first place: one can add, subtract, multiply, or divide them meaningfully); however, the underlying dimension of intelligence is not, as far as one can tell, equal interval. What can be meaningfully said is that the student whose IQ is 120 is at the 91st percentile compared with students his or her own age, whereas the student who scores 60 is only at the .4 percentile for his or her age. The first student obviously ranks higher than the second (even taking the SEM into account), but he or she does not rank twice as high as the second student, because the underlying mental energy is simply not equally distributed, nor does it have a zero point.

Grade-Equivalent Scores

If what I have said about IQ scores makes their measurement seem "fuzzy" and imprecise, the situation is even worse for so-called grade-equivalent standard scores. These scores are not used in interpreting IQ scores, but because they are used in almost all standardized achievement tests, it is worthwhile spending a little time discussing them.

For example, the *Peabody Individual Achievement Test–Revised* (PIAT-R) (Markwardt, 1989) is a well-standardized achievement test, which means that many students from a variety of age, sex, and socioeconomic groups from across the United States were used in the standardization sample. Different norms for different age groups are found in the PIAT-R manual. Unfortunately, grade-equivalent norms are most frequently reported, but almost never with the accompanying SEM, even though they should be. This is the examiner's responsibility.

Consider, for example, that 8-year-old Li-Shing achieved a raw score of 51 on the PIAT-R Reading Comprehension subtest when tested in October of the school year. The manual provides tables that allow the examiner to report grade-equivalent scores, age equivalents, percentiles, and/or standard scores. In Li-Shing's case, a raw score of 51 is converted to a grade-equivalent score of 3.1, or the beginning of Grade 3, which is where the student is actually placed. The corresponding standard score is 100, which means her score falls above 50% of the students her own age; also, it is the midway mark in terms of ranking.

Most likely, the examiner will choose to report Li-Shing's results using the grade-equivalent scores, and Li-Shing will be reported to be reading at the beginning Grade 3 level. This statement is misleading in a number of ways. The SEM, for instance, is almost never reported. In the case of the PIAT-R and most achievement tests, this is very significant. The PIAT-R manual provides the SEM for standard scores for each of the subtests at different grade levels. In this case, the SEM for the standard score is ±4 (age-based). That means that there is 68% confidence that the standard score from 96 to 104 contains Li-Shing's "true" standard score. This means her score on Reading Comprehension could be anywhere from the 39th to the 61st percentile, which is quite a range. In terms of grade-equivalent scores, the range of confidence is from 2.8 to 3.6—almost a full grade level! (And the 68% confidence level is regarded as quite low!) To increase the confidence level, the confidence range must be increased. So, to achieve the 95% confidence level, the range of confidence is changed to ±8 for the standard score, and the range of confidence in the equivalent percentiles is now 30 to 70! For the grade-equivalent scores, the range of confidence is now 2.5 to 4.0. I suppose the lesson to be learned is that test scores are not very precise, even though educators work under the illusion that they are.

Additionally, the PIAT-R items, like the WISC-III items, are chosen for their "discrimination power," not their match to any particular third-grade curriculum. Li-Shing may or may not be reading third-grade material at her school. It depends on what is being taught, and where. Canadian students, for example, typically score higher than their U.S. counterparts on achievement tests. (Thus, for Canadian students, I recommend the *Canada Quick Individual Educational Test*, Wormeli & Carter, 1990.)

Based on this information, is Li-Shing functioning at grade level? This question is not easy to answer because the test results have a large error band, and the test content does not necessarily match the school's curriculum. Thus, a grade-equivalent score of 3.1 on the PIAT-R does not necessarily mean that Li-Shing comprehends third-grade reading material. Obtaining a more accurate picture of where she does comprehend requires a more in-depth reading assessment. Usually, an informal reading inventory is used for this purpose. However, no matter what reading test is used, formal or informal, someone has made a judgment of where the student stands, relative to some standard or criterion. A criterion-referenced test is one that specifies how a student performs against that criterion, whereas a norm-referenced test, such as the PIAT-R, compares the student's scores against a norm. Both kinds of achievement tests are useful, despite these interpretation problems. However, the results of norm-referenced tests should be reported with the same care and caution that IQ tests should be. "One-shot tests"—either IQ or achievement—can be terribly abused, and so can the results.

I think it is very important to get some idea of what children can be expected to be doing by way of reading and mathematics at different grade levels. Check your local, state, or provincial curriculum guides for assistance. I have found the *Barbe Reading Check Lists* (Barbe, 1961) to be very useful.

The last point worth mentioning is that a grade-equivalent score of 3.1 on the PIAT-R is a midpoint if the student is tested at the beginning of the third school year. That means that 50% of all students in the beginning of the third-grade year will score below 3.1 on the PIAT-R when administered at the beginning of the third-grade year. Unfortunately, this fact has often been misinterpreted to mean that any student who scores below grade level must be underachieving, perhaps even learning disabled. However, as discussed in the next section of this chapter, notions of underachievement and the diagnosis of learning disabilities are complex issues. In the meantime, remember that 50% of all students will score between the 25th percentile and the 74th percentile—the average range—on any achievement test.

Despite their drawbacks, I strongly urge the use of percentile scores rather than grade-equivalent scores on achievement tests when results are being discussed with parents or teachers. However, because the practice of using grade-equivalent scores is very entrenched, if they are used in feedback to teachers and parents, the audience needs to have some understanding of the large confidence intervals that are involved.

Many kinds of reading and achievement tests are used in the United States and Canada. However, these tests, like IQ tests, should never be used alone for major decisions such as placement in special classes. They can be helpful to the classroom teacher for screening pupils who may have remedial needs, and to assist in flexible grouping for classroom instructions. Results can also be entered into regression equations (see Reynolds, 1989) and, again, prove helpful in placement decisions, but they should not be used alone for such decisions.

DIAGNOSING LEARNING DISABILITIES IN NORTH AMERICA

The question of whether a student is learning disabled is one that school psychologists must regularly answer. To tackle this question, the school psychologist must be very sophisticated in understanding the major issues involved. A thorough discussion of the matter would take me too far off my main topic, however, so I deal here with only a few of the most relevant issues.

The first issue is to define *learning disabilities*. There are four key components found in almost every definition of the term. The following definition is currently used by the Learning Disabilities Association of Canada (1991):

- Learning disabilities is a generic term that refers to a heterogeneous group of disorders due to identifiable or inferred central nervous system dysfunction. Such disorders may be manifested by delays in early development and/or difficulties in any of the following areas: attention, memory, reasoning, coordination, communicating, reading, writing, spelling, calculations, social competence, and emotional maturation.

- Learning disabilities are intrinsic to the individual, and may affect learning and behavior in any individual, including those with potentially average, average, or above-average intelligence.

- Learning disabilities are not due primarily to visual, hearing, or motor handicaps; to mental retardation, emotional disturbance, or environmental disadvantage; although they may occur concurrently with any of these.

- Learning disabilities may arise from genetic variations, biochemical factors, events in the pre- to perinatal period, or any other subsequent events resulting in neurological impairment. (p. C-5)

The key concepts found in this definition and in many others of learning disabilities are that (1) learning disabilities involve a *discrepancy* between the student's (average) ability and achievement in one or more academic areas or (2) thinking (processing) skills. *Difficulties in information processing* or other psychological processes, such as attention, perception, memory, reasoning, and conceptualization, are also part of the problem. (3) This definition also contains an *exclusionary clause* stating that learning disabilities are not to be confused with mental handicaps, emotional disturbances, or other handicapping conditions. Also, (4) a presumed *central nervous system dysfunction* is specified. Every one of these four key concepts has at some time posed tremendous difficulty to legislators, school administrators, school psychologists, special educators, and parents.

The second major issue in this area, and an even more difficult one, is the ability to meaningfully operationalize and measure learning disabilities. An extremely helpful article on the complexity of the measurement issues was written by Cone and Wilson (1981). In it, they identified eight variables that must be considered in using any expectancy formula, which is the usual method whereby a diagnosis of learning disabilities is made. Also very helpful is an article by Reynolds (1984–1985) in *The Journal of Special Education*. His state-of-the-art (as of 1989) computer software program for severe discrepancy analysis is available from Trainware (Neshaminy Plaza II, Suite 101, Bristol Pike and Street Road, Bensalem, PA 19020). I have found it to be quite helpful in some cases.

Until there is some consensus regarding a standardized format for the diagnosis of learning disabilities (and there may never be), school psychologists involved in this tricky business can only follow their own existing state or provincial guidelines. Some of these guidelines are more sophisticated than others. The Iowa Department of Public Instruction, for example, has gone a long way in the right direction for their own school population. School psychologists in North America should support any efforts made in their own areas for adoption of similar procedures.

As it stands right now, however, the diagnosis of a learning disability is almost whimsical in many places. Almost everyone who is assessed could be labeled learning disabled, simply because of the broadness of the definition. The classification also depends on who does the assessment, what tests are used, and how the results are interpreted in light of local guidelines. Most often, only one or two of the eight critical variables identified by Cone and Wilson are incorporated into the diagnosis, which makes the task of the school psychologist even more arduous, aside from all the "political" ramifications of making such a diagnosis. The process is complex and can be extremely frustrating to professionals and parents alike. Therefore, when discussing results with parents, the school psychologist must be sure to tell them which definition of learning disabilities and which guidelines are being used to make the judgment. Also, the school psychologist must become very familiar with the intricacies of discrepancy assessments. The diagnosis of learning disabilities is not like a medical diagnosis of, say, appendicitis, in which the "patient" presents certain "symptoms," which then require a specific course of action, such as an operation. That kind of precision simply does not exist in the field of learning disabilities. Also, the psychologist should try not to become too embroiled in the political issues or to "take sides." His or her primary role is to assist the child.

Affective Considerations in WISC-III Testing and Reading Success

School psychologists regularly receive referrals on students who exhibit behavioral and academic problems. As part of the assessment process, the psychologist often administers the WISC-III. This basic test provides valuable information about a student's cognitive functioning in relation to his or her peers. Equally important, however, is how the student reacts to the structure of testing itself. Students' dispositions, attitudes, and reactions during the testing are as much clues to remediation as the test scores themselves. In addition, teachers and parents often provide extremely valuable observations about the student's behavior and reactions to academic tasks.

THE EFFECT OF STRESS

It is very important for the school psychologist and special educator to have some grasp of how the student's cognitive and affective states interrelate. For this purpose, I have organized this discussion using *stress* as the umbrella term. Other theoretical frameworks for discussing a student's behavior may be equally valid, but stress is an area in which I have some expertise, and with which I am comfortable. I will digress into a number of areas that are only indirectly related to WISC-III testing, per se, but that certainly belong to the broader category of the psychology of reading. The school psychologist

should be aware of these areas because, directly or indirectly, they come into play when making recommendations about a specific student.

In Chapter 2, I suggested that intelligence is a kind of mental energy, a sort of primary substance that guides actions in orderly and purposeful ways. This energy is fueled by the emotions. Thus, intelligence and emotion are closely intertwined, giving rise to observed behavior. From the behavior, we infer the *valence* of the emotion and the purpose of the action. This valence may be positive or negative. Every time a student sits in front of an examiner to be tested on the WISC-III, both intelligence and emotions are being tapped.

In this respect, mental energy is closely akin to Hans Selye's (1974) concept of "adaptation energy." Selye was a pioneer in the area of human stress research. He suggested that humans are all born with a finite amount of such energy, which could be squandered quickly, or used appropriately to prolong lives. He also discovered that, in response to stress, humans go through three distinct stages:

1. Alarm reaction
2. Resistance
3. Exhaustion

These stages constitute the general adaptation syndrome, or GAS. People all have a level of homeostasis, or balance, that they try, at all times, to maintain. When homeostasis is threatened, the stress response is triggered automatically. The body mobilizes its resources to "fight, flight, or freeze"— whatever the appropriate response is to the situation. Continued triggering of the stress response uses up more adaptation energy.

Stress, itself, is the amount of adaptation energy required to adjust to change. Stressors trigger stress. Stressors that are strictly environmental in nature, such as excessive noise, are limited in number. By far the largest class includes the psychological stressors, in which the stress response is triggered primarily when the environment is perceived as threatening. The key word is *perceived*, because people perceive and interpret their environments very differently. In a classroom situation, for example, a teacher or a student may feel comfortable and at ease, or very uncomfortable and stressed. Because of the individual differences in interpretation of environmental stressors, Selye said that stress, like beauty, is in the eye of the beholder.

Because stress is self-perceived, Selye's work can be linked to phenomenologists such as Carl Rogers (1951) (and, more recently, James Battle, 1982), who view behavior as the result of the person's perception of reality. This point of view is helpful when it comes to trying to understand what at times seems to be very irrational behavior on the part of the student. Try to remember that all behavior has a purpose, even if the student is unable to express it. As a school psychologist, your task will frequently be to make sense of a host of behavioral concerns that the teacher or parent has about the child. Helpful sources are the *Systematic Training for Effective Parenting* (STEP) (Dinkmeyer & McKay, 1976) and *Systematic Training for Effective Teaching* (STET) (Dinkmeyer, McKay, & Dinkmeyer, 1980) programs from American Guidance Service (in Canada, this material is available from Psycan), and the book *You Can Handle Them All* (DeBruyn & Larson, 1984). I find the latter useful, even though it is quite a cookbookish format. The model used in the book's introduction is very helpful and is actually an extension of Rudolph Dreikurs's (1950) work.

In my experience, it is better if teachers have the opportunity to actually practice some of the techniques that arise from any theoretical viewpoint, rather than simply reading about them. I teach practicing teachers an accredited in-service course called Self-Esteem and Discipline at the University of Calgary. The approach I use is largely phenomenological, and I have structured it in such a way that teachers must implement and keep track of strategies they learn in the course over a period of time in their classrooms. The positive results that the teachers experience are very encouraging to me and to them. When implementing some of the ideas from this book, school psychologists and teachers should remember that they are going through a process. If an idea is not working out, they should try to fine-tune it in some way before abandoning it. Also, they should try talking to colleagues about it, since their feedback often helps immensely.

Everyone requires some stimulation to function. Because the environment constantly makes demands on people, even when sleeping, some degree of adaptation energy is always required. Therefore, people are always under some degree of stress. Too much stress on a continual basis could lead to burnout, whereas too little stress can lead to "rustout." In my book, *Teacher Burnout and What to Do About It* (Truch, 1980), I discuss the effects of stress on teachers and students.

The concept of stress is one I find useful when discussing students with learning difficulties. Anxiety is, of course, related to stress—a close cousin, one might say. Some people, including children, can be described as high-anxious or low-anxious. Too much anxiety can interfere with good performance in school when the student perceives the situation as threatening, such as during a test. Some anxiety is helpful, as long as it is not too much. Of course, test anxiety can affect performance on the WISC-III as much as on academic tests. It is important that students be made to feel as comfortable as possible during the WISC-III administration, to optimize their performance. The examiner needs to keep in mind, however, that too little anxiety may be equally debilitating. The examiner should note any subtests on which anxiety obviously affects performance. (Anxiety is more likely on the timed subtests than on the untimed ones.) If anxiety is a factor, then the Full Scale IQ is likely to be an underestimate of the student's ability, and this should be strongly stated in the report.

Excessive stress also can reduce students' ability to concentrate, thus affecting their learning and academic performance. The result becomes a vicious circle. A lack of success in reading, for example, would automatically lead to the perception of threat on the part of the student. When the stress response is triggered, then the student is "alarmed," and energy is required to resist the stressor. This requires much expenditure of energy (both intellectual and emotional) to "fight" or "run away" or "freeze" ("block") the reading task. Such students spend vast amounts of energy avoiding the task. Their concentration is impaired. They may become excessively active in the threatening situation, or they may withdraw and "play dead." Abrams and Smolen (1973), two researchers who have related the GAS to reading failure, stated, "The child who experiences initial reading failure . . . is ultimately subjected to emotional stress. If the reading failure persists, it is almost inevitable that frustration, reduced attention, anxiety, and a real sense of helplessness will be involved" (p. 465).

Students with reading disabilities may take flight or play dead (regarding the reading task), as already mentioned. Psychologically, this behavior can be measured through arousal levels. Reichurdt (1977) found that the running-away group was the less seriously handicapped in reading. The most disabled readers were the playing-dead group, who showed a sharp drop in arousal as they progressed into a reading task. What develops is what Downing and Leong (1982) called the "failure–threat–anxiety syndrome" or "emotional blocking," a phenomenon that every school psychologist and special educator has witnessed. This syndrome leads to four major categories of emotional reaction:

1. Overt fear reactions—these include anxiety, depression, the fear of making mistakes, of failure, and of people discovering how poorly the student has read.

2. Nonspecific emotional behaviors—these reactions include submissiveness, indifference, inattentiveness, laziness, daydreaming, and evasive actions such as joining gangs or playing truant from school.

3. Escape behaviors—these include withdrawal, psychosomatic disorders, rigidity, and various avoidance strategies. The student who makes an irrelevant remark

(showing that he or she was not paying attention to the task) fits in here. Another escape behavior is to "play stupid."

4. Attack behaviors—these reactions include restlessness, antisocial behavior, and a rebellious attitude, as well as aggressiveness. (Downing & Leong, 1982, pp. 242–243)

School psychologists need to be very cautious about attributing every negative emotion/behavior that a student has to reading failure. Not every case of reading failure is accompanied by such reactions, for one thing. For another, sometimes antisocial behavior is quite independent of reading failure. Finally, home factors may be equally important, if not more so, than the reading failure per se. Many students model aggressiveness or daydreaming or any of the reactions listed above on what they see at home. Also, the intense disappointment and anxiety that a parent feels in reaction to a slower reading child is almost always conveyed to the child, aggravating the situation immensely.

Lansdown (1974), for example, mentioned three negative parenting styles in relationship to reading:

1. Expecting too much of a child and . . . communicating this to the child. Children faced with this attitude see themselves as constantly failing to meet parental demands.

2. . . . Being actively hostile towards a child. . . . Given this situation, the child is likely to fail at everything, except possibly crime, since [he or] she has so firmly received the message of [his or] her worthlessness.

3. . . . Being indifferent. (p. 103)

I have met all these kinds of parents in my consulting work. Although some parents can be excessive in their parenting styles, most of them merely want their children to be able to read.

Although school psychologists and educators must be careful about attributing every negative behavior to reading failure, it is equally important to become aware of how damaging it is to a child's psyche to be unable to read. Children can resort to some rather extreme behaviors to avoid or cover up the reading disability. The behavior itself is then seen as "the problem," when in fact it is the *result* of the problem.

SUCCESS–PROMISE–CONFIDENCE: BREAKING THE STRESS CYCLE

The opposite of the failure–threat–anxiety cycle, according to Downing and Leong (1982), is the success–promise–confidence one. I feel that this cycle is very aptly named.

Reading or arithmetic failure undoubtedly can cause untoward—and in some cases extreme—stress for many students. The emotional factors can be either secondary or primary in reading failure. In either case, more use of the student's adaptation energy is required. Such failure almost always destroys self-confidence, and cannot be ignored when developing Individualized Education Programs.

A number of methods can be used to break into the vicious stress cycle and make it a more "virtuous" one. The focus of these interventions can be on the student or on the teacher. I will discuss the following general categories, with which every school psychologist needs to be familiar:

1. Classroom atmosphere

2. Success

3. Setting goals (purposes) for reading

4. Attitudes

5. Self-efficacy

6. Deep relaxation

In addition, the reader should be aware of an excellent publication called *Stress and Reading Difficulties* (Gentile & McMillan, 1987) from the International Reading Association. The book's authors succinctly described the effects of stress from students' reading failure (primarily in terms of fight or flight), provided an informal means of assessing such behaviors, and suggested a detailed lesson plan for reading intervention with appropriate guidelines for the flight-and-fight type of student.

Classroom Atmosphere

Any classroom, particularly a special education one, needs to convey a sense of security to the student. This responsibility rests primarily with the teacher, but may be tied in to the general atmosphere of the entire school. Not only should the atmosphere be comfortable, but it should convey a sense of purpose and mutual respect in which learning can and does take place. The classroom atmosphere also is related to teacher effectiveness. Effective teaching can be described as follows:

> Effective teaching involves "direct instruction," which refers to academically focused, teacher-directed instruction using structured materials. Teaching goals are clear to pupils, time allocated for instruction is sufficient and continuous, coverage of content is extensive, performance of pupils is monitored, feedback to them is immediate, and questions are easy enough that they can produce many correct responses. High-achieving classrooms tend to be convivial, democratic, and warm. (Taylor & Taylor, 1983, p. 370)

Effectiveness is very difficult to measure, but one way is simply to rate one's teaching behaviors. In Appendix 3A, I provide three self-rating scales that break the larger concept of effectiveness into three smaller components: classroom management, instructional organization, and teaching presentation. All the variables listed in the scales have been shown in research studies to relate to teacher effectiveness. The scale itself is not standardized, however, so no cutoff scores have been established for the various categories. However, any teacher wishing to use the scale will find most of it self-explanatory. Low scores on any one variable suggest that it is an area in which improvement can take place. I have found that even excellent, experienced teachers have found the rating exercises useful.

All of the variables in the scales are behaviorally oriented. If a teacher practiced all of them faithfully, but did not like students, that teacher would be an effective technician. However, nothing substitutes for human sensitivity when it comes to reducing stress for a student. Although all of the variables listed are under a teacher's direct control, the motivation to change one's teaching practices must come from a genuine desire to help the student.

Success

Another cornerstone of reading rejuvenation is success in reading. The threat of failure must be reduced for the student experiencing difficulty. This is vital during those few precious weeks of beginning reading instruction. Most remedial teachers and school psychologists, however, meet the student after 2 or 3 years or more of the failure–threat–anxiety cycle, when it is well established. The student's sense of self-efficacy (the "I-can-do-it" feeling) is sometimes severely disrupted by this point.

The following are several key ingredients to success with a student:

1. Material must be used that the student can handle. This is important in both the remedial and the regular classrooms. A number of approaches to teaching reading may be successful, including radical, mainly bottom–up departures, such as DISTAR (Engelmann & Osborn, 1987). A variety of approaches can be used, however, and, in view of recent research evidence, much more attention needs to be given to restoring decoding for students with learning disabilities.

2. No approach will work if it is implemented without regard for the student's delicate feelings. Therefore, feedback and the correction of false self-attributions are very important. The student should have some visual form of feedback, such as a chart that focuses on the student's success. Because students and teachers live in a day-to-day world, it is difficult to keep a broader perspective and appreciate gains being made unless some form of feedback is implemented. The teacher should also stress, whenever the opportunity arises, the student's strengths, new interest in reading, and differences in personality and behavior. Such feedback is vital to strengthen or rebuild a weak self-concept. Smith (1969) found that

students who charted their progress in word recognition and comprehension performed as well as students who received money as a reinforcer, and better than those who received reinforcement in the form of teacher praise and free time. However, reinforcers may be necessary for some students in the short term, and school psychologists and teachers must continually seek new reinforcers, as they tend to lose their potency with time. One system that can help is a "reinforcement menu" for each student. (Appendix 3B is an example menu of potential reinforcing activities.) If reinforcers are to be used with students, they can be asked whether they find each listed activity to be something they "Like," something they "Don't Like," or something that is "OK." With such a list, most students will indicate several activities that they would work for. Although the general aim is to have students enjoy reading for its own sake, not for anything else, the initial step sometimes cannot be taken unless the vicious stress cycle is first broken.

3. Communication with parents about a student's success is also very important. Too often, parents of special students hear only negative reports about their children. Some parents will no longer even come to the school, and many others who do come do not want to. They, too, are caught in the failure–threat–anxiety cycle. Remember that positive feedback takes time. A student or parent will not change overnight. Relapses into old thinking, feeling, and behavior patterns will occur.

A weekly or even daily report card can provide the school–home communication that is vital in some situations. Figure 3.1 shows one that I have occasionally recommended. Happy faces or check marks can be placed in the columns. Sometimes, contracts or contingencies are attached. For example, a student who achieves 6 of 12 possible marks receives a hug and 15 minutes of "private time" with Mom and/or Dad in the evenings. Three

Daily Report Card

Name _____

Period	Academic OK	Academic Not OK	Social/Behavioral OK	Social/Behavioral Not OK
1	_____	_____	_____	_____
2	_____	_____	_____	_____
3	_____	_____	_____	_____
4	_____	_____	_____	_____
5	_____	_____	_____	_____
6	_____	_____	_____	_____
7	_____	_____	_____	_____
8	_____	_____	_____	_____

Comments:

Figure 3.1. Example of a daily report card.

"good" days out of the week might mean a special treat, such as breakfast at a fast-food restaurant on Saturday. These numbers are arbitrary, of course, and depend on the student's baseline behavior.

Such feedback systems can work well, provided all parties are willing to participate. The standards must be set low enough initially that the student can achieve and feel successful, but they should not be so low as to be without challenge. The standards can gradually be increased as the weeks go on. Reinforcers can also be varied.

One frequent problem with such systems, however, is that the student may tell the parent that he "forgot" his report card at school when a "bad day" has occurred. The parents should be warned about this possibility beforehand and asked to call the teacher by phone if it happens.

Such incidents should be dealt with in a matter-of-fact way, such as by saying to the student, "Well, yesterday wasn't such a good day, but today is a new day. Let's try again." Unfortunately, I have seen many teachers and parents abandon these systems after one or two bad days. Persistence is the key to success, and so are expectations. By abandoning a workable system at the first hitch, participants are showing that they expect instant and

permanent results. There is no such thing. (Such systems do require parent cooperation, which in some cases is not possible. In such situations, school personnel must do what they realistically can within the school environment.)

If the system is obviously not working, something else is needed. Sometimes more can be accomplished by focusing on the class as a whole, rather than an individual student. Teachers often complain that setting up a reward system for one student is unfair to the rest of the class. The "Good Behavior Game Plus Merit" bypasses this objection because it involves the whole class. This approach has been shown to be effective in (a) reducing disruptive behaviors and (b) increasing academic output (Darveaux, 1984).

Implementing this game is reasonably easy. The class is divided into three or four teams, with approximately equal numbers on each team. If two or three disruptive students are in the class, they can be distributed equally among the teams. (One teacher who used this game had three teams, called W, I, and N.) The students are then told that they will be playing the game for a special treat at the end of each day. Usually, 15 minutes of free time is a reinforcer that most students will gladly work toward. They are told that each time a student breaks a classroom rule, a mark is made on the chalkboard against that person's team. The majority of classrooms I have seen have had lists of classroom rules. The list should be short, and it is best if the students are involved in devising the rules initially. As a rule of thumb, every team should strive for five marks or less per day. This criterion approach is very important. Do not turn this game into a competition to see "who gets the least marks." Every team should be able to win by getting five marks or less each day. In fact, all teams can win, some might win, or none may reach the daily criterion.

What saves this approach from being strictly a demerit system is the introduction of "merits," which are handed out by the teacher any time during the day for academic or academically related work. For example, the teacher could announce a merit to a student who raises a hand to answer a question (especially if the student rarely does so), or to anyone who completes the math assignment or achieves some other relevant academic task in the classroom. Merits can be recorded by a team captain (students can take turns being captain). For every five merits earned by a team, one mark made against the team for violating a classroom rule can be erased. Thus, even if a team has more than five marks against it in a day, the team still has a chance to earn free time by earning merits.

This system covers the two major components of every classroom—behavior and academics. I have recommended use of the game in a number of situations where one student in a classroom was particularly disruptive. Because the system treats that student as a member of the entire class, and does not focus on that student, it can have effective results. Many teachers in my self-esteem courses have used this game (or variations of it), the majority with very good results. In the classroom research study from which the game was developed, the effects were dramatic and very positive in improving on-task and limiting disruptive behavior for the target students, and for the class as a whole. Results were equally dramatic in terms of improving assignments completed.

However, this system can break down and may need "fine-tuning" from time to time, especially if there is a "bad" day for everyone, or if the teacher is insensitive, or if a disruptive student continues to be disruptive. Remember not to throw out the baby with the bath water.

Setting a Purpose for Reading

According to Downing and Leong (1982),

> To become flexible readers, students must know the purposes of reading and must learn to adjust their skilled acts to different purposes. . . . The reading process actually changes with the purpose of the reading act. Hence, children need to practice reading for different purposes, and they need to practice changing from one type of purpose to another if they are to develop that flexibility of timing that is such a noteworthy feature of superior skill performance in reading. (p. 254)

Mature, adult reading serves various purposes, such as diversion and escape, information getting, and self-development, but these differ from the purposes given to students in a classroom, which include the following:

1. See how fast you can read a passage

2. Look for the specific sequence of events

3. Look for specific details or content

4. Read for general comprehension

5. Look for specific wording

6. Read for spelling errors

Setting a purpose, however, also influences what a student will remember from a text. A student who is asked to read a passage for the sequence of events will remember those better than any other aspect of the story, and will forget other aspects. Asking questions in advance focuses a student on getting only certain information.

Smith (1972) listed five very general suggestions for training students to be purposeful readers:

1. Pupils should be fully aware of the purposes of materials they have been asked to read. They should know what they are expected to obtain from their reading.

2. Pupils need to learn how to set their own purposes. For some pupils, this will be a gradual process. Teachers will need to continue setting purposes for such pupils and guiding them in setting their own goals. Help the student verbalize the purpose if he or she has difficulty.

3. Pupils should be given a wide variety of purposes for reading, both in their reading periods and in their content-area subjects.

4. The kinds of questions should be asked in harmony with the purposes for which students have been asked to read.

5. Students should be taught how to read for different purposes. In this respect, students could be asked to read a passage several times, each time for a different specific purpose, such as

   a. To grasp the main idea

   b. To note the important details

c. To answer specific questions, which are posed in advance

d. To evaluate what is read

Helping students to set goals and listen for certain details has been shown to be very helpful for listening comprehension of students with learning disabilities (Maier, 1980). Thirty-two learning disabled students between the ages of 8 and 12 showed a significant improvement in their ability to recall a story (a folk tale was used) with higher-level understanding over another group of learning disabled students who were simply asked to listen to the story. The procedure was simple. Each child was asked to focus on three things: what the problem was, how it was solved, and what lesson was to be learned from the story. The reading of the story was broken into three parts, each introduced by the comment, "Now, in this part, watch for. . . ."

This simple procedure is an excellent way for the teacher to help build meaningful cognitive structures and sustain attention for a group of students with learning disabilities. It is an example of a highly structured, teacher-directed strategy. As with many such procedures, students eventually need to learn to internalize the process for themselves.

In summary, then, setting a purpose for reading reduces a student's stress because it reduces the uncertainty that often accompanies reading. In the long term, mature readers need to be able to read for a variety of different purposes, depending on the text. The strategies for this must be directly taught for students who have difficulty. Reading purpose and reading comprehension are closely related, because purpose affects what is remembered and comprehended. John McNeil's (1984) book, *Reading Comprehension: New Directions for Classroom Practice,* provides excellent reading comprehension strategies for the classroom or remedial teacher. His strategies are all language-immersion oriented (see Appendix 2A). McNeil divided the strategies into those for the prereading phase of reading, those that can be used during reading, and those that can be used after reading a passage. He suggested different strategies for narrative and expository texts.

The teaching of reading comprehension strategies is of maximum benefit, however, only when the student can already access the print (i.e., can decode effectively). I will discuss this point in more detail in the next chapter.

Attitudes

Attitudes on the part of students, parents, and teachers alike, are very important in trying to establish a success–promise–confidence cycle. Attitudes of hostility, of passivity, toward task persistence, toward certain social situations, toward authority, and so on, frequently surface during administration of the WISC-III. The examiner needs to follow up on any noted, important attitudes by discussing them with the teacher or parents. In this section, I am mainly concerned with attitude (defined by Downing and Leong, 1982, p. 260, as "a tendency to behave in a particular manner toward a certain object or situation") toward books and reading. There is a surprising dearth of research on the topic, despite the fact that every teacher and parent mentions its importance. What has been done has focused on sex differences, home background, and school experiences, all of which tend to shape attitudes in some way.

In North America, girls typically have more positive attitudes toward reading than boys, and typically score higher on attitude scales (Kennedy & Halinski, 1975). Also, more boys than girls have reading problems. That difference is not found in all cultures, however. In England, Morris (1966) found no differences in attitudes toward reading between 10- or 11-year-old boys and girls. I feel it is important, especially in the beginning stages of reading, for teachers to try to select materials that are interesting to each child. Therefore, a wide range of materials, with boy and girl protagonists and a wide range of interests, should be present in the classroom and supplemented by the school's library. Even physical surroundings convey attitudes. Surroundings that include reading corners, reading lofts, pillows, couches, paperback racks, and so on, may encourage reading. A pleasant environment for reading should be a consideration for remedial classes, as well as for regular classes.

One factor that may be more important than all others in developing a child's attitudes toward reading, is the home environment. Hansen (1973) provided some detail as to which home environment variables make a difference:

> The one factor that stands out from all the others is the role of the parent in being involved with his child's reading activities. Working with homework; encouraging, helping select, and discussing his reading; reading to him; assistance in looking things up in dictionaries, and encyclopedias; and setting reading goals were more important than the mere provision of materials. (p. 98)

Also, very surprisingly, Hansen found that parents themselves did not have to be avid readers to have children who were. Their *active interactions* with the child's reading made the difference.

Teachers and school psychologists are continually asked by parents what they can do to help at home with a student who has a reading problem. I have taken some of the research findings I have discussed and composed a letter that might be useful for parents of elementary-age students (see Appendix 3C).

Of course, the school is a vital factor in students' development of good reading skills and positive reading attitudes. A host of studies have been done on teacher attitudes, methods, materials, school characteristics, and so forth, and their effects on reading achievement and attitudes. Downing and Leong (1982, Chapter 13) provided an excellent discussion and summary of the findings. The following is a list of some of the more important considerations. (Details and the supportive research studies can be found in Downing and Leong's book.)

1. Physical features of the school:

   a. There is a significant correlation between good reading attainment and better physical facilities, such as size of classroom, type of furniture, presence of a sink, storage space, type of lighting, playground equipment, general appearance, and noise pollution.

   b. Urban schools and large schools were found to have better reading attainment.

   c. Poor reading is associated with poor provision of books.

2. School system characteristics:

   a. Despite popular belief, there is evidence that people learn languages better when they are older, rather than younger. Children do better on almost all aspects of language acquisition when they are older. Reading readiness, then, is the gap between the child's level of development and task difficulty, and has little to do with mental age, per se. Children can be prepared for the reading task, and the task can be modified so that the reading readiness "gap" can be narrowed at any time. After all, we can teach chimpanzees some elementary reading. Very young children can be taught to "read," provided that the task is sufficiently modified. On this point, Taylor and Taylor (1983) made a very interesting observation: Because reading is a receptive language task, then it should be easier for a child to learn to read than to speak!

   In any case, there is no optimal age, it seems, for learning to read. Public law in North America demands that all children enter school by the age of 6. Some of these children will already be reading, many will learn to read at age 6, and some will have difficulty. Nothing would change if the entrance age were raised or lowered. No matter what the age, the child has to be prepared and/or the task modified so that success can be experienced and stress reduced.

   b. Class size *can* make a difference to reading attainment, as long as teachers individualize instruction and actually spend more time interacting with pupils. Reducing class size, even to as low as 15 to 1, by itself, makes no difference to reading achievement and attitudes. It makes a difference only if teachers take advantage of it.

c. The lock-step grade system seems to be damaging to pupils who lag behind. Multiage groupings of various kinds, along with individualized instruction, are better alternatives.

3. Teacher characteristics:

a. Teachers need to be aware that their own beliefs regarding gender of the pupils (the boys-versus-girls problem), desirability of the language spoken by the pupils, and the pupils' apparent "brightness" or "dullness," might have an influence on actual reading attainment. This is the so-called Pygmalion Effect. How it operates is explained by Downing and Leong (1982):

> Under normal conditions, teachers' perceptions of their pupils may be in some way signaled to the children as feedback about their behavior, progress, and so on. In this way, pupils may be guided (or misguided) about the effectiveness of their responses in the tasks of reading instruction (294).

So the message seems to be: "Watch your expectations. Your students will live up to them."

Despite contradictory research about this, my experience has taught me that expectations are indeed very important—if not on reading or cognitive scores, then certainly in behavior. Some temperamental students who may be difficult to begin with, most assuredly act much worse when the message, overt or covert, is: "I don't like you!" I have repeatedly had pupils referred to me where the teacher is quite prepared to describe the student in very negative terms. This is a signal to me that at least part of the problem lies in negative expectations and beliefs the teacher has about the student, as in actual behavior. Somehow, this vicious circle must be interrupted. The teacher must be involved in a corroborative way in the planning and implementation of a program designed to change such attitudes. A sure sign of frustration is when the teacher says: "I've tried everything. Nothing works!" In these situations, try to get the ball rolling in a more positive way.

b. According to Downing and Leong, "Teachers teach best when they are teaching by what they believe to be the best method." They also wrote,

> There is no real consensus of research conclusions on the comparative advantages of the various alternative [reading] methods described.... Usually, research evidence is selected to support the current fashion when its latest method comes into vogue. Then, a new series of researches tends to develop to "prove" the value of the "new" trend. The reader will find little help from research quoted in support of current methods from one country to another.
>
> So, whether a teacher emphasizes a "meaning-based" or "code-based" approach to reading depends on whether she feels that reading is "taught" or "caught." At this moment, there seems to be much research to support the view that a "code-base" in the early stages of reading is vital. (p. 295)

At any rate, the important message to be gleaned from this section is that teacher beliefs about how reading should be taught are more important than any theories about how it should be taught, or any administrator's or consultant's beliefs or edicts or policies or government laws about how it should be taught. There is no way to change a teacher's methods, then, unless the teacher is receptive to the changes suggested, and is directly involved in planning and implementing such changes. Many reading consultants and school psychologists are frustrated when their best planned prescriptions are ignored or bypassed. Part of this problem comes from the fact that the teacher is not the initiator. Follow-up of all referrals is one way to help ensure that recommendations are followed. The other way is to have an administrator in the school take charge and see that recommendations are carried out in the absence of the consultant. Schools that have such a mechanism in place, do, in my experience, initiate more positive individual change for students than those that have no such mechanism. Such schools are more positive places for consultants, also, because the consultants know their work is taken seriously. (This Pygmalion Effect operates at all levels!) However, the best method is when the consultant works with a teacher. The school psychologist must be prepared to make a variety of suggestions from different theoretical perspectives. Together, the consultant and the teacher arrive at a plan of action. If teachers are involved in the planning, they will more likely implement change.

An effective approach that incorporates this principle is to have a school-based intervention team whose purpose is to work in consultation with the teacher who makes the referral. The team (comprised of appropriate people from the school) brainstorms a variety of alternative intervention strategies to solve the problem. The strategies are arranged according to priority, the resources needed to implement it are identified, and the teacher attempts to carry them out. The intervention plan is written, and a date is set for reviewing its effectiveness. Only after all school-based alternatives have been exhausted, is a referral made for in-depth assessment and intervention from resource personnel outside the school. The concept is very exciting in terms of professional development for the teacher, and assures that school psychologists will receive referrals only after a number of pre-referral strategies have been attempted. Readers interested in pursuing this idea in depth are urged to consult the docu-

ment, *Intervention Assistance Teams: A Model for Building-Level Instructional Problem Solving,* by the National Association of School Psychologists (1986).

c. A teacher's personality has some bearing on both effectiveness and reading achievement. Enthusiasm is a very important ingredient, as is the ability to develop a sympathetic, friendly, and understanding relationship with pupils. In one extensive review of the literature on this topic, Hamachek (1975) concluded,

> Effective teachers appear to be those who are, shall we say, "human" in the fullest sense of the word. They have a sense of humor, are fair, empathetic, friendly, enthusiastic, more democratic than autocratic, and apparently more able to relate easily and naturally to students on either a one-to-one or group basis. Their classrooms are something akin to miniature enterprise operations in the sense that they are more open, spontaneous, and adaptable to change. Teachers who are less effective apparently lack a sense of humor, grow impatient easily, use cutting, reducing comments in class, are less well integrated, are inclined to be somewhat authoritarian, and are generally less sensitive to the needs of their students. (p. 304)

According to Downing and Leong (1982), students who have reading difficulties make better progress in classes where teachers "more frequently displayed behaviors allowing for student freedom of expression, use of pupils' ideas, and praise" (p. 297). In other words, less stress makes for better learning.

Self-Efficacy

Self-efficacy is the personal judgment a student has about how well he or she can perform in certain situations that might be ambiguous or stressful. The student who lacks a good sense of self-efficacy usually displays it sometime during WISC-III administration. This is the student who says, "I don't know," too quickly, or the one who says, "I can't do this," after making a feeble effort on Block Design or Object Assembly. The examiner must observe how the student reacts when task difficulty increases.

Many students give up before they even start a task. Such students are "blocking." *It is more comfortable for such students to fail a task by never making an effort, than it is to make the effort and fail.*

The student's perception that "I can't do it" may or may not be accurate, depending on the task's difficulty. These students, however, have a poor sense of judgment in terms of matching their perceptions of their ability to do the task with the task itself. It is possible to realign such faulty perceptions.

First, devise an "I Can Do It" scale of some type, with a 0 to 100 grading, perhaps like the one shown in Figure 3.2. Because the student says, "I can't do it," immediately upon seeing a task, this perception needs to be the focus of change. Next, teach the student how to use the scale. It is best to initially use a nonacademic task, such as trying to jump a real or imagined line. Make sure the first jump is so easy that the student is certain to jump it. Then, have the student make a guess on the "I Can Do It" scale. Of course, she should circle the 100% certain line. Then have the student jump the line. If the student does so, *praise her correct perception.* It is not important whether the student actually can broad-jump; what is important is to "align" her perception with her efforts. Keep moving the line back

so it becomes more difficult for the student to jump it, but each time before she jumps, have her take a guess and commit herself to paper on the scale. If this is all done in the context of a fun game, then its novelty alone is sure to attract the interest of any student.

Once you are certain that the student can use the scale correctly, the next step is to apply it to academic tasks. Arithmetic problems may be easier, initially, than others, but the method can be used with basically any short task. If the task is very long, such as a research project, then the student may be overwhelmed. In that case, break down the task into smaller steps, and have the student apply the scale to each sequence of steps.

Prior to the student's doing the task, have her make a prediction, as with the jumping, as to how certain she is that she can or cannot do the work. In each case, praise her whenever she is consistent with her appraisal, and reward her with a point. Let her accumulate points toward a self-selected reinforcer. In most cases, students go from about 40% certain to 70% or 80% certain. It is also appropriate to introduce goal setting and rewards (the combination of the two works better than either one alone) into this program. The important point is that the student must begin to feel some degree of self-competence and confidence in her own predictions (Schunk, 1984).

Closely allied to self-efficacy are self-attributions. What kind of "self-talk" is a student using when he feels he cannot do a task? In more severe cases, the student simply puts down his head and refuses to do it. The self-talk is probably very simple—"I can't do it"—although the message to the teacher

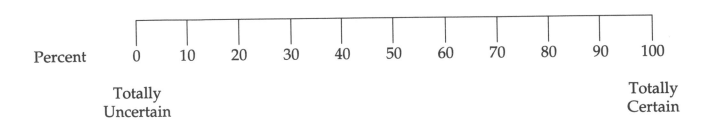

Figure 3.2. Sample "I can do it" scale.

might be, "I won't do it" (it is very important that the student not be labeled as lazy because of this behavior).

Such students may begin to respond more appropriately through modeling. A fairly detailed procedure that I have found to be quite helpful is given in Appendix 3D. Using this procedure twice a week (in half-hour sessions) for 3 weeks, Shelton, Anastopoulos, and Linden (1985) found that it made a very significant difference in helping learning disabled students persist in the face of difficult reading tasks. By changing the self-attributions (internal self-talk), it is possible to change the student's persistence on given tasks. The work becomes less stressful, and the vicious circle is broken.

Deep Relaxation

Deep relaxation is an important component of an anxiety/stress-reduction program for students. Physiologically, deep relaxation is the opposite of the stress response (Benson, 1975). During stress, the body's natural response is to prepare to fight or run. Heart rate, blood pressure, oxygen consumption, and breathing rate increase. Even brain-wave changes occur, with high-frequency beta waves predominating. This response, or parts of it, can be activated many times in the course of a day, and each time, some use of adaptation energy is made.

Unfortunately, there is no automatic relaxation response. The relaxation response must be taught, learned, and practiced frequently for it to become natural for a person. The relaxation response, which is the opposite of the stress response, is measured physiologically by lowered breathing rate, lowered heart rate, and "de-excited" brain waves.

A number of techniques can produce the relaxation response. I classify them somewhat arbitrarily as inside–out or outside–in, although top–down and bottom–up might be equally appropriate terms. An inside–out (top–down) technique is one that uses primarily a mental or conceptual device to produce a physiological response of deep relaxation. A mental or conceptual device might be a mantra, such as is used in the transcendental meditation (TM) technique, or it might be an imagined scene, such as those employed in various visualization techniques. The primary reason I call such

techniques inside–out or top–down is because the major focus is on the mental side. The physiological aspect of deep relaxation is a by-product of the process.

An outside–in (or bottom–up) technique, on the other hand, focuses primarily on the physiological process to eventually produce a state of deep relaxation. A good example is Edmund Jacobson's (1938) progressive relaxation. In this technique, the person learns to tighten and relax various major muscle groups in the body in a progressive, systematic way. In so doing, the relaxation response is elicited.

Although many techniques are a combination of inside–out and outside–in procedures, usually one or the other predominates. All the techniques have the potential to bring a host of positive changes. The choice of technique is an individual one. Evidence indicates that the effectiveness of a technique is enhanced when a person has the choice of which one of several options to use. (My preference is the TM technique.)

A number of studies have been done showing the effectiveness of relaxation techniques for a variety of student problems. Of special interest here is a study from Germany (Frey, 1980) that showed that reading improvement was better when a deep relaxation technique was added to a remedial program than when the remedial program was used alone.

Appendix 3E includes two deep relaxation scripts that originally appeared in my book, *Teacher Burnout and What to Do About It* (Truch, 1980). Because no teacher who hopes to use deep relaxation with students or classes should do so without having some personal experience, the first script is basically for teachers themselves (and for older students). The second script is useful for younger students.

If a teacher decides to use deep relaxation, it should be incorporated on a regular basis into the daily routine of the classroom. Several teachers with whom I have worked in establishing such procedures with their classes, found that first thing after opening exercises in the morning and first thing in the afternoon after lunch break were good times to use deep relaxation with the whole class. All the teachers reported good to excellent results, particularly with more restless students. The calming influence in the class as a whole was very positive, they found.

A number of programs introducing deep relaxation to students are available commercially. One program, *Coping for Kids* (Herzfeld & Powell, 1986) is a valuable resource, particularly for counselors. Deep relaxation and numerous other topics related to stress reduction are covered in a very practical format.

Three Reading Models and Some Links to WISC-III Testing

Reading is the magic key that unlocks the door to the wonderland of stories and information.

(Taylor & Taylor, 1983)

In this chapter, I digress somewhat from direct WISC-III interpretation for a discussion of the reading process. School psychologists need to be aware of the reading process for obvious reasons. However, I will stress again that neither is the WISC-III a reading test nor is the school psychologist necessarily in the best position to make judgments about a student's reading. That is usually the province of the reading specialist, although not all school districts have reading specialists (or even school psychologists, for that matter). Thus, if information regarding the student's reading is required, then an informal reading inventory (together with miscue analysis) will reveal much about how the student actually reads. At best, the WISC-III can complement such testing, so WISC-III results and observations should, when possible, be combined with the reading specialist's test results and observations to provide the most creative, useful recommendations and programming for a particular student. In reality, the knowledgeable school psychologist sometimes makes recommendations about reading, and the knowledgeable reading specialist

sometimes makes recommendations that are more the province of the psychologist. Teamwork always brings better results for the student.

When the WISC-III is administered, some underlying cognitive processes are being tapped. To the extent that these processes also underlie the act of reading, then there may be some direct overlap between reading and the WISC-III. I will discuss some of these "links" in this chapter and in the remaining chapters of this book. Forging such links, however, is an art, not a science. Although all attempts to directly diagnose specific reading problems from particular profiles have not been very fruitful, that does not mean that individual profiles should not be carefully examined to see what fruits may be there.

WHAT IS READING?

Reading is an act of "language." It *is* language, specially coded via a particular alphabet. The purpose of reading is to derive meaning from print. Whether material is read for leisure or for information, meaning is paramount. The same is true of oral language. People do not listen for sounds of language, but rather for meaning. Nevertheless—and this is a very important point—we do have to learn the sounds of our language prior to speaking it.

Unlike the learning of language, which is acquired and developmental, and which seems to unfold in an incidental way, reading is more directly taught. Although for some children, reading seems to unfold in a process similar to the learning of oral language, these children definitely form a small minority. Various studies have shown that only about 1% to 4% of children read prior to school entry. On the average, such students have measured IQs of around 120 (percentile 91), although a very few children with IQs in the 80s also may read prior to school entry.

Taylor and Taylor (1983) pointed out that reading is an act of receptive language. Because receptivity precedes production, it should be possible to teach children to read before they speak. To further support this claim, congenitally deaf children have been taught to "sign" their first words at 6 months of age, months before normal children utter their first words. Indeed, there are recorded cases where parents have taught their children some sight words before they spoke. (Note, however, that this strategy does not involve actual decoding.) The desirability of children's learning to read at such an early age may be another matter. Where the parent is extremely motivated and the child quite bright, then perhaps no harm is done. For the vast majority of children, however, reading must be directly taught. In North America, this happens at age 6, although there is nothing magical about that age. For some students, perhaps, waiting until they are 8 or even 9 might be better.

Learning to read, then, is learning to extend oral language through the special code of the written language. Taylor and Taylor (1983) described four levels of learning to read (adapted from pp. 354–355):

1. *The Letter and Word Recognition Level*— This level comprises two sublevels. The "lower" sublevel involves matching a visual pattern, a "word" or logograph, to an object. Chimpanzees can be taught to read at this level, as can 10- to 12-month-old human infants. One of the earliest and most common examples of reading at this level would be recognizing the "golden arches" (the McDonald's hamburger sign). The "upper" sublevel involves matching the visual pattern of the whole word with a sound pattern and recognizing its meaning through language. Thus, when the child sees "car," he or she also knows that this particular letter combination represents something that can be identified in the real world. This stage can also be called reading "environmental print." If the child is actually decoding, then true reading can begin.

2. *The Sentence Reading Level*—This level can occur quickly, once a child knows only a few words, even only two words (e.g., "She ran"). Chimpanzees can attain this level of reading, and some of the sentences they can produce are quite complex—an eloquent testimony, I think, to the mental energy (*g*) that is common to purposeful beings. (Perhaps it is even possible to "speak with" and "read" many forms of life, once the correct "codes" are discovered.)

3. *The Story Reading Level*—At this level, children can read stories with plots, and prediction, which is such an integral part of mature reading, enters the picture. Children can anticipate a particular sequence of events and guess what comes next.

4. *The Independent Reading Level*—This is reading for its own sake. Once a person has learned to read, he or she can read to learn. This level of reading is probably not open to chimpanzees, but it is open to humans as young as 3 years old in some cases. The mature reader at this level is constantly making predictions and deriving meaning. At this level of reading, the meanings of words and phrases are primary. The process of decoding is very automatic, and understanding or comprehension becomes paramount.

Reading at this level also involves thinking. "Thinking" is a larger universe than "speaking," and larger still than "reading," although all are related. In terms of relating reading to intelligence theory in general, I have already discussed how language is largely related to intelligence—indeed, is an integral part of it. Therefore, reading would be expected to be largely related to intelligence as well, and it is. As I have pointed out, reading and intelligence are correlated, but not in any one-to-one way. There are some intelligent children who have never learned to read very well, and some children who read well but are not very intelligent. However, all children can learn to read, even though the level of reading that is open to, say, a child with a measured IQ in the lower trainable mentally handicapped range may be considerably lower than for someone with an IQ in the gifted range.

The process is similar, however, for people at all levels of intelligence. Mature reading, according to advocates of whole language, involves an interaction of top–down and bottom–up strategies, as well as an interaction between the reader's knowledge (schemata) base and the text itself. For example, the student who does not know anything about coyotes has either no "script" or a weak "schema base" to draw upon when asked to read and answer questions related to any text about these animals. Reading comprehension depends on this interaction between concept-driven and data-driven processes. According to John McNeil (1984),

> A concept-driven process is a "top–down" strategy in which the reader's goals and expectations determine what is said. In contrast, data-driven processing occurs when the reader attends to the text and then searches for structures (schemata) in which to fit the incoming information. The reader monitors the information from the bottom–up, replacing initial expectations with new ones triggered by the text. Different words and sentences suggest new expectations.
>
> Good readers approach text with top–down strategy, and then use selected schemata to integrate the text, discarding schemata that are inappropriate. Less able readers tend to over-rely on either a top–down strategy or a text-driven process, which has a deleterious effect on comprehension. An overemphasis on top–down processing—staying close to the print—results in word calling. (p. 4)

Learning to read, then, is a very complex act, and some radically different approaches exist for teaching reading. In this chapter, I consider three models of reading and draw out some educational implications of each. I discuss the psycholinguistic (PL) model first because it is widely subscribed to at present. Then I discuss dual coding (DC) theory. I discuss the relationship between each of these two models and the WISC-III. Finally, I introduce the bilateral cooperative (BLC) reading model and some of its educational implications. I make little reference to the WISC-III and the BLC model because of the model's similarity to dual coding.

THE PSYCHOLINGUISTIC MODEL OF READING

The PL model of reading (Pearson, 1976) emphasizes that efficient, mature reading involves the use of three types of information, working in concert (see Figure 4.1). *Semantic information* is provided by a person's knowledge of the meanings of words in the real world, including their meanings in various contexts. "Schema development" is an important asset the student brings to the act of reading. Specific schemata may be well developed or poorly developed in individual children. *Syntactic information* comes from a person's knowledge of how word order affects meaning (e.g., a "blind Venetian" versus a "venetian blind"). Every child knows that "There girl went the" does not make sense, but that "The girl went there" does. *Grapho-phonemic information* (i.e., sound–symbol relationships) is the knowledge of phonics, or how sounds and print go together. It is not the same as being able to state phonics rules; it is being able to use the rules when reading, even if the person cannot state them explicitly.

According to Pearson (1976),

> Real reading occurs when all three kinds of information are utilized in concert. Efficient readers maximize their reliance on syntactic and semantic information in order to minimize the amount of print to speech (call this decoding, phonic, or grapho-phonemic analysis) they have to do. They literally predict what is coming and get enough grapho-phonemic information to verify their predic-

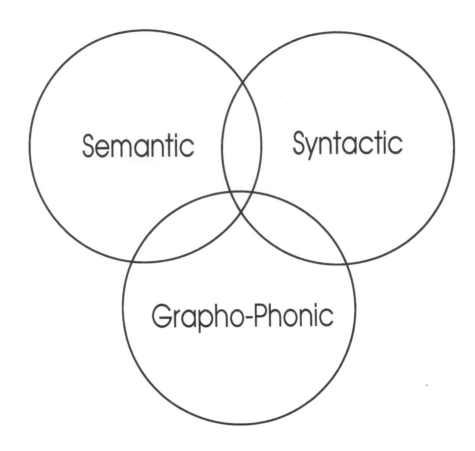

Figure 4.1. Schematic diagram of the psycholinguistic reading model. From "A Psycholinguistic Model of Reading" by P. D. Pearson, 1976, *Language Arts, 53,* p. 310. Copyright 1976 by National Council of Teachers of English. Reprinted with permission.

tions. A single letter or a single syllable may be enough information to verify their predictions. For example, it doesn't take much visual or grapho-phonemic information to confirm the hypothesis that "telescope" fits into the sentence, "The astronomer looked through the ____." Readers must vary the amount of attention they pay to the graphic information according to their familiarity with the content. . . .

Novice or poor readers are so bound up in their search for phonic information that they have little chance to attend to meaning. Good readers, on the other hand, because they attend to meaning, may often make unimportant errors in decoding words accurately. (p. 310)

As you can see, the model views top–down and bottom–up skills as occurring in concert, but places more emphasis on top–down processing.

Indeed, one aspect that is given little attention in this model, but emphasized in others, is auto-

maticity. "Automatic" behavior can be performed without attention, once it is learned. For example, like all drivers, when I first learned to drive a car, my attention was directed to the gear shift, clutch, brake, and listening to instructions. I had no attention left for listening to the radio. Once driving became an automatic habit, however, I was able to do several things at once—listen to the radio, flip stations, converse with a passenger, and drive. My "automatic pilot" took over. There are many examples of automatic habits in everyday life, including reading. The fluent reader, for example, may read a passage but not attend to its meaning. His decoding skills are on "automatic" at that time, but his mind may wander, perhaps to the nice-looking girl he met that morning in class. Samuels (1976) stressed the need for automatic behavior in reading:

For years, teachers of beginning reading have been satisfied if their students were accurate in decoding words. While it is true that accuracy in decoding is necessary in reading, it is not a sufficient condition. In order to have fluent reading and good comprehension, the student must be brought beyond accuracy to automaticity in reading. (p. 323)

The bottom–up skills, then, in the PL model, usually are given secondary importance. Indeed, most reading specialists who subscribe to this model take it as axiomatic that no skills should be taught in isolation. Thus, they feel that phonics worksheets, in and of themselves, have little value.

Closely allied to the PL model is the *language experience approach*. The skilled teacher of reading is the one who brings the knowledge of language the child *already* has to the learning of reading. For example, an average 6-year-old has a speaking vocabulary of about 5,000 words, but a reading vocabulary of next to nothing. The teacher's job is to bring the strong semantic and syntactic base the child has to the task of reading. Reading is much easier if it relates to the child's own language. Thus, children might be encouraged to tell a story about an experience they just had, such as a visit to a zoo. The teacher writes the story the child tells about the experience, and then reads the story with the child. Sight vocabulary, prediction, sequencing, and phonics are integrated into the one lesson, but the primary focus is always on meaning and prediction. Any bottom–up skills training is drawn out of the lesson and practiced from it.

Prediction is an integral part of reading, from this perspective, because that is exactly what we do when we listen to someone. We listen and predict what the person is going to say next. Thus, anyone who uses language is capable of predicting. Prediction is routinely practiced, according to Kenneth Goodman and Frank Smith, by both beginning and fluent readers. Two conditions must be met by teachers to help the student to use prediction in reading. The first is that the material itself must be at least potentially meaningful for the student. If it is not, then it is nonsense and therefore more difficult for the student. The second condition is that the student must feel free to predict and to make intelligent guesses and occasional mistakes. "The worst strategy for any reader who is having difficulty understanding text," said Smith, "is to slow down and make sure that every word is identified correctly" (p. 310). Therefore, anxiety and fear of

failure, as discussed in Chapter 3, apply to the process of prediction.

Prediction is not reckless guessing. The guesser is trying to get every word right to please the teacher, with little emphasis on whether it makes sense. The guesser also overrates accuracy. Errors, says Smith, either distort meaning or they do not. If meaning is not distorted by a reading error in context (e.g., "home" for "house"), then it is of no consequence.

Prediction can be encouraged in at least four ways:

1. "First skip, and second, guess" according to Smith. That is the preferred strategy to encourage a student who meets an unfamiliar word. Striving for meaning is critical in the act of reading. The teacher can determine if the student is doing this by seeing if the student is self-correcting reading errors, using logical substitutions, indicating dissatisfaction in some way with a passage or word that does not make sense, or using his or her own dialect to substitute without distorting meaning. The students who accept nonsense—and many students with reading difficulties and disabilities do—must go back to square one. Such a student perhaps feels that, as long as he or she says anything when reading, as long as an attempt is made, the teacher will be happy.

2. Deemphasize correcting a student who has made a reading error. The student may well go back during the next sentence and self-correct, which is to be encouraged. The teacher should not say the correct word immediately.

3. If the student asks what the word is, turn it around by asking, "What do you think it is? What makes sense?"

4. Play reading games with the student. The teacher should stop suddenly when reading, or leave a word out, or make a deliberate mistake, thus encouraging the student to predict and correct while following along.

According to the psycholinguistic reading model, predicting and intelligent guessing are to be encouraged. Everything is to be "meaningful," because if it is not, the process of predicting is upset. Although the four recommended strategies may be helpful to some aspects of the comprehension process, my experience is that, in the absence of well-developed phonemic processing, they are in fact damaging to the student who struggles with decoding.

Smith's and Goodman's influences in the development of the whole language approach has been enormous. According to proponents of this approach, the following generalities about the teaching of reading have emerged:

1. Good readers do not attend to individual words of text.

2. Good readers do not process individual letters.

3. Spelling–sound translations are irrelevant for readers.

4. Little time should be spent teaching phonics.

The school psychologist should be aware that research support for the above statements is nonexistent. In fact, each of the generalities has been shown to be false (Adams, 1991). Although some of the whole language principles can be very helpful to students who already have mastered the code, the same principles can be very harmful to the disabled reader. A thorough discussion of these points can be found in my book, *The Missing Parts of Whole Language* (Truch, 1991). The importance of decoding to the act of beginning reading and its basis in phonemic processing, together with a discussion of the top–down processes, can be found in Adams's (1990) excellent book, *Beginning to Read*.

Although predicting and guessing may be helpful to someone who can already decode, in my experience these strategies are counterproductive to the student who has a decoding impairment. Because the whole process of decoding is not functioning for that student, much of his or her reading turns out to be nothing but reckless guessing. The student cannot predict or make intelligent guesses from context because he or she cannot decode the surrounding words. Apparently, then, bottom–up processing is important.

BEGINNING READING— ANOTHER LOOK

In my teaching and consulting work, I am frequently struck by the fact that, no matter what particular reading *model* a teacher or specialist adheres to, many youngsters are still unable to read, even after many years of excellent teachers. It seems to me, then, that no matter what particular theoretical position one adheres to, something is missing.

What can it be? I have said repeatedly in this book that I favor a language-rich or language-immersion approach, in both the regular and the remedial classrooms. Although I believe that top–down processing occurs in the mature reader, I believe it is possible only because of a very fluent basis in the bottom–up processes, in particular the quick deciphering of the phonics code of the language. In other words, reading is an interaction between the top–down and the bottom–up, as stated in the PL theory, but often forgotten in practice.

What is necessary in beginning reading? It is necessary for the student to crack the code. However, we know from years of experience that exposure to phonics instruction is a necessary, but not a sufficient, condition for learning to read. What, then is missing? What could be more basic than phonics?

In recent years, some articles have appeared in the research literature that have, I think, some profound implications for the teaching of reading in its initial stages. These articles have to do with the role of phonemic analysis as a necessary prerequisite to reading. Phonemic analysis is the ability to recognize and manipulate the underlying basic sound units (*phonemes*) of our language. Once that skill is mastered, the student is able to link the sounds with the symbols (*graphemes*). Thus, the ability to recognize, discriminate, and manipulate *sounds* comes first. Perhaps this is why phonics instruction is not as successful as it could be. Phonics teaching actually proceeds from the grapheme to the phoneme, and *assumes* that the child can manipulate the phonemes at an adequate level. If that ability is not present (and for many children of all intelligence levels, it is not), then the child will never become a fluent reader. The child may be able to make some progress in reading because of the variety of ways in which he or she can learn to extract meaning from print (including guessing), but may not become a fluent, self-correcting reader or a good speller (because a thorough knowledge of the sound–symbol connections is necessary for spelling).

Thus, encouraging poor readers to guess, is not the most fruitful approach. The important debate regarding a strictly top–down approach to reading, versus a bottom–up approach, has recently been discussed by Nicholson (1986). I urge the reader to consult Nicholson's article regarding the "great debate," as he calls it. The essence of the debate is this:

Goodman sees reading as a sophisticated guessing game where the efficient reader uses linguistic knowledge as much as possible, and print as little as possible. . . . Gough, however, takes the opposite view, that the reader is not a guesser, and that linguistic knowledge only comes into operation after the print has been decoded. As he puts it:

A guess may be a good thing, for it may preserve the integrity of sentence comprehension. But rather than being a sign of normal reading, it indicates that the child did not decode the word in question rapidly enough to read normally. The good reader need not guess; the bad should not. (p. 198)

Nicholson then reviewed the recent studies, which indicate that context cues do not improve word recognition. He wrote, "The irony is that poor readers, not the good, are the ones most likely to guess, simply because they are less able to decode, and have to rely on context clues to help them" (p. 199). I think that there is much to be gained from this particular analysis. In the initial stages of reading, the child may pick up a number of sight words from environmental print, as mentioned earlier. However, this particular strategy becomes inefficient as the number of words rapidly increases and the number of distinctive visual cues from the words themselves decreases. The child must then make the transition from environmental print to cracking the code (which Gough calls the cipher). To break the cipher, four conditions must be met:

1. The child must be aware of the letters in words, and their order, that is, the cipher text;
2. The child must be aware of the abstract sound segments, or phonemes, in words, that is, the plain text;
3. The child must recognize the nature of the cipher problem, that print is encoded speech, and try to solve it; and
4. The child must have sufficient data to work with—for example, the child need not only to see the printed word cat, but also to hear its spoken form. (Nicholson, 1986, p. 200)

Each of these four conditions is somewhat unnatural for the child, but must eventually be met before fluency in reading can be attained.

Condition 2, phonemic segmentation ability, seems especially important. Nicholson wrote,

To me, the value of phonemic awareness training in the context of reading instruction is that it generates an explicit awareness of the nature of the cipher, and how to solve it. Although it is only one of the four conditions for breaking the cipher, it acts like fluoride in water. That is, it seems to prevent the teething problems of learning to read.

Even more importantly, there is evidence to suggest that early attention to phonemic awareness will lead to better reading comprehension. (p. 200)

This may sound like more process training because, in a way, phonemic analysis training *is* a type of process training. However, there is much better evidence of the direct connection between this process and reading that there ever was with, say, perceptual training and reading. In fact, in one important study, Bradley and Bryant (1983) showed a causal connection between early training in phonemic awareness and reading progress. Such studies have quietly been going on since about 1972. A good body of research now supports the idea that lack of phonemic awareness and facility is linked directly to reading difficulties, and that training in phonemic processing corrects them.

There are a number of ways to teach phonemic segmentation, also called linguistic awareness or linguistic insight. One of these ways, and in my experience the most effective, is the *Auditory Discrimination in Depth* (ADD) program (Lindamood

& Lindamood, 1975). The ADD program has been the subject of some research, and the results are encouraging.

For example, the Santa Maria Bonita School District in California started their students on the ADD program in kindergarten, and continued it through the second grade. The district was able to complete the program over a 3-year period with only 15- to 20-minute daily lessons for all students. Students were instructed in small groups for the lessons by trained aides and back-up consultations.

Results have been most impressive. On the *Stanford Achievement Test,* students made very substantial gains over previous years on their reading scores. The kindergarten students jumped from the 50th to the 75th percentile on the average. Similar gains were posted in Grades 1 and 2. "The primary grades have shown the biggest increase in reading I've seen in ten years," Doug Palmer, the school psychologist, was reported as saying.[1]

Bob Howard, the principal of Arco Elementary School in Arco, Idaho, wrote in an open letter:

> I am writing to urge your consideration of the Lindamood Program, Auditory Discrimination in Depth, as a proven tool for ameliorating problems learners may have in reading, and as an excellent way to teach beginning reading. . . .
>
> The program has proven its effectiveness in improved reading scores in many ways. Students taught with the program in kindergarten enter first grade with significantly better reading skills ($p < .001$) than students in our district who did not receive such training. Students taught with the program in the first grade have significantly better reading skills ($p < .001$) than students who did not have the ADD Program techniques added to their curriculum. As the children progress through elementary school (grades two through eight), those who had ADD Program training in the first grade do better in reading than students in our district who did not have such training ($p < .0001$). . . .
>
> As you can tell, we strongly promote the Lindamood Program as a valuable teaching technique for use with all children. Our support is based on long-term experience, careful monitoring of the program's results, and the trust school and community members feel for the program.

It would seem, then, that a very valuable key for the beginning stage of reading has been found. I believe that phonemic training is a concept whose time has come. (I will have more to say in Chapter 5 on the relationship between the WISC-III Digit Span subtest and phonemic processing.)

DUAL CODING THEORY

For a decade, reading research and practice has been enormously influenced by whole language proponents. In turn, much of what has been said by whole language proponents has been driven by schema theory, which hypothesizes that abstract memory structures exist for representing knowledge. The top–down part of reading involves the employment of schemata to aid in the prediction and learner–text interaction processes.

Although many whole language theorists admit that decoding is important in the reading process, the notion of teaching phonics is given secondary importance. They fear that if a child's attention is given to the code itself, comprehension will suffer.

Indeed, in my opinion, it is possible to be a "word caller" in terms of reading. This peculiar combination of good, automatic decoding coupled with little or no text comprehension is very challenging, in terms of both understanding the phenomenon and remediating the problem. In fact, some researchers deny its existence altogether. The following case example illustrates the complexities.

I first assessed Jody when she was in Grade 2. On the WISC-R, which was used at that time, she obtained a Verbal IQ of 125, a Performance IQ of 126, and a Full Scale IQ of 128, which placed her in the top 2% of children her age in terms of cognitive functioning. On the Verbal Scale, her subtest scaled scores were all in the superior range, except Comprehension (11) and Digit Span (12). On the Performance Scale, she obtained elevated scores on all the subtests except Object Assembly (10) and Block Design (12). A note on her WISC-R protocol indicates her frustration with the Object Assembly subtest. She became fixated on the pieces and had great difficulty seeing the whole. One would not predict from the pattern of scores, however, or from the enriched background from which she came, that this child would develop academic problems. In fact,

---

throughout elementary school, she did quite well, consistently performing at the top or near the top of her class.

In Grade 7, when Jody entered junior high school, her grades began to fall, not dramatically at first. By ninth grade, however, her marks were near the middle of the class, and she was getting failing grades on some of her tests. Toward the end of ninth grade, her parents were beginning to wonder if something more was going on besides Jody's entering the teenage years. When I reassessed Jody, I found that her pattern of scores on the WISC-III had changed somewhat. Her Vocabulary score had dropped from 15 on the WISC-R to 11 on the WISC-III, Block Design and Object Assembly were again very frustrating for her, and her Full Scale IQ had fallen by 13 points to 115. This large of a drop is unlikely even in going from the WISC-R to the WISC-III.

When I looked deeper into the reading process, I discovered through the battery of tests that I administered that Jody was an excellent decoder and speller, but that her comprehension was very problematic once she was challenged by material much more complex than a Grade 4 or 5 level. She was a classic word caller. Her strong language base carried her through the elementary school years, when she could rely on language and memory, but her processing began to fall apart when the information load became much greater and the complexity of the material increased substantially. To understand Jody's problem, we need to understand how dual coding works.

Dual coding theory has been developed over the years by a number of theorists, most significantly by Allan Paivio. Figure 4.2 shows a schematic diagram of the theory.

According to Sadoski, Paivio, and Goetz (1991),

dual coding theory holds that linguistic representations can be interpreted in relation to other linguistic representations (e.g., synonyms, paraphrases, syntactic alternatives) or in relation to nonlinguistic representations of the objects, events, or feelings for which they stand (e.g., images, affects). . . . We can trade goods and services for other goods and services, or for money. Similarly, dual coding also posits associative processing within the nonverbal system (images evoking other images) and referential processing from the nonverbal system to the verbal system (images evoking languages). (p. 474)

In other words, language at any level (word, sentence, multisentence, etc.) can be stored (coded) in the verbal and/or the nonverbal system. Cross-linkages between and among the systems can then occur.

Sadoski et al. continued,

Processing in dual coding theory includes external and internal variables. External contexts, situational constraints, instructions, and so on, interact with a person's two existing symbolic systems, as determined by prior experience and individual differences. Processing can be conscious or unconscious, and often involves the transformation and recoding of representations. An important point here is that the theory does not include any *separate* abstracted structure such as a schema. Processing consists of the probabilistic activation of particular verbal and or nonverbal mental representations by external stimuli or by previously activated representations. Because dual coding does not assume the necessary existence of a schema, or processing under the guidance of a schema, it can better account for the great detail found in memory for events, as well as the flexible construction and reconstruction of events in memory. (p. 475).

Dual coding also can account for the struggle that Jody was showing with information once she hit the higher grades, and quite possibly for her drop in Vocabulary scores. Here was a student who decoded well. From about Grade 5, most people experience a substantial increase in vocabulary because they read. Many words occur in print that are not heard in speech. Contextual cues and the search for meaning help the person to infer the meaning of a word from the context. Something more must be involved, however, because even though Jody read frequently (contrary to many word callers who do not like to read), her vocabulary was not growing. When I questioned her on this point, she said that she liked reading and could get enough out of a story to enjoy it, but that she would have to reread information many times if she was asked to give specific details or draw conclusions. That is a common characteristic of most word callers who are still interested in learning.

Dual coding theory postulates that both oral and written language can be coded in the verbal system or the nonverbal system. If Jody was relying exclusively on the verbal system for meaning, then

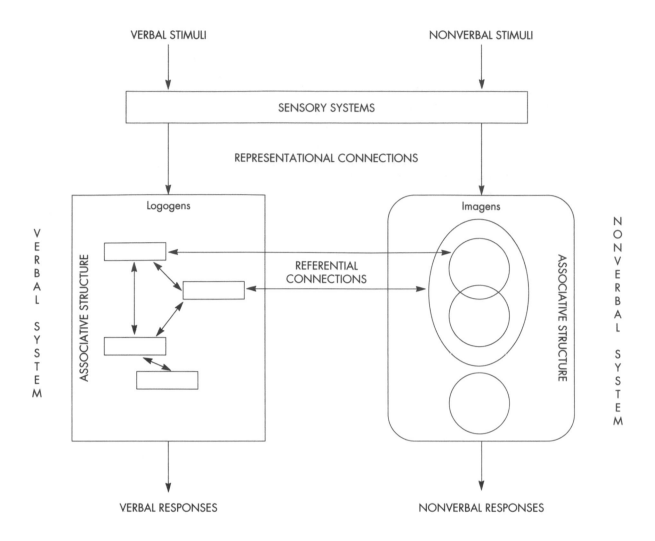

Figure 4.2. Dual coding theory: verbal and nonverbal representation systems. From *Mental Representations: A Dual Coding Approach* (p. 67) by A. Paivio, 1986, New York: Oxford University Press. Copyright 1986 by Oxford University Press. Reprinted with permission.

the richness and depth of nonverbal coding is not open to her.

From a clinical perspective, Nanci Bell of the Lindamood–Bell Clinic in San Luis Obispo, California, developed a program that links the verbal and nonverbal processing systems for more integrated processing for readers such as Jody. Bell (1991) wrote,

> Language comprehension is the ability to connect to and interpret both oral and written language. It is the ability to recall facts, get the main idea, make an inference, draw a conclusion, predict/extend, and evaluate. It is the ability to reason from language that is heard and language that is read. It is cognition.

Unfortunately, my clinical research and experience ... [suggest] the existence of a specific *language comprehension disorder.* This comprehension disorder underlies the reading process and goes beyond use of context, phonological processing, word recognition, vocabulary, prior knowledge, and background experience. It is a disorder in the comprehension of both oral and written language and is based in the sensory system. It is a weakness in creating a gestalt. (p. 13)

Bell went on to define gestalt:

> Gestalt is defined as a complex organized unit or whole that is more than the sum of its parts. The whole may have attributes that require a certain

function for each part in the whole; these attributes are not deducible from analysis of the parts in isolation. In the case of a language comprehension disorder, the weakness in creating an imaged gestalt—whole—interferes with the *connection to* and *interpretation of* incoming information. (p. 13)

The lack of dual coding, in other words, interferes with the full interpretation of the information that is possible. This leads to the bits-and-pieces reading, as I call it, of the word caller. Many bright students have described the symptoms to me as "words going in one ear and out the other." They complain of great distractibility in listening to conversations or lectures, and they tell me they must reread material many times. They often complain that they must hear instructions repeatedly before they get the idea, or that they must write down everything if someone is talking in order to rely on it later. They also can have a poor sense of direction and time, and often appear quite confused. Parents and teachers sometimes comment that such students have poor social relationships. I see all these symptoms as connecting to the oral language processing dysfunction that Bell postulated.

Indeed, I find it most interesting to see the large symptom overlap between what is currently called attention deficit disorder and an oral language processing dysfunction. At this point, however, no research study has provided information on the overlap between these conditions and their possible treatment. Based on experience, I do not feel that attention is the primary issue with children said to have attention deficit disorder. I feel it is the lack of *connection* to oral language processing that makes them so distracted. That lack of connection comes from poorly developed dual coding. The lack of visual imagery processing is a critical feature in their individual information processing.

According to Bell, one creates a gestalt through imagery:

Gestalt imagery is the ability to create an imaged whole. Readers or listeners construct mental models of the situation a writer or speaker is describing. This is the basis of language comprehension. A number of great thinkers, most notably Albert Einstein, professed to rely heavily on imagery in their work. Consider these words of Einstein: "The psychical entities which seem to serve as elements of thought

are certain signs of more or less clear images which can be voluntarily reproduced . . . this combinatory play seems to be the essential feature in productive thought—before there is any connection with logical construction of words or other kinds of signs which can be communicated to others." (p. 14)

She continued,

Imaging is a *sensory link* to language and thought. Gestalt imagery connects us to incoming language—both oral and written—and links us to and from prior knowledge, accesses background experiences, establishes vocabulary, and creates and stores information in both long term and short term memory. Vivid gestalt imaging may even be considered a "vicarious experience." Researchers in reading and imagery have produced direct evidence linking reading and mental imagery as well as studied the relationship of imagery to prior knowledge and thinking processes. (p. 14)

Bell's process of visualizing and verbalizing is a practical means of treating those students who are word callers. In this process, treatment is best accomplished by trained clinicians who work in an intensive one-on-one fashion with the student.[2]

In Jody's case, about 75 hours of treatment produced a dramatic impact on reading comprehension. When she entered 10th grade, she required further part-time tutoring from the clinicians to help her make the links between the visualizing and verbalizing process and the content areas. Her marks have risen dramatically, and she is feeling much better about herself.

In the following sections, I discuss some of the implications for school psychologists in terms of WISC-III assessments and the psycholinguistic and dual coding models.

THE WISC-III AND THE PSYCHOLINGUISTIC MODEL

In terms of the WISC-III and the PL model, the Verbal Scale and the Verbal Comprehension Index are very important in showing whether the student

---

2. For more details on the procedures and training, contact the Lindamood-Bell Clinic, 416 Higuera St., San Luis Obispo, CA 93401, phone (805) 541-3836, or The Reading Foundation, #250-200 Rivercrest Dr. SE, Calgary, AB T2C 2X5, Canada, phone (403) 279-8639.

has a well-developed language base. They also provide some clues to the student's schema base. The content of the responses the student makes often reveals in a general way his or her knowledge of semantic and syntactic structures. Any difficulties the student is having with such structures should be pointed out to the teacher and reading specialist so that accommodations and/or remediation may take them into account. The school psychologist administering the WISC-III will find that Level V analysis will be very helpful. Although I discuss this type of analysis more fully in Chapter 7, I provide one example here. Suppose the student's answer to why an apple and a banana are the same is that they both have peels. This response is not as abstract as answering that they are both fruits. By doing a language arts activity that is semantic based, such as categorization games, the teacher will help the student to "stretch" his or her categorization skills to a higher-level, more abstract way of verbal processing. Various reading activities using word banks can help to accomplish this (see Appendix 5A).

The WISC-III examiner also can observe how anxious the student is, and to what degree the student displays risk-taking and fear of failure. The student who is anxious and/or afraid to take risks may be reacting to failure experiences. The examiner who notes such behavior during the WISC-III should confirm with the teacher or determine whether it also occurs during the act of reading. If it does, then the suggestions in Chapter 3 for providing a sense of purpose in reading might be helpful. The relaxation exercises also may be useful. Determinations as to what suggestions will be best for a particular student must ultimately be made on an individual basis, taking into account each student's reactions and needs. The examiner also needs to find out whether the student has trouble decoding and/or comprehending, which can cause a major disruption in the reading process, which can in turn lead to much anxiety about reading. Poor decoding may be the result of a lack of phonemic processing skill, and poor comprehending may be the result of a lack of dual coding.

Another way in which the WISC-III and the PL model are linked, is in regard to background knowledge (schema base). Again, the WISC-III Verbal Scale may be helpful. In particular, the Information subtest provides some insight into whether the student's knowledge base is appropriate for his or her age.

The examiner can do an *item analysis* of the Information subtest to determine which items the student is actually getting wrong. In this respect, Cooper (1982) provided a valuable grouping of the content of the 30 items of the WISC-R Information subtest, which I have adapted to the WISC-III as follows:

Grouping	*Item Numbers*
Numeric Content	2, 3, 10
Divisions of Time and Sequential Processing	4, 7, 8, 9, 11, 15
Directionality/Space/Distance	14, 16, 18, 29
Self	1, 2, 12
Environment	3, 6, 17, 19, 24, 30
People	13, 20, 22, 28
History/Geography	13, 14, 16, 18, 21, 23, 25, 29
Science	5, 17, 19, 20, 26, 27

Note that some items fall into overlapping categories. In my experience, many younger students with learning disabilities who score poorly on the Freedom from Distractibility factor also do poorly on the first two categories. Nevertheless, a low score on the Information subtest does not necessarily indicate weak background knowledge. Indeed, the student's schemata may be well developed in many areas, but weaker in specific areas, as suggested by item analysis. Specific static bits of information in certain areas may not have been learned well by some students, but more dynamic background information, such as required on the Comprehension subtest, for example, may be very well developed. Remedial strategies, such as semantic mapping and semantic feature analysis, should also be considered when weak background knowledge is hampering a student's reading (McNeil, 1984).

The PL and related models, then, have much to contribute to reading instruction and remediation. The PL model is practical at the classroom level, and considerable research has been generated from it. Nevertheless, this model has its limitations and the school psychologist needs to be aware of other possibilities.

THE WISC-III AND DUAL CODING THEORY

Many school psychologists will discover a striking parallel between dual coding theory and the Wechsler scales. From the beginning, Wechsler conceived intelligence as an overall ability. He thought that intelligent behavior should be sampled from many different domains, including both verbal and non-verbal reasoning.

Dual coding theory seems to be an elaboration of Wechsler's conception, and the Verbal and Performance IQs are direct measures of reasoning and making representational connections between the verbal and nonverbal coding systems. These two systems, according to Paivio (1986), can work independently of each other, in parallel, or in an integrated manner.

For years, psychologists have seen profiles like the one in Figure 4.3 on the Wechsler Scales. This sort of profile makes the examiner wonder if he or she added the scores correctly.

Note the large discrepancy between Nicole's Verbal and Performance IQs. The difference of 29 points is statistically, and in this case diagnostically, significant. This young girl has some severe processing problems, which can best be understood in terms of dual coding theory.

First, her verbal system is very strong (relative to the nonverbal system) and appears to be about average for her age. On the WISC-III, the Verbal Comprehension Index is 93, which is in the average range. On the WISC-R, this may not have been as apparent, because one had to "tease it out" from the subtests. The WISC-III norms tables make it much easier to determine. On a first level, then, this student's Full Scale IQ is a gross underestimate of her potential.

This student can neither count nor read, yet she can discuss topics (for limited times) that show an interest and language base that is well advanced. For example, she may suddenly ask what the hottest planet in the solar system is, and then provide the correct answer as well as detailed knowledge about the solar system. She is very interested in pyramids, history, and scientific matters. However, her severe processing problems interfere greatly with basic math and with reading.

Nicole's academic needs (and they are many) can be better met if the teacher realizes that one coding system (the nonverbal) is severely hampered. Unless better linkage between the two systems occurs, much of what is done with Nicole is unlikely to have an impact. Nicole is a prime candidate for some direct therapy in the visualization–verbalization process. She needs to learn how to evoke imagery to represent language, and vice versa. Because she is so distractible, she will likely respond to short remedial "bursts" and then build up to longer periods as her processing improves. She also has a severe phonemic processing disability that is interfering with her learning of the alphabet code and that also requires some intense therapy. For Nicole, the prognosis is guarded at this point because a great deal of therapy is required before any measurable success can be expected.

According to Paivio (1986), information in the verbal system is generally organized in a sequential and syntactic way, whereas information in the nonverbal system is processed in a more parallel manner. However, interconnections between the systems allow for great variety in cognitive activity. Sadoski et al. (1991) wrote,

> a logogen [see Figure 4.2] could correspond to a phoneme, grapheme, morpheme, word, phrase, or a larger familiar unit, and an imagen could represent a natural object (or sound, etc.), a part of that object, or a natural grouping of objects. These representations form hierarchical organizations within each system. (p. 473)

Dual coding theory also explains how the major processes of decoding and comprehension might interact *separately* in the act of reading, leading to a "splitting" of the processes. Figure 4.4 demonstrates how I have schematized this splitting (Truch, 1991). The schematic simplifies the process into only four quadrants. Many readers are in between on a continuum, however, particularly in terms of the decoding process, so in this respect, the schematic is oversimplified. Nevertheless, it states the point.

Good decoding can occur without comprehension (Quadrant 2); I label this word calling. The problem of poor comprehension in the presence of good decoding may be more common than not. Unfortunately, these students often get by because they are not immediately noticeable, as I mentioned with Jody's case example. Such children do indeed "bark at print," which strikes mortal terror into the hearts of all good whole language advocates. For these word callers, the top–down approach and strategies that whole language promotes are very much needed, but can be greatly enhanced with the addition of visual imagery to the process.

Name _Nicole_ Sex _____

School _____ Grade _____

Examiner _____ Handedness _____

WISC-III™
Wechsler Intelligence Scale for Children–Third Edition

Subtests	Raw Scores	Scaled Scores					
Picture Completion	11		5		5		
Information	10	8		8			
Coding	7		1				1
Similarities	11	8		8			
Picture Arrangement	8		3		3		
Arithmetic	6	1				1	
Block Design	8		3		3		
Vocabulary	26	12		12			
Object Assembly	5		1		1		
Comprehension	13	7		7			
(Symbol Search)	N/A		(—)				—
(Digit Span)	6	(3)				3	
(Mazes)	6		(2)				
Sum of Scaled Scores		36	13	35	12	4	—
		Verbal	Perfor.	VC	PO	FD	PS

Full Scale Score   OPTIONAL

	Year	Month	Day
Date Tested			
Date of Birth			
Age	9	2	28

	Score	IQ/Index	%ile	% Confidence Interval
Verbal	36	84	14	–
Performance	13	55	.1	–
Full Scale	49	68	2	–
VC	35	93	32	–
PO	12	59	.3	–
FD	4	55	.1	–
PS				–

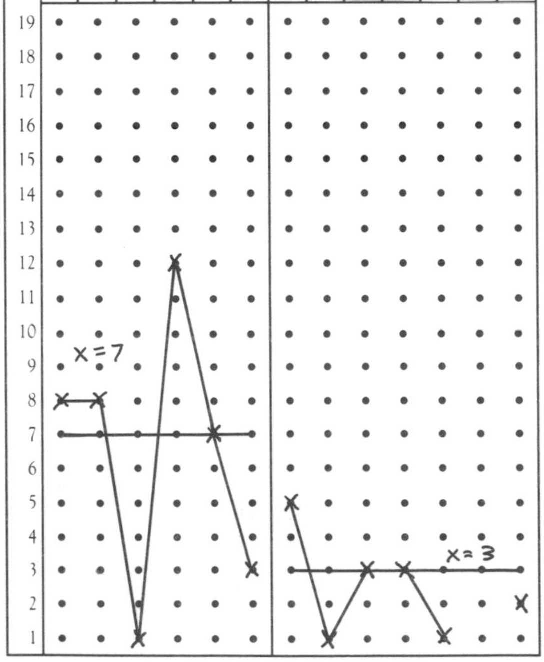

IQ Scores **Index Scores (Optional)**

VIQ	PIQ	FSIQ	VCI	POI	FDI	PSI
84	55	68	93	59	55	

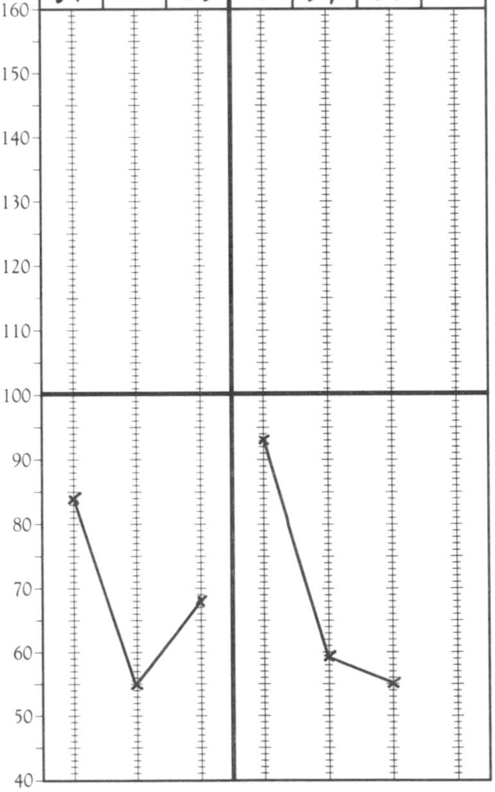

Subtest Scores

Inf	Sim	Ari	Voc	Com	DS	PC	Cd	PA	BD	OA	SS	Mz
8	8	1	12	7	3	5	1	3	3	1	—	2

THE PSYCHOLOGICAL CORPORATION®
HARCOURT BRACE JOVANOVICH, INC.

09–980004

Figure 4.3. Nicole's profile.

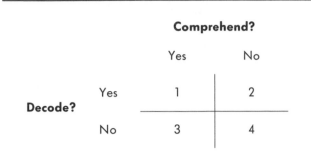

		Comprehend?	
		Yes	No
Decode?	Yes	1	2
	No	3	4

Figure 4.4. Classification of reading problems. From *The Missing Parts of Whole Language* (p. 37) by S. Truch, 1991, Calgary, Alberta: Foothills Educational Materials. Copyright 1991 by Steve Truch. Reprinted with permission.

Some students have difficulty with *both* decoding and comprehension (Quadrant 4), and different combinations of techniques are necessary to remediate the problems. Quadrant 3 represents the readers who cannot decode but who can to some extent comprehend. These students have to work hard at reading and utilize their magnificent top–down processing to their potential. However, these readers (and those in Quadrant 4) are usually the ones in resource programs. For Quadrant 3 readers, stimulation of the logogen at the phonemic level is desperately needed.

Dual coding theory provides a powerful tool to examine the needs of disabled readers in Quadrants 2, 3, and 4. It helps psychologists and teachers to understand these students' processing problems and direct the course of treatment.

Sadoski et al. (1991) stated,

Contemporary reading research has been greatly influenced by schema theory. By focusing attention on the constructive nature of comprehension and on the role of the reader's prior knowledge, schema theory has inspired a wealth of empirical research and has enriched our understanding of the nature of reading. However, because of the dominance of schema theory, the reading field has perhaps lost some of the benefits of the theoretical plurality enjoyed by the broader field of cognitive psychology. An unfortunate pattern in the development of our knowledge about reading and the teaching of reading has been a tendency toward an overemphasis on one theory or another. (p. 481)

In my estimation, dual coding theory is a powerful alternative to schema theory and dovetails nicely with the WISC-III.

CASE EXAMPLE

To this point, I have discussed a number of important considerations related to learning in general and to reading specifically, including affective states, cognitive processes, schemata, predictions, automaticity, phonemic processing, and dual coding. These factors overlap, of course, when it comes to sorting out the processing difficulties of any individual.

To illustrate this overlap, I have chosen a case from The Reading Foundation clinic in Calgary, of which I am director. This clinic offers intensive short-term therapy in the reading processes. We begin with an assessment to determine a student's processing needs, and then see that individual one-to-one for 4 hours daily for about 4 weeks. Therapy is directed to each student's primary need. For some individuals, the greatest problem is disrupted decoding; for some, it is disrupted comprehension; and for others, it is a combination. Decoding restoration begins at the phonemic level. The clinic hires professionals who have been trained and supervised extensively in the ADD program, and provides individuals with an in-depth immersion in the program. Overlap to reading and spelling improvement occurs as phonemic judgments progress.

Some cases at the clinic are extremely severe and require much more follow-up than do individuals whose processing difficulties are in the mild to moderate range. One such case is Darwin, who came for an initial assessment when he was 15 years old. His parents did not speak English well, but were very successful businesspeople. Their son was born in Canada and educated in the public school system. He had never learned to read, at least not to any appreciable degree. He had received every conceivable form of remediation, including intense and long-term resource assistance from his school, a variety of tutors, vision and eye-tracking exercises, and anything else that the parents felt might make a difference.

Darwin's WISC-III profile is shown in Figure 4.5. The profile suggests that his verbal and nonverbal systems were reasonably well developed, at least

WISC-III™
Wechsler Intelligence Scale for Children – Third Edition

Name: Darwin Sex: ____
School: ____ Grade: ____
Examiner: ____ Handedness: ____

Subtests	Raw Scores	Scaled Scores					
Picture Completion	24	10		10			
Information	14	5	5				
Coding	56	7					7
Similarities	23	10	10				
Picture Arrangement	40	10		10			
Arithmetic	21	10				10	
Block Design	56	10		10			
Vocabulary	45	11	11				
Object Assembly	35	10		10			
Comprehension	28	10	10				
(Symbol Search)	25	(7)					7
(Digit Span)	12	(6)				6	
(Mazes)	24	(10)					
Sum of Scaled Scores		46	47	36	40	16	14
		Verbal	Perfor.	VC	PO	FD	PS

	Score	IQ/Index	%ile	95% Confidence Interval
Verbal	46	95	31	89 – 101
Performance	47	96	39	88 – 104
Full Scale	93	95	31	90 – 101
VC	36	95	37	89 – 102
PO	40	100	50	92 – 108
FD	16	90	25	82 – 101
PS	14	86	18	78 – 98

Age: 15 2

VIQ	PIQ	FSIQ	VCI	POI	FDI	PSI
95	96	95	95	100	90	86

Figure 4.5. Darwin's profile.

to an average extent compared with his peers. He had processing difficulties, however, with auditory and visual input when the material was abstract and relatively meaningless, as on Digit Span, Coding, and Symbol Search. Although he did poorly on the Information subtest, one could hardly count his background as impoverished. It is more likely that he missed some of the information due to a lack of reading.

Darwin had no interest whatsoever in reading. He was so frustrated in his attempts at having people "help" him with this problem that he simply became passive, and sometimes passively oppositional. He was extremely sensitive about his reading problem.

On the screening battery used at this clinic, we found that Darwin had a severe phonemic processing dysfunction. He obtained a score of 52 on the *Lindamood Auditory Conceptualization Test* (LAC) (Lindamood & Lindamood, 1979). This score is considered minimally acceptable at about a beginning Grade 1 level. Darwin had difficulty manipulating even two sounds. His sound–symbol connections were also very weak, despite the many phonics programs he had been exposed to. His decoding of regularly spelled nonsense patterns, as on the Woodcock Word Attack (Woodcock, 1973) subtest, was at about a beginning Grade 2 level. He obtained equally dismal scores on the *Wide Range Achievement Test–Revised* (WRAT-R) (Jastak & Wilkinson, 1984) Reading and Spelling subtests (standard scores of 59 and 62, respectively, both of which are at the first percentile or less). Contextual cues were of some assistance to Darwin, as he was able to read meaningful passages at a Grade 2 level. At the Grade 3 level, his decoding was extremely weak. He took an inordinate amount of time to read the few sentences that were involved; however, his recall and understanding of the information were excellent. In fact, his listening potential was appropriate to his grade placement.

Darwin's case was extremely severe and would normally involve extended therapy time. Therapy took place during the summer months for 4 consecutive weeks. Posttest results were not particularly impressive, but nevertheless some processing gains were very evident. One major change was in Darwin's attitude toward reading. Although his reading was still well below his potential, he showed, for the first time in his life, some interest in read-

ing. He remained quite shy, but his family reported that they saw a more relaxed individual who would now at least try to pick up a magazine and read.

Darwin then entered a private school for students with learning disabilities in the Calgary area. This school works closely with our clinic in terms of follow-up. The school's teachers are well aware of our procedures and are able to reinforce them in their classrooms. Additionally, they are able to provide many strategies that help bridge the gap between the clinical processes and transfer to academic areas.

Darwin settled into the school nicely. About mid-year, he began to "take off" and is now reading, writing, and spelling at a level only slightly below his potential. The marked discrepancy between his potential and his performance has been greatly closed, and I am confident that by the end of the school term, it will have been closed almost completely.

Darwin's story is not unusual in terms of the success of these procedures. The combination of intensive stimulation and appropriate follow-up has, in my experience, produced processing gains that I would never have believed possible based on my previous experience with learning disabilities. This combination also has provided a basis for more optimism about outcomes, even for students with severe learning disabilities. Much more research is needed, however, to achieve greater understanding of this stimulation, and more work is needed to fine-tune some of the procedures.

THE BILATERAL COOPERATIVE READING MODEL

The BLC model was designed to provide a framework for every aspect of reading, from letter recognition to understanding whole texts. As such, it is much more complete and complex than the PL model and seems to dovetail nicely with the dual coding model.

Taylor and Taylor (1983) described the BLC model in this way:

> Reading involves two parallel streams or "tracks" of interacting processes. The left track deals with functional relationships, sequentially ordered material,

phonetic coding, syntax, and most functions we commonly think of as "linguistic." It is the analytic and logical track. The right track performs pattern matching functions, seeks out similarities between the input patterns and previously seen patterns, evokes associations, and relates the meanings of words and phrases with real-world conditions. Its functions tend to be global, parallel and passive. Left and right tracks cooperate in extracting the meaning from marks on a page (and indeed from speech as well . . .). The two tracks interact. . . . The right track makes quick guesses, and the left corrects the guesses as well as linking the results into phrases, clauses, and larger units. (pp. 233–234)

The BLC model, then, is similar to the PL model in terms of the importance it gives to the language base and to prediction. Although it seems to be more bottom–up than the PL model, closer inspection indicates that it is very much an interactive model. Both top–down and bottom–up processes are essential to reading (and speech) in the BLC model. The PL model seems to be more a reading-only model, with language production already assumed, whereas the BLC model is more explanatory, and includes speech production in various languages in its explanatory process—an interesting feature.

A skeleton diagram of the BLC model for the first 1 second of reading is shown in Figure 4.6. Taylor and Taylor (1983) listed the following as important features of the diagram:

> The processes on both left and right tracks can operate independently of one another between interconnecting points.
>
> The interconnections occur only at discrete points between which the processes on the two tracks perform related tasks on similar data. Five crossover points have been postulated, but the actual number is unimportant.
>
> It takes longer to transfer data from one track to the other at the higher stages because of an increase in processing required to translate the representations of one track to those of the other. The crossovers require complicated processing in their own right, especially at higher levels.
>
> The processes in each track have a family resemblance: The low-level processes resemble the high-level processes within the same track much more closely than they resemble the same-level processes in the other track. [The diagram] lists some of the

major differences between the left and right processes. . . . In each track, the lower levels deal with simple things such as letters or words; the higher levels with complex matters such as syntax or meaning. The left track links words together, in the manner discussed in grammar books. The right combines the ideas behind the words and connects them with the current real-world context; it fleshes out the skeleton built by the left. Both tracks are heavily dependent on context, although it may not be evident from patterns or rules active in the higher stages. Each stage is thus firmly linked to higher and lower stages in its own track, and to parallel stages in the other track. (p. 235)

In addition, Figure 4.7 specifies the functions of the left and right tracks. It is important to note that the left and right tracks do not correspond directly to the left and right hemispheres of the brain; however, at the higher comprehension levels, the parallel between tracks and hemispheres is much closer. Readers should also note the similarities to the simultaneous–successive distinction and to dual coding. As with dual coding theory, readers might already have noticed the parallels between the left and right tracks in the BLC model, and the WISC-III Verbal and Performance Scales, respectively.

The BLC model, according to Taylor and Taylor (1983), is supported by research on normal readers, those with brain damage, and split-brain patients.

There are implications of the BLC model to reading disabilities (which the Taylors called developmental dyslexia):

> A deficient left track leads to poor phonetic coding, poor syntactic integration, poor sequencing, and poor STM [short term memory]. A deficient right track leads to poor visual word recognition, poor comprehension of associations and real-world relationships, and perhaps poor LTM [long-term memory]. (p. 421)

That statement certainly describes many of the students in resource rooms. Where does it leave the teacher, however, in terms of how to teach a student? The Taylors provide this overall suggestion:

> Familiar words are recognized wholistically using a fast pattern-matching process, which can be done by both brain hemispheres, but is usually done by the right. Unfamiliar words and pseudowords are

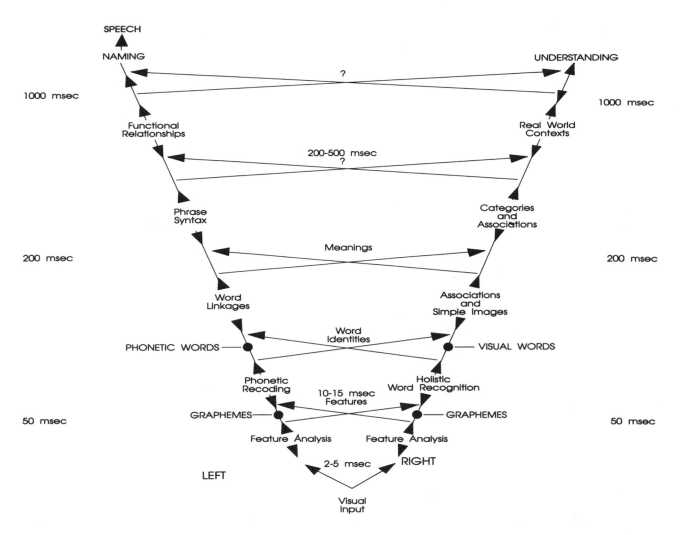

The two tracks are connected at a few discrete levels but otherwise are independent. The RIGHT track works by global pattern matching and association, ultimately linking the sense of items to the state of the real world; the LEFT works by analysis and rules, selecting appropriate pattern matches developed by the RIGHT and inhibiting inappropriate ones. The LEFT track is responsible for syntactic relations and phonetic coding of words.

Figure 4.6. Left and right tracks and their interactions in the bilateral cooperative reading model. From *The Psychology of Reading* (p. 234) by I. Taylor and M. M. Taylor, 1983, New York: Academic Press. Copyright 1983 by Academic Press. Reprinted with permission.

coded from their letters using a slow, analytic-phonetic process in the left hemisphere.

In learning to read both sets of processes must be developed and integrated, using whole-word and phonics methods. Learning proceeds in a series of three-phased cycles: recognizing a unit as a whole; analyzing it into subparts; and recognizing it as a whole again, based on securer recognition of its subparts. Poor or disabled reading results from failure to develop some part of the cycle. (p. 429)

More specifically,

The BLC model suggests that the learning sequence should have three phases: Learn a handful of words by their visual shapes (right whole-word recognition based on visual features); learn to analyze words into their parts (left analysis); learn once more to recognize the wholes, based on the securer knowledge of parts (right whole-word based on letter identities). Chinese children learn characters in the three phases, Swedish- and English-speaking preschoolers pick up reading in three phases, and German children are taught to read at school in the three phases. School children in the United States

	LEFT track	RIGHT track
Cortical location	Left hemisphere	Both hemispheres, but mainly right in normal reading
Specialty	Labels, symbols, functional relationships, sequences	Patterns, colors, pictures associations, collections
Processing style	Active, under attentional control Analysis into sub-units Seeks out differences Exact Unique result Serial, slow Handles material presented sequentially Time order Syntactic, rule based Pattern analysis Phonetically based Good short-term memory Speech output	Passive, automatic Global, wholistic Looks for similarities Approximate Many acceptable results Parallel, fast Handles material presented as a group Associations and spatial relations Meaning centered Approximate pattern matching Visually based Poor short-term memory Nonspeech output
Letter	Abstract letter identities Kanji phonetic and radical Hangul and Kana	Isolated but not embedded letters Single or nonsense pairs of Kanji
Morpheme	Syntactic components Abstract elements	Content components Concrete elements
Word	Unfamiliar words Abstract words Embedded words Pseudowords	Familiar words Concrete, high-imagery words Words marked off by spaces
Sentence	Syntactic relations Make verbal gist	Meaning relations Visualization
Text	Functional and logical relations	Speed reading Humor and poetry

Figure 4.7. Functions in the Bilateral Cooperative Model. From *The Psychology of Reading* (p. 236) by I. Taylor and M. M. Taylor, 1983, New York: Academic Press. Copyright 1983 by Academic Press. Reprinted with permission.

are often taught by an eclectic approach mixing whole-word with phonics.

Three-phased learning applies not only to words, but also to letters and to higher units of reading such as phrases, paragraphs, and whole texts. At the letter level, the child learns several letters by their gross shapes; then she notes the same and different features (configurational or fragmental) in the letters; and in the third phase she recognizes the whole letters again, now based on secure knowledge of the features.

At the word level, teach a child a handful of words by look–say, ensuring that the vocabulary contains enough words with letters in common that the child can begin the analysis procedure. When the child notices that there is something similar between *cat* and *hat,* the analysis procedure should be encouraged, while at the same time, more look–

say words are introduced to teach other letter–sound relations. By this means, the children develop both analytic and wholistic routes to word recognition. As fluent readers, they will read a familiar word as a whole visual pattern, and an unfamiliar word by phonetic analysis.

At the passage level, the child already knows from speech something about elementary syntax and semantic associations among words, so that reading presents few problems of a new kind. But the syntax of writing can be more complex than that of speech, requiring a repeat of the same kind of three-phased learning. The three phases here are simple exposure to written syntax, its analysis into constituents and the direct recognition of how words in common patterns fit together.

Three-phased learning will happen no matter what a teacher does, but the teacher can encourage all three of the phases. At all levels, the analytic second phase is probably the one that can benefit most from formal training; the first phase requires exposure; and the third phase will follow the second automatically. If our observation is true, teachers should concentrate their efforts on phonetic word analysis, syntax and story structure, but should allow the children to practice whole-word recognition, association and story reading.

Effective learning requires not only the development of the analytic–phonetic left track and the wholistic right, but also their full integration. (pp. 385–386)

The BLC Model and Automaticity

Although Taylor and Taylor (1983) believed that reading is best learned by doing a lot of reading and practicing, they took issue with the primarily bottom–up approach that emphasizes teaching each subskill to an automatic level before progressing to the next. They wrote,

Subskills may be mutually facilitative rather than independent. . . . Instead of training each subskill to the level at which it becomes automatic before tackling the next one, . . . we believe in training a few related subskills together, emphasizing one or another as conditions demand. The grounds for our belief are: (a) There is no clear boundary where the need for one subskill ends and another starts; (b) The smaller and lower the subskill, the less meaningful and interesting it tends to be; (c) The more finely and definitely is word decoding divided into subskills the more difficult it will be to integrate the subskills again; (d) When one skill is learned, a cluster of its subskills may be partially acquired. For example, selecting, scanning, and unitizing letter features seem to be acquired largely spontaneously in the learning of letters and words. Calfee and Drum (1978) point out that prereading kindergartners handle graphic symbols in much the same way as do adults when allowance is made for the role of memory and encoding, and that programs for enhancing visual perception are seldom effective. Sensitivity to orthographic structure might be considered as one of the subskills involved in word recognition. But is it sensitivity that facilitates word recognition, or vice versa? (pp. 390–391)

From what I have discussed previously regarding phonemic processing, it is obvious that both the PL and the BLC models do not go into the necessary depth in this "sublexical" area. Sensitivity to orthographic structure develops as the child learns to read, but only in those children who do not have a problem with phonemic processing in the first place. For those who do, sensitivity to orthographic structure develops in a very spotty fashion.

In addition to their excellent review and insights on word recognition, Taylor and Taylor (1983) provided a succinct summary of comprehension skills, where *comprehension* simply means extracting an idea conveyed in a sentence or passage. They wrote that

Similar comprehension subskills are involved in whatever languages or scripts children, or adults for that matter, may read.

In reading sentences children must learn to

Recognize words

Assign syntactic and case roles to words

Construct a message based on content words, with the help of function words, if necessary

Identify the referents or anaphora

Organize words into larger syntactic units, such as phrase and clause

Extract the gist from a sentence

In reading stories children must learn to

Identify the motive of a hero or heroine

Follow the sequence of events or plot

Anticipate an outcome or climax

Extract a theme or moral

In reading expository prose, children must learn to

Identify the topic

Distinguish important from unimportant idea units, processing the former more than the latter

Follow a sequence of directions or logical ideas

Draw inferences or conclusions

Sort out cause/effect relations; Extract the gist of a passage

A reader has other, higher-level tasks. She must separate facts from opinions; evaluate the relevance of materials to the author's thesis or to her reading goals; appreciate the beauty, aptness, or novelty of expressions; grasp the point of a joke, irony, or sarcasm; and above all, retain at least the main points of what has been read. (pp. 393–394)

When I became a school psychologist, I had no idea how complex the job was and the degree of understanding required for even seemingly simple tasks such as reading. I hope that, by discussing these three reading models, some of the complexity is more comprehensible to other school psychologists and, more importantly, that useful teaching strategies become apparent. The models are complementary in many ways, although some obvious divergences are likely to surface with more thought and research regarding the implications of each model. Also, all three models have some serious shortcomings I believe, with respect to the beginning stages of reading.

REMEDIAL TEACHING STRATEGIES

This is a good place at which to discuss some generalizations regarding teaching strategies for remedial readers. These generalizations seem to arise in many studies of good and poor readers:

1. Good readers benefit under almost *any* instructional procedure. The "almost" is important here, because some conditions will not be as good as others. Good readers seem to learn even *despite* some kinds of instruction.

2. On the other hand, poor readers will benefit *only* under some instructional procedures and strategies. Unfortunately, the gap between good and poor readers is not necessarily narrowed. The reason for this is that both good and poor readers will benefit from an instructional strategy, good readers usually more so.

3. Some readers will remain behind, *despite* various teaching methods.

School psychologists and remedial teachers, then, need to continually evaluate their reading programs and strategies, and change them for poor readers through such practices as flexible groupings, diagnosis and program development, and the test–teach–test method, among others. More importantly, they need to remain open to new possibilities (e.g., phonemic analysis), but *without* jumping on bandwagons.

WISC-III Interpretation: Levels I and II

Sattler (1982, p. 193) suggested that the WISC-R can be interpreted in successive levels:

Level I—The Full Scale IQ

Level II—Verbal and Performance IQs (I also include factor splits in this level)

Level III—Subtest strengths and weaknesses

Level IV—Patterns within a subtest

Level V—Analysis of content response styles

This levels approach to interpretation works equally well, in my experience, with the WISC-III. In fact, the renorming and Scale Indexes on the WISC-III greatly facilitate the process of interpretation.

This interpretive approach corresponds closely to Vernon's (1979) hierarchical model of intelligence, with the primary emergence of *g* as the mental energy common to all human endeavors. It also corresponds to the complex statistical work known as factor analysis that has been done extensively on the WISC-R, and more recently on the WISC-III. Additionally, this successive-level approach considers the difficulty associated with subtest reliability: When a student is retested on the WISC-III, the Full Scale IQ will be the most stable score, whereas the subtest scaled scores will vary. Therefore, beginning a WISC-III interpretation from the

bottom, up, with a subtest-specific interpretation, is the least reliable approach. On the other hand, Level I interpretation alone is not terribly helpful in terms of generating educational implications, because all that can be determined at that level is how the student ranks on overall ability (*g*) compared with the standardization sample. (However, in some cases, that is only as far as one can legitimately go.)

Some combination of top–down and bottom–up interpretation is therefore desirable. One way around the bottom–up problem is to combine subtests into meaningful clusters, because combined subtests are statistically more reliable than a subtest by itself. Readers should be familiar with the approach taken by Kaufman (1979) in *Intelligent Testing with the WISC-R,* as his detective-work approach is very similar to and complementary with what I am advocating here and applies to the WISC-III as well as the WISC-R.

Other valid interpretive approaches have used this successive-level model. For example, Blaha and Wallbrown (1984) reviewed a number of hierarchical factor solutions of the WISC-R. They found considerable confirmation of Vernon's model as discussed in Chapter 2. Figure 5.1 shows how the model looks in relation to the WISC-R.

As one can see, Figure 5.1 presents Blaha and Wallbrown's interpretation of the WISC-R factors (in particular, Coding does not load on the Free-

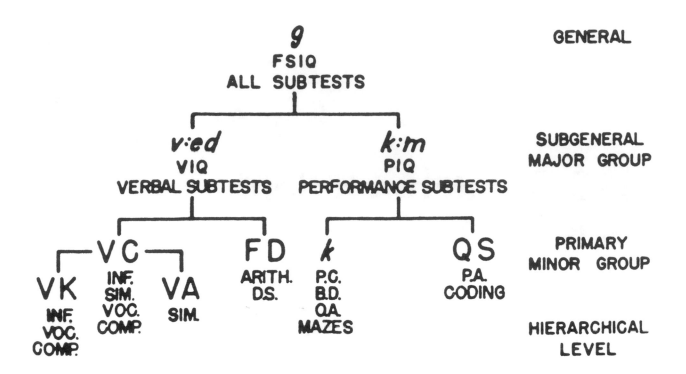

Figure 5.1. Hierarchical factor structure of the WISC-R. Composite heirarchical factor structure of the WISC and WISC-R derived from hierarchical analyses of 13 normal and atypical samples. (As of this printing, such a data synthesis has not been completed on the WISC-III; however, this does not change the substance of the interpretive process.) g = general intelligence; v:ed = verbal–numerical educational; k:m = spatial–mechanical–practical; VC = verbal comprehension; FD = freedom from distractibility; k = spatial; QS = quasi specific; VK = verbal knowledge; VA = verbal abstraction. From "Hierarchical Analyses of the WISC and WISC-R: Synthesis and Clinical Implications" by J. Blaha and F. Wallbrown, 1984, *Journal of Clinical Psychology, 40,* p. 563. Copyright 1984 by Clinical Psychology Publishing Co., Inc. Reprinted with permission.

dom from Distractibility factor in this approach), which varies somewhat from Kaufman's (1979) factor analysis. However, I believe that it is necessary to be eclectic, and not get stuck in one model. (This caveat is particularly important in factor analysis, which can be performed in several ways.) With the variety of possible student patterns, examiners must be knowledgeable about a number of interpretive systems, each of which has some merit.

Blaha and Wallbrown presented four important implications for clinical interpretation of the WISC-R (and that apply equally well to the WISC-III). They suggested that profile interpretation be performed as follows. First,

Account for child performances in terms of the broadest or highest-order factor(s) possible. (p. 567)

In other words, work from the top, down. When a profile is relatively flat, then further calculation of factor scores may be redundant. Interpretation would have to stop at this level. However, if there is considerable variability among the subtests, the Full Scale IQ should be deemphasized and the lower-order factors emphasized. Within each Verbal or Performance Scale, variability is also important. For example, if there is a 12-point (or greater) difference between the Verbal and the Performance Scales, but there is much variability within each scale, then the discrepancy may not be as important as the variability.

The second step is to

Determine the internal validity of a factor by examining the factor's variance. The greater the variance of the subtests that comprise a factor, the less valid that factor is in accounting for the child's performance. (p. 567)

As an example, Blaha and Wallbrown wrote,

If the scaled scores for Arithmetic and Digit Span are 11 and 13, respectively, one can conclude that the student is above average in the ability to maintain numerical items in short-term memory and manipulate them without being distracted by extraneous stimuli. However, if the scaled score is 7 for Arithmetic and 17 for Digit Span, it would not make sense to consider the two scores together and relate them to other information about the child. Regardless of the weighting procedure used, we still would end up with a mean score on the FD [Freedom from Distractibility] factor and mask the huge differences (variance) between the two subtest scores. (p. 569)

The third step is to

Determine the external validity of a factor by examining the degree to which the factor estimate agrees with other information about the child. (p. 567)

This is a point I have emphasized throughout this book.

The fourth major step in the analysis is as follows:

If a higher-order factor analysis does not provide a valid estimate of a child's performance, then move down the hierarchy and attempt to account for the child's performance in terms of lower-order factors. (p. 567)

Blaha and Wallbrown elaborated on this point by stating,

If the variability among the six subtests that compose either the v:ed or k:m factors is noteworthy, then it makes sense to move down the hierarchy of the major group factors whose validity is questioned and investigate the primary factors under its domain. Therefore, if the Verbal subtest variability is substantial, then attention should be drawn away from the VIQ [Verbal IQ] and toward the Verbal Comprehension (VC) and Freedom from Distractibility (FD) primary factors. The Information, Similarities, Vocabulary, and Comprehension subtests should be used to evaluate performance on the VC factor, and Arithmetic and Digit Span should be used to evaluate performance on the FD factor. (p. 568)

Finally, when substantial variability exists within any of the primary factors, then and only then should one rely on a subtest-specific interpretation.

The approach advocated by Blaha and Wallbrown, then, is an elaboration of Sattler's (1982) Levels I and II. For the remainder of this chapter, I discuss Level I and II interpretations and some of the educational implications.

LEVEL I—THE FULL SCALE IQ SCORE

Although the Full Scale IQ is the most valid and reliable of the WISC-III scores, it should always be reported with its *confidence band*. The confidence band will be larger or smaller, depending on what level of confidence is desired for the score. The level of confidence can be increased by increasing the confidence band, but doing so results in a confidence band that could be so large that it becomes useless for educational purposes. Therefore, a reasonable trade-off is necessary. Usually, the 95% confidence level is required for educational purposes. However, the WISC-III manual allows the examiner to choose either the 90% or the 95% confidence level. The *confidence interval* is also conveniently provided in the norms tables.

Each Full Scale IQ score has a corresponding percentile, which enables the examiner to see how each student ranks at a particular time against the standardization sample. The WISC-III is a norm-referenced, not a criterion-referenced, test. There is no zero point for intelligence test scores, so *there are no absolute criteria for discriminating individuals in terms of intelligence—only relative ones.*

The confidence band for percentiles is larger than that for the standard scores. For example, if a student scores a Full Scale IQ of 100, the 95% confidence interval for the standard score is from 94 to 106. The corresponding percentiles are from 34 to 66! This range is substantial, and should be mentioned when interpreting results to teachers and parents.

Educational Considerations of the Full Scale IQ

General considerations. Certain cautions must be considered in interpreting the Full Scale IQ. The first, as already mentioned, is the confidence level; the other is the fact that, for any individual student, a picture of his or her cognitive profile applies only to a specific point in time. The picture is neither complete nor unchanging.

One of the widest uses of the WISC-III is to help determine a placement in a special education program. Such decisions, however, should never be made *exclusively* on an IQ score. Such scores are only part of the picture. Also, any cutoff points that are used for placement are entirely arbitrary and depend on how states and provinces best feel they can meet the needs of particular groups. One classification of IQ scores is provided on page 32 of the WISC-III manual. However, each examiner needs to become familiar with the classifications used in his or her local area.

Ignoring confidence levels for the moment, I generally have found that Full Scale IQs in the 80s (when there is little scatter on the subtest) are too low to be considered average. Placing an average expectation on such students, I feel, does them a disservice. Many such students are considered learning disabled (LD), and are therefore assigned to programs in which an implicit expectation of "catching up to grade level" is made in reading and/or other subjects. As these students grow older, they are denied an opportunity to participate in an excellent alternative program, such as a vocational one, because the LD label has stuck. It is much more difficult, in such cases, to convince parents that a nonacademic program is better for their children. Table 5.1 provides a list of expectations for various levels of mental handicap based on Full Scale IQ scores.

In practice, I have found educational systems quite flexible, so, even if a student *is* placed in a nonacademic program, he or she usually has the opportunity to switch to a more academic route later on, if circumstances change. Even if a person does not complete an academic program during the school years, he or she has ample opportunities to do so as an adult. For example, many colleges and universities open their doors to mature students who never completed an academic program in high school, but who now wish to continue their education at the university level.

High intelligence and good grades, then, are not *necessarily* prerequisites for university entrance, profession, or success in life. In fact, intelligence correlates very poorly with income level. However, intelligence does have an important bearing on occupational status. When average IQ scores are calculated for various occupational groups, results such as those reported in Table 5.2 are common. These are extremely important general educational implications of Level I WISC-III interpretation. School psychologists and teachers must remain flexible in their thinking, however, and remember that

1. All expectations based on IQs are very rough guidelines only. Individual variation is considerable, and can change dramatically with time.

2. Individual students should never be labeled or placed in special education programs and forgotten. Periodic updating of scores and review of placements are vital.

3. Students should never be placed in special education programs based on IQ scores alone.

4. The goal of mainstreaming students should be upheld where feasible and desirable.

Full Scale IQ scores *do* change as a result of many factors, including cognitive growth and stimulation, and extraneous factors, such as measurement error and regression effects. The value of a Full Scale IQ score is to help set reasonable expectations based on the individual's overall ranking at a particular point in time, and not to label that person.

Implications of the Full Scale IQ for teaching reading. In this section, I discuss some general implications of Full Scale IQ scores for teaching reading to mentally handicapped students. The group with learning disabilities is dealt with separately. Another special needs group, the gifted, typically do not have difficulty with reading, although gifted underachievers might. I will discuss

TABLE 5.1. American Association of Mental Deficiency Classifications

AAMD Classification	Degree of Mental Handicap	Preschool Age 0–5: Maturation and Development	School Age 6–20: Training and Education	Adult 21 and Over: Social and Vocational Adequacy
IQ 55–69	Mild	Can develop social and communication skills; minimal retardation in sensorimotor areas; often not distinguished from normal until later age.	Can learn academic skills up to approximately sixth-grade level by late teens. Can be guided toward social conformity. "Educable."	Can usually achieve social and vocational skills adequate to minimum self-support, but may need guidance and assistance when under unusual social or economic stress.
IQ 40–54	Moderate	Can talk or learn to communicate; poor social awareness; fair motor development; profits from training in self-help; can be managed with moderate supervision.	Can profit from training in social and occupational skills; unlikely to progress beyond second-grade level in academic subjects; may learn to travel alone in familiar places.	May achieve self-maintenance in unskilled or semiskilled work under sheltered conditions; needs supervision and guidance when under mild social or economic stress.
IQ 25–39	Severe	Poor motor development; speech is minimal; generally unable to profit from training in self-help; little or no communication skills.	Can talk or learn to communicate; can be trained in elemental health habits; profits from systematic habit training.	May contribute partially to self-maintenance under complete supervision; can develop self-protection skills to a minimal useful level in a controlled environment.
IQ below 24	Profound	Gross retardation; minimal capacity for functioning in sensorimotor areas; needs nursing care.	Some motor development present; may respond to minimum or limited training in self-help.	Some motor and speech development; may achieve very limited self-care; needs nursing care.

From *The Problem of Mental Retardation* by the U.S. Department of Health, Education, and Welfare, Office of the Secretary, Secretary's Committee on Mental Retardation, 1969, Washington, DC: Government Printing Office.

TABLE 5.2. Mean IQ of Different Professional and Occupational Groups

140	Higher Professional, Top Civil Servants, Professors and Research Scientists.
130	Lower Professionals, Physicians and Surgeons, Lawyers, Engineers (Civil and Mechanical).
120	School Teachers, Pharmacists, Accountants, Nurses, Stenographers, Managers.
110	Foremen, Clerks, Telephone Operators, Salesmen, Policemen, Electricians, Precision Fitters.
100 +	Machine Operators, Shopkeepers, Butchers, Welders, Sheet Metal Workers.
100 −	Warehousemen, Carpenters, Cooks and Bakers, Small Farmers, Truck and Van Drivers.
90	Laborers, Gardeners, Upholsterers, Farmhands, Miners, Factory Workers and Sorters.

From *The Measurement of Intelligence* (p. x) by H. J. Eysenck (Ed.), 1973, Baltimore: Williams & Wilkins. Reprinted with permission of the author.

some strategies appropriate to this group elsewhere in this chapter.

It should be kept in mind that the group of students with mental handicaps comprises *individuals.* These students are as heterogeneous (despite the fact that their measured IQ scores might fall below some arbitrary cutoff level) as, say, students with learning disabilities or any other group of students. As such, careful individual diagnosis and good record keeping, preferably using a criterion-based system, are essential. I have found the *Brigance Diagnostic Inventory* (Brigance, 1978) to be especially useful in this respect.

For teaching reading to students with mental handicaps, no one best method exists. Each student has his or her own learning style and achievement level. Therefore, IEPs are essential, and structured programs may form part of the overall educational process for this group. I have seen, for example, the *Auditory Discrimination in Depth* (ADD) program (Lindamood & Lindamood, 1975) used successfully with this group, although it was presented at a *much* slower than usual pace.

For these students, materials should be as concrete as possible, and much repetition is usually required. Students with mental handicaps typically have difficulty transferring what is learned from one context to another. Thus, not only is more repetition required, but so is more teaching in a variety of contexts. Task analysis and teaching for transfer become particularly important for this group.

The Full Scale IQ is a good predictor of overall academic achievement, including reading. Brighter children tend to read better; slower children, including those with mental handicaps, tend to read much more poorly. However, the relationship is by no means perfect, and there are always individual differences.

Nevertheless, for students whose overall WISC-III IQ falls in the borderline or intellectually deficient ranges, and who are placed in special classes, expectations and objectives for their reading program must be adjusted—in some cases, considerably so. Their overall cognitive handicaps may limit the levels of reading they eventually attain, but the teacher should always aim to stretch each student as far as possible.

In some states and provinces, the reading objectives are subsumed within the general language arts or communications curricula. To provide an example of some communications objectives and expectations at the educable mentally handicapped (EMH) level, I have included some from the Alberta Department of Education's (1980) *Curriculum Guide (EMH)* in Figure 5.2. In Alberta, the regular language arts curriculum is based on six primary modes of communication—listening, viewing, speaking, reading, spelling, and writing. The *Curriculum Guide (EMH)* (pp. iii–iv) describes the characteristics of the EMH student in each of these six areas. A few specific objectives and strategies for reading comprehension are listed in Figure 5.3.

The Alberta *Curriculum Guide (EMH)* is extensive and has been very valuable in the special education of this group of students with mental handicaps. There is a similar guide for students with trainable mental handicaps (TMH) (Alberta Department of Education, 1982). The guides are thorough and extremely useful references.

In the previous chapter, I discussed the psycholinguistic (PL) and bilateral cooperative (BLC) models of reading. For persons with severe mental handicaps, the BLC model (see Figure 4.7) has one very important implication: Even students in the low TMH range (Full Scale IQs below 45) should be able to acquire some Level I reading skills by emphasizing the *right* track (although a severely deficient *left* track, which many students have, will hinder progress). To do so, some form of logog-

raphy would be most appropriate. Simple line drawings and rebuses have been used successfully.

Both models also emphasize that a strong language base is necessary in reading. This is very pertinent for students with mental handicaps, because language disorders are far more prevalent in this group than in other handicapped groups. Therefore, a language-immersion approach, as outlined in Appendix 2A, is very appropriate for this group. This approach should include even more discussion, sharing experiences, development of basic verbal classification skills, semantic mapping, and development of background experiences and information. The sublexical levels, including phonemic processing, also cannot be ignored. However, all of this must be modified to the level of each student.

Predicting is just as important a process in reading for students with mental handicaps as for any other group (assuming decoding skills are in place). A language experience approach serves this purpose very well. Fagan (1980) wrote,

> Using this approach, the teacher transcribes a child's story or account of his experiences. Attention may be drawn to certain word sequences that could be modified or elaborated in further instruction. For example, the sentence, "I was at the party," could be modified by the child in response to questions read: "Bob was at the party"; "Jane was at the party"; and "I was at the party that the teacher gave." Sentences might be printed on strips and cut into words or phrases and scrambled. With direction, the child could be asked to put various sentences together. The word cards "Bob" and "was" may be presented and the child then asked to read these and state (predict) what comes next. The words "at the party" could then be found to complete the sentence.

The word bank (see Appendix 5A) can also be modified for readers with mental handicaps. I would also include a good number of rebuses and extensive use of visualization processes, because many studies have shown that mentally handicapped populations do better on spatial tasks, such as Picture Completion, Object Assembly, and Block Design, than they do on acquired knowledge tasks, such as Arithmetic, Information, and Vocabulary. Any relative strength in these subtests for an individual student should be noted and woven into instructional programming whenever possible.

Characteristics of Educable Mentally Handicapped Students' Communication Skills

Many characteristics are common among EMH students in terms of the degree of development and level of competency of their communication skills. Age-appropriate materials and activities should be used.

1. *Listening*—Due to the lower level of reading ability found in many EMH students, it is very important to develop other receptive communication skills. It is necessary to teach these students to become competent and discriminative listeners. It is through listening that much informal and practical learning takes place. Therefore, the ability to listen and interpret what is heard is a very crucial skill to develop in the EMH student.

2. *Viewing*—Again due to limited reading skills, EMH students rely heavily upon the visual media to obtain information about their world. They watch more television than the average student and are often found to be more gullible in accepting the standards and values of what they see on television or in movies. Reliance on pictures to get the context of a story, a news happening, or an advertisement further justifies the need to teach these students how to interpret information experienced visually.

3. *Speaking*—Speaking is one of the communication skills that is utilized each day. For the EMH student, difficulty in expressing himself and verbalizing his wants and needs is a common problem. Part of this problem is often due to specific articulation deficits or maturational lags in language development. Regardless of the nature of the deficit, a specific sequential language development program should be followed daily to assist these students in their speech and language development.

4. *Reading*—EMH students generally learn to read at a later age and at a slower pace than their nonhandicapped counterparts. They often have great difficulty generalizing concepts and rules associated with reading skills. Although these students can learn the various reading skills in the same order and through similar teaching methods as regular students, they often require more teaching time and extensive practice in the various skills. The approach utilized in teaching to these students should emphasize a practical or functional point of view.

5. *Spelling*—There is often a relationship between reading ability and proficiency in spelling. Therefore, the extent of development of reading skills of the EMH student has a direct bearing on the student's ability to master spelling skills. Cognitive functions such as discrimination, perception and memory must be developed within the spelling program to assist the EMH student in learning to spell competently. Often a pattern of ''says, points, reads, and writes'' is most effective in the teaching of spelling to these students.

6. *Writing*—For the EMH student, learning to print and write is sometimes slower to develop due to a slower rate of motor development or deficits in cognitive functions such as perception and discrimination. It is recommended that both manuscript and cursive writing be taught to EMH students. The teaching of cursive writing, however, should not be dependent upon mastery of manuscript writing.

Figure 5.2. Characteristics of educable mentally handicapped students' communication skills. From *Curriculum Guide (EMH)* (pp. iii–iv, Communication Section) by the Alberta Department of Education, 1980, Edmonton, Alberta: Author.

Meaning associations are usually very weak for students with mental handicaps. Therefore, associations must be taught in the context of the reading program. Procedures such as semantic mapping, to be discussed later, could be adapted and used in a class. Associations can also be encouraged by oral discussion, using examples and nonexamples of the concept in question. For example, if the student's task is to learn to read a "No Smoking" sign, then

A picture with signs incorrectly placed may be used for pupils to tell what is wrong with the picture. For example, pictures might show "No Skating" in an airplane, or "No Smoking" on an ice-covered lake. (Fagan, 1980, p. 237)

Although the Full Scale IQ is a good predictor of reading achievement, I repeat that the scores should not be cast in concrete. Teachers should neither allow the Full Scale IQ to become a self-fulfilling prophecy nor give up on a student with a low IQ score. The Full Scale IQ is usually a realistic *starting point* for educational planning. For those with low IQ scores, the programming must be

Learning Approaches

The needs of the EMH student to function adequately within society do not differ greatly from those of a regular student. However, due to the fact that these students' rate of progress in learning is much slower and their potential for mastery is not as great, programs designed in the teaching of communication skills must be modified in terms of instructional approaches and techniques.

It is recommended that an eclectic approach be utilized with these students. This approach necessitates that the teacher be adept at utilizing a variety of teaching techniques and methods (e.g., language experience, kinesthetic, phonetic) within each program. The eclectic approach makes use of the most appropriate program in terms of methods and materials to facilitate each student's maximum growth and development.

When teaching communication skills to EMH students, the teacher should relate instruction whenever possible to the tangible and concrete. In addition, one should not assume that a particular skill or concept is learned or has been mastered simply because the student can apply the use of the skill in one situation. By utilizing a wide range of instructional techniques, the teacher can facilitate generalization of skills across various situations. The rate of learning for the EMH student is very often much slower than one would expect of a regular student. When teaching communication skills to these students, then, repetition of instruction is often necessary. Maintaining interest is essential for the students.

Reading: Comprehension Development

Objectives	*Teaching Strategies*
The student:	
Finds main idea in a story or paragraph.	Duplicate paragraphs. Have students either find or draw pictures to illustrate them. Have pictures pasted on cards which the student can use for this activity. Have student summarize the paragraph he has read by choosing a suitable picture.
Organizes events in proper sequence.	Cut story into paragraphs. Paste the paragraphs on cardboard and code so that the students may correct their work with a key. Have students read the paragraphs and place them in proper sequence.
Predicts outcomes from material read.	Paste short stories on cardboard sheets. Place conclusions of these stories on another card. Have students read the stories and the conclusions and then match the stories with the endings.
Uses the index to find specific information.	List words from the reader's index on the chalkboard. Have students find each word in the index and write the number of the page on which information about each subject is found.
Skims to locate specific information.	Have student reread a story to answer specific questions.

Figure 5.3. Learning approaches and reading comprehension objectives for educable mentally handicapped students. From *Curriculum Guide (EMH)* (pp. 34, Communication Section) by the Alberta Department of Education, 1980, Edmonton, Alberta: Author.

intense and directive. Teachers must not get caught in the "label trap." Carnine (1983) cautioned,

> Several researchers have found that when students are given a special education label, teachers rate behaviors more negatively. A description of a child is more likely to result in the label "mentally retarded" if the teacher is told the child is from a low-income background.... Poor attitudes and expectations for children can also affect peers' attitudes and the behavior of teachers, leading to segregation as well as fewer and less effective instructional interactions. (pp. 19–20)

In the same article, Carnine provided some very impressive and compelling data on the effects of the direct instruction model on some 8,000 "high-risk" students from low-income homes in 20 U.S. communities. The major building blocks of this model are the DISTAR programs (Engelmann &

Osborn, 1987). Many professionals I know cringe at the very term "DISTAR," because they view it as too rigid and too structured a program. More recent criticisms attack the bottom–up approach that DISTAR uses in teaching reading. I see the criticisms as lacking substance for certain exceptional groups. Carnine (1983) discussed some impressive research evidence to show how effective implementation of the direct instruction model can be. About expectations, Carnine wrote,

> One of the most important findings from [Direct Instruction Follow-Through] was that students entering kindergarten who would typically be expected to fail in school could achieve at close to the national average. Direct Instruction Follow-Through students, all of whom were from economically disadvantaged homes and who were over 90-percent minority, scored about as well as the median of the test's norming sample. This finding and similar ones with special education populations is important because it justifies higher expectations on the part of educators. (p. 19)

Those concerned about the rigid, bottom–up approach of DISTAR should remember that most approaches have merit depending on the situation and the individual student. The great fear that a bottom–up approach will produce only word-callers does not appear to be true. Carnine (1983) described a "miscue analysis" that he and his co-workers did of the reading of students in Grades K through 3 who were taught using direct instruction principles:

> Even though the children continued to work on the analysis of words in isolation, teacher-directed exercises on sentence and story reading led to a covertization of a set of reading skills; the children anticipated meaning, self-corrected words that apparently made no sense, and made the kind of mistakes that are possible only if the semantics and syntax of the passage are understood. (p. 35)

Carnine (1983) compared direct instruction with eight other major instructional approaches in a 6-year study of using them with various economically disadvantaged groups across the United States. I do not discuss the different approaches here; a brief description of each can be found in Carnine's article. What is important for current purposes are the results comparing the programs on a complex

set of measures collectively called the "Index of Significant Outcomes," as shown in Figure 5.4.

Of these results, Carnine (1983) wrote,

> Direct Instruction is the only model that shows consistently positive outcomes across measures. The more open-ended, child-centered programs show consistently negative outcomes.
>
> These findings concerning Direct Instruction deserve particular attention. First, Direct Instruction students achieved well not only in basic skills ... but also in cognitive skills—reading comprehension, math problem solving, and math concepts. Second, Direct Instruction students' scores were quite high in the affective domain, suggesting that competence enhances self-esteem and not vice versa. (pp. 13–14)

Although I am not a strong advocate of the DISTAR program per se, I do feel that there is a place for direct instruction *principles,* many of which have already been discussed in the "Classroom Atmosphere" section of Chapter 3. This is particularly true for disadvantaged and mentally handicapped students, whose present Full Scale IQs would otherwise suggest a poor academic prognosis.

In any case, this is the 20th century and *anything* is possible. Who knows what new and exciting developments will yet develop for those students who are currently more limited because of cognitive handicaps.

LEVEL II—VERBAL AND PERFORMANCE IQS AND FOUR-FACTOR SPLITS

The Verbal and Performance IQs

The Verbal and Performance Scales of the WISC-III measure two separate factors or underlying cognitive abilities. On the Verbal subtests, the student listens to the questions and responds to them verbally; the Performance subtests measure a student's ability to solve unique problems. The output on the latter is primarily motor (use of hands) and the materials are primarily nonverbal (pictures, blocks, puzzles), but some verbal explanation is required on the part of the examiner. The student does not reply verbally except on Picture Completion,

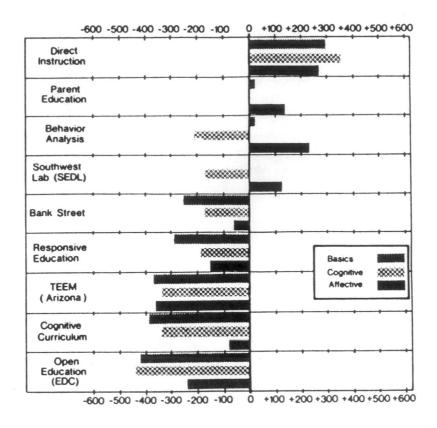

Figure 5.4. Index of significant outcomes for basic skills, cognitive skills, and affective measures. From "Direct Instruction: A Successful System for Educationally High-Risk Children" by D. Carnine, 1979, *Journal of Curriculum Studies, 11,* p. 31. Copyright 1979 by Taylor and Francis. Reprinted with permission.

although, even on this subtest, the student may simply point. Nevertheless, the examiner should watch for rapid, automatic naming on the student's part. Rapid, automatic naming is a correlate of good reading, and is often part of the student's response style on the Picture Completion subtest. I discuss this in more detail in Chapter 7.

In summary, then, the WISC-III Verbal Scale is quite broad in its sampling of verbal ability (v:ed). Blaha and Wallbrown (1984) summarized v:ed as follows:

> The Vernon definition of v:ed may be applied as follows: Verbal information as indicated by Vocabulary and Information, the application of verbal skills and information to situations that require judgement as indicated by some items from Comprehension and Similarities, the retention and manipulation of verbal information in short-term memory as indicated by Digit Span and Arithmetic. This illustrates the breadth of this major group factor directly below *g* in the hierarchy, which is somewhat less broad than the *g* factor. (p. 559)

They describe the Performance Scale as

> a gross estimate of a child's ability to think in terms of visual images and manipulate them with fluency, flexibility, and relative speed. In the classroom, one might expect that a child with a high Performance IQ would respond to visually oriented modes of instruction such as graphs, charts, diagrams, and pictures. (p. 559)

Much attention has been given over the years to Verbal–Performance discrepancies (i.e., when one scale is significantly higher or lower than the other). The key word is "significantly." According to the WISC-III manual, the difference between the Verbal and the Performance Scale IQs should be 11.3 (rounded to 11) points or more in either direction to be significant. Such a difference forms the basis for a number of educational hypotheses important for the student's educational program or placement. The WISC-III manual provides tables (Appendix B) that are very helpful for determining statistical differences among scores.

Discrepancies of 11 points or more suggest a broad preference for one or the other mode of reasoning and suggest other differences, such as in cognitive style, in information-processing strengths or weaknesses, in difficulty in working under time pressure, or in differences in aptitudes and interests. Consideration also has to be given to the possibility of brain damage or emotional disturbance (Sattler, 1982). However, because discrepancies of 11 points or more occur in a significant number of students in the normal population, the discrepancy, by itself, should never be used to make such a diagnosis. If other corroborating evidence exists, then further testing becomes imperative.

This discussion brings me to a small but important digression. Much has been made of the fact that Verbal–Performance discrepancies (and other WISC-III clusters) occur so frequently in the normal population, that their diagnostic value is nil. I do not agree with such interpretations. It is true that Verbal–Performance discrepancies occur frequently in the normal population. Additionally, in the old WISC-R standardization sample, it was found that

> Verbal/Performance IQ differences were not related significantly to either sex or race, but were related significantly to parental occupation and to intelligence level. Children of professional parents tended to have higher Verbal than Performance IQs, while children of semiskilled and unskilled workers tended to have higher Performance than Verbal IQs. More Verbal/Performance differences were observed in the brighter groups than in the duller groups. At all levels of intelligence, it was about as likely that Verbal IQ would be higher than Performance IQ, as that it would be lower. (Sattler, 1982, p. 198)

These are important facts of which every school psychologist should be aware. They suggest to me that a combination of genetic and environmental factors influence the development of the two major factors tapped by the WISC-III.

As for the validity of interpreting such differences, Sattler made a statement that I think is very pertinent:

> Verbal/Performance differences may be significant and yet occur with some frequency in the population. Thus, the discrepancy may be a reliable one but not a unique one. The probability-of-occurrence approach is dependent on the correlation between the two Scales, while the reliability-of-difference approach is based on the standard error of measurement of each Scale. I recommend that when reliable (significant) differences occur between the child's Verbal and Performance scales, hypotheses about the child's cognitive strengths and weaknesses may be formulated. This recommendation is made because discrepancies may provide a meaningful profile (or pattern) of abilities, even though they may occur in a large segment of the population. (p. 198)

Thus, the examiner should always carefully consider a number of possible hypotheses when the Verbal–Performance discrepancy is 11 points or greater. Besides the ones already mentioned, Sattler (1982) also suggested the relationships between Verbal and Performance Scale scores listed in Figure 5.5.

In my experience, the student with the Verbal > Performance pattern is less likely to have a problem with academic subjects than the student with the Performance > Verbal pattern. For example, two students obtained the following WISC-III IQ scores:

Michele
Verbal IQ: 85
Performance IQ: 115
Full Scale IQ: 99 ±6

David
Verbal IQ: 115
Performance IQ: 85
Full Scale IQ: 99 ±6

Both students obtained the same Full Scale IQ, and both had markedly discrepant Verbal–Performance patterns (30 points). However, Michele is far more likely to have problems with reading, because language facility is such an integral part of it. In the upper years, if the pattern remains, Michele may benefit far more from a placement in a vocational school, because the hands-on training she gets in such a setting is far more matched to her strengths. Students such as Michele are likely to be classified as learning disabled or dyslexic; however, the underlying assumption is that, somehow, she can "catch up." This may or may not be true. Many factors are involved.

David may encounter some problems in school as well, but they are likely to be quite different from Michele's. David's verbal strengths will likely lead teachers and parents to have higher academic

Verbal > Performance	Performance > Verbal
1. Verbal skills better developed than performance skills.	1. Performance skills better developed than verbal skills.
2. Auditory processing mode better developed than visual nonverbal mode.	2. Visual nonverbal mode better developed than auditory processing mode.
3. Possible difficulty with practical tasks.	3. Possible difficulty with reading.
4. Possible performance deficit.	4. Possible language deficit.
5. Possible limitations in motor nonverbal output skills.	5. Possible limitations in auditory conceptual skills.

Figure 5.5. Illustrations of hypotheses developed from Verbal–Performance discrepancies. From *Assessment of Children's Intelligence and Special Abilities* (2nd ed., p. 200) by J. Sattler, 1982, Boston: Allyn & Bacon. Copyright 1982 by Allyn & Bacon. Used with permission of the author.

expectations of him. They are bound to notice his verbal facility and expect him to match it in academic tasks. If the situation requires oral discussion, he may very well do so. His reading may also be consistent with the Verbal IQ. However, he could have problems organizing himself on paper. Therefore, his written output may be more akin to his Performance IQ than to his Verbal or Full Scale IQ.

Again, such generalizations are not perfect, so caution must be observed in such interpretations. Behavioral observations and teacher comments about how the student works under different task demands are very important considerations in each case.

For students whose Verbal–Performance discrepancies are also associated with written output problems, the written expression compensations suggested in Appendix 5B may be applicable. Some research also supports the use of electromyographic biofeedback for improvement in handwriting, other academics, and self-concept (Carter & Russell, 1985). The improvements occurred in as little as ten 1-hour sessions. One practical drawback, however, is the special biofeedback training required.

For most school situations, then, the Verbal–Performance discrepancies merit careful attention. Remedial attention in the Performance > Verbal profile should focus primarily on language and reading development in the elementary grades. This pattern also corresponds closely to the one that Wallbrown, Blaha, and Vance (1980) called "Pervasive Language Disability." The prognosis, according to these authors, for the student who received 3 to 5 hours per week of individual instruction in a reading clinic for 2 years, is very poor in terms of catching up to grade level. Thus, the objective of having the student catch up may be unrealistic in such cases. That does not mean that the effort should not be made, or that other techniques could not produce better results.

Language development, especially as applied to reading, becomes a major objective for such students in the primary grades. In the following sections, I discuss some strategies for vocabulary development in reading. They require the student's background of information, abstract reasoning, and lexical knowledge. As such, the strategies draw on many of the language aspects tapped by the Verbal Scale of the WISC-III.

Vocabulary Development Strategies

Building associations among words requires building a meaning base, that is, stretching and expanding the student's schemata (internal cognitive structures). However, as I discussed in Chapter 4, schema theory is not as powerful an explanatory model as dual coding theory. Besides building schemas, the educator's job is to link language to an internal visual representation of it. The internal visual representation forms an additional way to store information. Thus, in addition to knowing the word *strawberry* based on one's experiences with strawberries, it is necessary to code the experience with a visual representation of it. Building vocabulary is an important part of every student's normal development and formal schooling. For those students whose Full Scale IQ scores are low, this is even more true. Before I begin discussing some vocabulary-building strategies in depth, however, an important caveat is necessary.

Reading vocabulary builds via reading. The paradox, then, is that good readers (those who can both decode and dual code what they decode) are the ones whose vocabularies grow by reading. From about Grade 5 on, a good reader reads at least a million words a year. That level of exposure introduces them to many new words, and, if their comprehension processes (both verbal and nonverbal) are intact, then vocabulary growth is automatic. Although a student's vocabulary can grow based on verbal stimulation alone, the growth is much more complete when the process of using mental imagery is simultaneously being applied.

With that in mind, a number of methods have been used to develop reading vocabularies. These methods are applicable, with modifications, at practically every level of intelligence that might be measured by the WISC-III.

Experience-based strategies. An experience-based strategy for vocabulary building emphasizes—just as might be expected—students' own experiences. These strategies are closely related to the semantic ones I discuss next, although some of the semantic strategies do not build on experience as a cornerstone.

Why is an experience base important for building vocabulary? According to Duffelmeyer (1985),

> The more firmly rooted in experience each schema is, the more integrity it has. Thus word meanings that are rooted in experience would result in more substantial schemata than word meanings that lack an experiential foundation.
>
> All of this suggests that vocabulary instruction should be experience-based. Otherwise, students are likely to end up with a store of words that Dale

refers to as "floating items unattached to real experience [where] the shell of meaning is there, but the kernel is missing."

Some research supports the notion that experience-based vocabulary learning is superior to non–experience-based approaches, such as using context or using the dictionary (Duffelmeyer, 1985). Duffelmeyer described four strategies using this approach in a teaching lesson. I quote only one of them:

Strategy 1: Synonyms and Examples

- Planning. Select a word you wish to teach. Decide on a simple synonym for the word, find several familiar examples that illustrate the concept, and write a sentence containing the word.

  Example:

  Word: renowned

  Synonym: famous

  Examples: Christopher Columbus, Reggie Jackson, Michael Jackson.

  Sentence: If you discovered a cure for the common cold, you'd be renowned.

- Teaching

  Teacher: (Displays *renowned,* pronounces it, and has students pronounce it.) *Renowned* means the same thing as famous. A person becomes *renowned* by doing something that no one else has ever done or by doing something very, very well. For example, Christopher Columbus is renowned for . . .

  Student: Discovering America.

  Teacher: Reggie Jackson is renowned for . . .

  Student: Hitting a lot of homers.

  Teacher: Another example of someone who is renowned is Michael Jackson. What is he renowned for?

  Student: "Thriller," that real scary video.

  Student: The millions of records he sold.

  Teacher: What other person do you know of who is renowned?

  Student: Sally Ride.

  Teacher: What is she renowned for?

Student: She was the first woman astronaut from the United States to go into outer space.

Teacher: (Displays a sentence.) Read this sentence silently. (Pause.) Why would you be renowned if you discovered a cure for the common cold?

Student: Because right now there is no cure.

Student: And it would help millions and millions of people all over the world. (pp. 7–8)

The other strategies mentioned by Duffelmeyer are positive and negative instances, example and definition, and definition and use. Each is discussed in the same practical detail as the one just quoted. Readers can refer to the article for complete details.

Another useful and related vocabulary-building strategy is the word bank, complemented by word sorts. In word banks, the student selects words from his or her own experience and language bases, writes or prints them on file cards, and keeps them in a "bank" of some sort. A number of teaching activities can be done with the words in the bank (see Appendix 5A). Note how the addition of visualization strengthens all of these strategies.

Semantic-based strategies. A number of general semantic-based techniques are used by regular and special education teachers for reading. Some are based on analysis of context clues, which can be used in isolation or in the act of reading itself. These strategies may not be as effective as the experience-based ones, but they need to be taught in any case. These strategies are commonly used and do not take nearly as much teaching time as the experience-based ones. Goodman (1973) provided the following seven strategies and principles, all of which are semantic based:

1. The way the word or phrase is used is a good clue to its meaning in the particular passage.

2. Authors frequently provide simple definitions right in the text: "To measure wind speed, meteorologists use an anemometer."

3. If a word is important, it will occur several times. Each subsequent occurrence will provide a new context to help the reader zero in on its meaning.

4. If the word is unimportant to the reader's comprehension, he will only need a vague notion of its meaning to go on. Usually its context provides that. Most proficient readers have learned to be undisturbed by a few unimportant words, the meanings of which are uncertain.

5. Dictionaries are most helpful for confirmation when the reader has formed a fairly strong notion of a word's meaning from the context.

6. If the word or phrase is a name difficult to pronounce or a foreign word, it may be sufficient to use a place holder to facilitate reading. Calling the character with the Slavic name Ivan may be good enough—and save a lot of time while avoiding distraction.

7. One need not be able to pronounce every word to get its meaning. Most proficient readers have many words in their reading vocabularies they do not use or have not heard used orally.

Our research has shown that less proficient readers dissipate a lot of energy working at every word while more proficient readers have the confidence that they can get the meaning without word-by-word accuracy. (p. 66)

These strategies are all derivatives from PL theory. They are excellent, day-to-day semantic strategies that can be used by regular teachers and, with modification, by special educators. Their intent is to help build reading vocabulary levels in all groups of students, regardless of intelligence level. However, in most special education classes, a good deal more structure is required to help students acquire the same strategies that good readers seem to pick up incidentally. This structure can be provided by modeling, a great deal of "thinking aloud" on the part of the teacher, and adding the process of visualization. For example, if a teacher is working with a student who comes to a word he does not know, the teacher could pause and think aloud by asking, "OK. Here's a word that's new (difficult) for you. What are some things you could do to figure out what it means?" Try to elicit the following kinds of strategies from the student:

- "I could read the other parts of the sentence. That's a good clue."

- "I could see if the word is used anywhere else in the paragraph. Sometimes that helps."

- "I could see if the author gives a definition."

- "I could ask the teacher." (This strategy should be used only infrequently.)

- "I could skip over it if it's not that important anyway."

- "If it's a name that's hard to pronounce, I could substitute an easier name for it every time I see it."

Whereas students who are good readers seem to pick up these strategies incidentally, the poor reader frequently needs to have them taught. If the student cannot verbalize the strategies as in the example just shown, the remedial teacher can do so first, and then have the student follow suit. The idea is to model first, then have the student eventually internalize the strategies. Many students with reading problems will learn to internalize such strategies with time, but they often must be encouraged to do so in a very direct manner by the teacher. Of course, I am assuming they can already decipher the word. If they cannot, the above strategies are too advanced and therefore meaningless to the students.

Additional factors must be considered at different levels of reading. For example, at the beginning stages of reading, children need to build a sight vocabulary for reading, again regardless of their intelligence level. (Most children in our culture are exposed to, and remember, certain signs such as "McDonald's" and "Exit," which become part of their initial reading vocabulary.)

When children are taught to read, basal readers are almost always used. These all have a controlled vocabulary, and the vocabulary is almost always selected on the basis of frequency of occurrence. That is the basis of the Dolch (1936) word list, for example. School psychologists should be aware of cognitive factors that can affect the "learnability" of a word. One such major factor is the categorization level of the word, which King (1984) explained as follows:

Children as well as adults have fairly stable hierarchies for concept and category members. That is, they are aware that *apple* and *banana* are related, and at some stage of cognitive development, know that both are fruit. A unique aspect of this approach is that within these hierarchies there exists a basic level of categorization which is more salient than category levels which are superordinate or subordinate relative to the basic level. *Chair, flower,* and *car* are basic level objects because they represent their respective categories at highly discriminable levels. Car cues are highly differentiated from chair or flower cues. *Furniture, animal, plant,* and *vehicle* are superordinate. They share very few salient attributes and therefore, comparisons between them yield little usable information. They have low cue validities. *Kitchen chair, poodle, petunia,* and *sports car* are subordinate. These more specific examples have many overlapping attributes with other category members at this level of categorization and therefore have a lower cue validity than the basic level objects. (pp. 130–131)

A number of studies show that categorization by *basic* levels is very facilitative. Therefore, *basic* words might be learned easier by sight than superordinate, subordinate, or high-frequency words. This prediction was confirmed by King (1984), who found that basic words were learned faster and recalled better after 24 hours.

Teachers of beginning readers and special education teachers dealing with students who have difficulty acquiring sight vocabulary, should try to develop their own basic word lists for their students and use them as needed. High frequency or concreteness is an insufficient criterion to include a given word.

The implications of King's (1984) study for school psychologists and teachers are the following:

1. Be aware that basic nouns in basal readers are much easier to learn than super- or subordinates.

2. Use super- and subordinate names with care for beginning readers.

3. Discuss the relationship between unknown nouns and known, basic nouns where appropriate in the reading lesson. Semantic mapping, discussed next, may be helpful in this respect.

4. Pictures that illustrate basic concepts should also be at a basic level. Thus, a flashcard with the word *chair* printed on it should be accompanied by a very *basic* generic illustration of a chair. A picture of a bean-bag chair, for example, would not be as appropriate as a picture of a dining chair.

5. Categorization and classification skills should begin with basic words and move to super- and subordinates. Children can classify from higher levels, but this is more difficult for them.

For children who have some difficulty on the Similarities subtest of the WISC-III, these findings might be useful.

Semantic mapping. Semantic mapping is a widely used, highly advocated method of developing reading vocabulary. This technique activates what students already know about a word. Students generate "maps" that link the unfamiliar or target word to existing words and concepts.

There are a number of variations of the technique. I present one example here, the steps of which might be employed in the construction of a semantic map on seasons of the year.[1]

1. Hand each child a piece of paper on which is written the name of one season of the year. Have each child write on the paper all the things that come to mind when he or she thinks of that season. Allow a short period of time for this.

2. Have the children read their lists. Compile these on the chalkboard in a manner similar to that shown in Figure 5.6.

3. The semantic maps may be expanded as the children think of additional items to be added.

4. The semantic maps can be refined and extended. For example, ask the children

if they could group any of the items related to winter. It may be necessary to ask such questions as, "What do cold, snow, and blizzards have in common?"

Thus, a refined semantic map for winter may look like the one shown in Figure 5.7.

Verbalizing. Discussion should be encouraged to go from the top, down (deductively), or from general to specific (i.e., there are four seasons of the year; one of them is winter; in winter, it is cold; etc.). They should also be encouraged to go from the specific to the general (inductively), or from the bottom, up (i.e., skating, skiing, and playing hockey are all things that you can do in winter; winter is one of the four seasons of the year).

Extension and practice. To make sure the child does understand the relationships, practice is needed. Many activities could be designed for this. For example, (a) Keep the structure of the map intact, but remove the words, and have children write them in the correct place (flashcards can be used if desired) or (b) after studying lessons, ask children to use their maps to help them write a paragraph about the topic.

5. Similar semantic maps can be constructed for the other seasons—or for virtually any other theme consistent with your program.

An important ingredient of semantic mapping is the group process involved between teacher and students. It is this very feature that makes semantic mapping a useful classroom procedure in both regular and special education classes with students of varying verbal abilities. Readers should keep in mind what I discussed earlier regarding basic versus super- and subordinate word learning. Perhaps basic words should most frequently be used as the target words in semantic mapping to facilitate learning.

One interesting variation of semantic mapping is the ENIGMA (Engineering Individual Growth through Manipulative Associations) program (Sachs & Banas, 1985). The teacher cuts a high-quality pic-

---

1. I extend my thanks to Marilyn Znider, reading specialist with Rocky View School Division, Calgary, Alberta, for preparing the example.

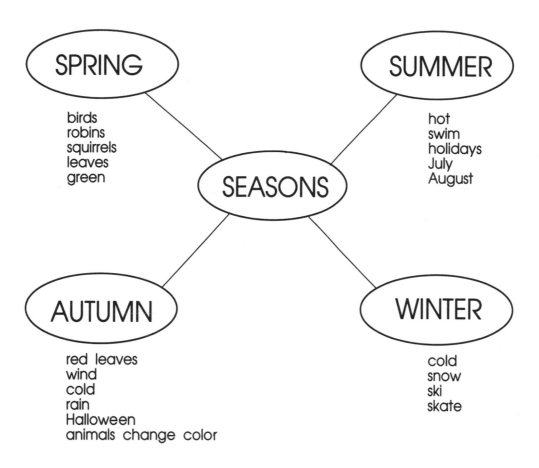

Figure 5.6. Seasons semantic map.

ture (e.g., from a magazine) into pieces. Vocabulary items are taken from the picture, and the teacher writes an appropriate accompanying story. The vocabulary items are printed separately on cards (concrete words can be placed on white paper, and more abstract words on another color), and can be repeated as often as possible in the story. In a small group, students are then given the picture puzzle pieces and asked to arrange the pieces correctly. Word cards are then matched to the picture. (This is not only a semantic map; it is a visual map.) Students then take turns reading the story. Difficult words can be practiced by the student for homework; the student also may draw an appropriate picture to accompany the difficult word. A number of other excellent activities can be developed that are appropriate to the student's age and reading level. More details can be found in Sachs and Banas's article.

Mnemonic-based strategies. Mnemonic-based techniques differ radically from the experience- and semantic-based techniques already

discussed. Their classroom use is not as well developed, but school psychologists and special educators should become aware of them and begin using them more often. Research shows that the mnemonic strategies are superior to the semantic ones for learning new words, particularly for low achievers and/or students with learning disabilities (Levin et al., 1984). This does not mean that they should be used exclusively. A combination of methods and approaches needs to be recommended by school psychologists and used by remedial teachers as they seem appropriate with individual students. Students with low verbal patterns on the WISC-III will benefit from an eclectic approach using a variety of procedures.

The major mnemonic strategy for vocabulary development is called the *keyword* approach. It is based on the idea that a word is better learned and stored in memory if it is more effectively encoded in the first place. The procedure for developing a keyword is to use a word that is acoustically similar to the target word. For example, if the new

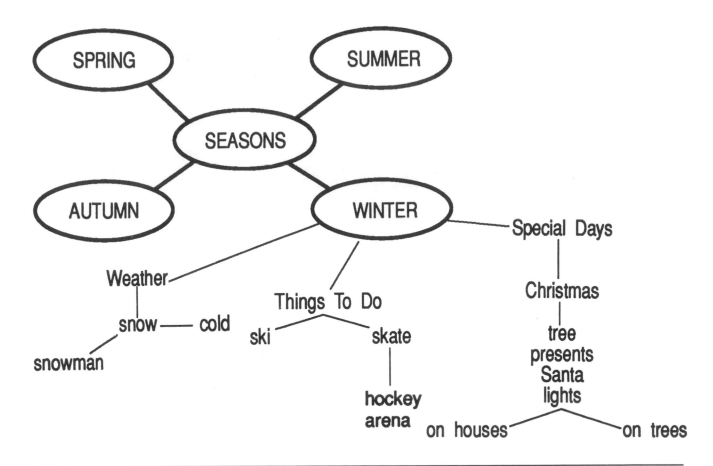

Figure 5.7. Refined semantic map of seasons.

vocabulary item to be learned is *angler,* an acoustically similar word such as *angel* might be appropriate. Then—and this is most important—the parallel acoustic word and the target word are illustrated together. They need to interact in some way. Thus, for *angler,* the drawing shown in Figure 5.8 might be appropriate.

If one were teaching new vocabulary in a foreign language, such as the Spanish word for *duck* (*pato*), a good, acoustically similar word in English might be *pot,* or perhaps *potato.* Then, the pot and the duck are drawn so that they are interacting, as in Figure 5.9.

The student must also be taught how to retrieve the appropriate response. For the example in Figure 5.9, Scruggs and Mastropieri (1984) suggested the following:

> When the student is asked what the meaning of *pato* is, he is told first to think of the keyword for *pato* (*pot*) and then told to think back to the picture with the pot in it, and what was happening in

that picture. In this case, the learner thinks of the picture of the duck with the pot on its head, and, therefore, is able to respond that *pato* means *duck.* (p. 160)

These authors also emphasized that

> The most important thing to remember, whenever using the strategy, is to think of a good keyword that sounds as much as possible like the word to be learned and to picture it in some interactive way with the information to be learned. Just to think of a duck and a pot together to recall the Spanish word *pato* is not sufficient. The duck and the pot must actually be doing something together. This makes retrieval much easier. (p. 162)

The keyword method has been used successfully in a variety of content areas. History, science, social studies, language, and foreign language concepts have all been taught using this approach.

A related method to the keyword approach is called *pegword.* The pegword strategy is best applied to learning sequenced information, such as

ANGLER (ANGEL) a person who likes to go fishing

Figure 5.8. "Angler" keyword. From "Vocabulary Learning Strategies" by J. Levin et al., 1984, *Reading Psychology, 5,* p. 4. Copyright 1984 by Hemisphere Publishing. Reprinted with permission.

the order of U.S. presidents or Canadian prime ministers, or the hardness level of minerals. Therefore, the strategy may be useful for those students who show sequencing difficulties on the WISC-III, and for whom sequencing is difficult on academic tasks. Scruggs and Mastropieri (1984) described the strategy as follows:

> This is a rhyming scheme in which a pictured word, which rhymes for each number, is given—that is, *one* equals *bun, two* equals *shoe, three* equals *tree, four* equals *door, five* equals *hive* . . . . Learners are told to memorize these pegwords. Then, if students need to learn any information in sequence, they tie each item to its associated pegword. In learning hardness levels of certain minerals, for example, learners can think of a keyword for the mineral and picture it interacting with the associated pegword. Therefore, to recall that bauxite is number one on the hardness scale, learners can think of a keyword

for bauxite, which could be box, and imagine a picture of a box full of buns. Then, to retrieve the information when they hear the word bauxite, they can think back to the box, remember that it was full of buns, remember that *bun* equals the number *one,* and respond with that number. (p. 163)

This method can be used in other ways, such as

> learning the order of the U.S. presidents. For example, to remember that Jackson was number 7, learners first think of a keyword for Jackson, which could be *jacks,* and associate it with its pegword for *seven,* which is *heaven.* An image could be pictured of angels playing jacks in heaven. . . . (p. 163)

If students have to learn more than 10 items, the pegword/keyword approach is limited. However, it can be extended by using the *method of loci,* which is actually a very old technique, used frequently by Greek orators. One method of loci

Mnemonic Illustration of pato = duck.

Pato (pot)   Duck

Figure 5.9. "Duck" keyword. From "Improving Memory for Facts: The Keyword Method" by T. Scruggs and M. Mastropieri, 1984, *Academic Therapy, 20,* p. 160. Copyright 1984 by Academic Therapy Publications. Reprinted with permission.

involves relating each season of the year to a decade of numbers. Thus, spring can include the numbers 1 to 10, and be associated with a spring garden scene. To complete the Jackson scene, the angels playing in heaven with jacks can be doing so above a spring garden. When the student retrieves this scene, because it includes the spring garden, he or she knows it must be in the first 10 numbers. For summer, the primary scene might be a summer beach scene. Summer would include the numbers 11 to 20. Thus, for example, to remember that Fillmore was the 13th president:

First, one thinks of a keyword for Fillmore, which could be *film,* and the pegword *three* plus its seasonal referent, which would be a summer beach scene to make it the second decade of three, or

thirteen. Therefore, to recall that Fillmore is president number 13, one could think of a film in a tree in a summer beach scene. (Scruggs & Mastropieri, 1984, pp. 163–164)

Including the seasons extends the number of sequences that could be learned to 40. However, the Greeks extended it to infinity by simply increasing the number of scenes in some integrated way. For example, if one had to memorize a great deal of information, such as to perform in a play, one could visualize a house with any number of distinct rooms. In each room, one could place a scene until one had the whole play covered. The Greek orators were said to memorize their speeches in this fashion, and were specifically trained in the method of loci.

Obviously, there are other ways to memorize text or sequences. However, this unique and intriguing method may be especially useful for students who have difficulty memorizing specific items.

Attribute learning. Another related mnemonic method is attribute learning. This strategy is similar to semantic mapping, but is primarily visually based, rather than verbally based. Semantic mapping delineates how words are related to each other in a verbal way. Attribute learning visually demonstrates and expands a concept. For example,

It may not be enough to know simply that bauxite is number one on the hardness scale. It may be important to know several other things about bauxite, such as its color and what it is used for. The learning of such attributes has also been increased with the use of the keyword method. For example, to remember that bauxite is number one on the hardness scale, white in color, and used in making aluminum, one could picture the keyword for bauxite, *box*. In addition, the box may be colored white to represent the color. Aluminum foil in the box with the buns can represent the use, and the buns themselves can represent the hardness level. Similarly, to recall that pyrite is six on the hardness scale, yellow in color and used for making acid, the learner can picture a yellow pie (keyword for pyrite) resting on sticks (pegword for six) with acid being poured into it. Other content areas for which attribute learning may be helpful include biology (for example, organs of the body and their functions) or social studies (for example, famous people and their accomplishments). (Scruggs & Mastropieri, 1984, p. 165)

Attribute learning goes well beyond vocabulary development. However, a big drawback at the present time to using the mnemonic strategies is the lack of commercially available, teacher-made materials. The method also takes for granted that the student can generate such imagery; however, some students cannot do so, and someone else must help them develop the imagery.

Comparing semantic to mnemonic strategies. In special education, it is important to know whether a strategy works, because time is such a precious commodity. However, comparisons are also important. If one strategy works better than another for a special education population, that strategy should be carefully considered for addition to the repertoire of strategies the special education teacher needs at his or her disposal.

When comparing semantic mapping to the keyword approach in research studies, the keyword approach wins. In one study, for example, the keyword method was compared with semantic mapping and contextual analysis (Levin et al., 1984). High achievers were compared with low achievers on the three methods. For the low achievers, the keyword approach was significantly superior to the other methods in all outcomes of recall tested. Indeed, except in one area, the low achievers *matched* the high achievers in all outcomes. This is strong evidence of a powerful tool!

In another study (Mastropieri, Scruggs, & Levin, 1985), junior high school students with learning disabilities (WISC-R Full Scale IQs ranging from 72 to 129) were taught the hardness levels of minerals using the keyword/pegword approach, a traditional teacher-questioning/drill method and a free-study condition in which students were shown how to study the hardness levels and given materials to do so. Results are shown in Table 5.3. The high achievers and low achievers in this group were those with reading comprehension scores on the *California Achievement Test* at or above the 40th percentile and below the 30th percentile, respectively. The mnemonic techniques were superior for both groups. Although mnemonic strategies generally require much more processing time, they may well be worth the time because recall after a 24-hour delay is substantial.

Strengthening and stretching recall ability: An appeal for an eclectic approach. I began this section by focusing on students with low Verbal compared with Performance WISC-III scores. These students are particularly difficult to remediate in terms of bringing them up to grade level; however, there are ways of building and stretching these students' vocabularies by a judicious use of both semantic and mnemonic techniques. Both are necessary, although some preference might be given to the mnemonic strategies in some circumstances for some students. Although these techniques are good for all learners, evidence suggests that they are especially effective for the lower achieving student.

Another factor that needs to be considered in teaching vocabulary is the multiple meanings of words. For example, even at the primer level, there

TABLE 5.3. Mean Percent Correct by Experimental Condition and Achievement Level

	Condition			
	Mnemonic	Questioning	Free Study	Across Conditions
Lower achievers	70.0	25.7	27.6	41.1
Higher achievers	80.5	30.0	44.8	51.7
Across achievement levels	75.2	27.8	36.2	

From "Mnemonic Strategy Instruction with Learning Disabled Adolescents" by M. Mastropieri, T. Scruggs, and J. Levin, February 1985, *Journal of Learning Disabilities, 18*(2), p. 96. Copyright 1985 by The Professional Press. Reprinted with permission.

are 37 meanings of the word *run,* 21 meanings of *sound,* 20 meanings of *play,* and 17 meanings of *cut.* About 90% of basal word lists in reading series have multiple meanings. The number of words a child knows correlates strongly with reading comprehension. In addition, the number of different meanings known for a single word and the ability to select a particular meaning in a given context relate to reading comprehension (Searls & Klesius, 1984).

How can a teacher help students recognize multiple meanings? A good part of every primary and special education teacher's time is spent on vocabulary development. Searls and Klesius offered some excellent instructional strategies to help the instructor teach multiple word meanings. Their list of the 99 most common multiple-meaning words is shown in Figure 5.10. These are all taught in first grade and occur frequently in later grades.

These authors suggest that multiple meanings can be taught using pictures and objects. For example, *duck* could be illustrated by a picture of a duck, or of a person who ducks going through a doorway. The student and teacher share an oral discussion and generate examples of their own. This, as previously discussed, is very important, because it draws in the experience base of the students. (In addition, the group process allows those students who have a weak experience base to profit from hearing students with stronger ones.) Definitions could be listed in various ways. Children could be encouraged to bring in their own pictures and have the other students guess which of the meanings the word represents.

A variation of semantic mapping could be used. Figure 5.11 shows a map for *run,* which illustrates some of its many meanings.

Students could be grouped and develop their own semantic maps for a particular word. Each

meaning could also be illustrated, acted out, or posted in some way. I believe this step is extremely important for the remedial student because it provides a direct link from experience to word. All the groups' words could then be shared and displayed around the room or school.

Context could also be used, because it provides clues to word meaning. Sentences such as the following could be created to show how syntax affects meaning (Searls & Klesius, 1984, p. 61):

—The *cook* will *cook* a delicious meal.

—Jane wants to *dance* at the *dance.*

—The *rain* may *rain* all afternoon.

Prepositions also have multiple meanings. These are best taught in context as well. Here are some examples (Searls & Klesius, 1984, p. 62):

—Bill was reading a book *by* the tree.

—The book was *by* his favorite author.

—Bob said he would come *by* my house.

—He said he would be there *by* three o'clock.

—We went to the football game *by* bus.

—Our team won the game *by* one point.

Searls and Klesius suggested that students be given blank playing cards, each with one multiple-meaning word. Various card games could be played. Furthermore, writing activities could be drawn out of the words.

One student can write a sentence in which one multiple-meaning word is used in two different ways. The sentence is read aloud omitting the target word. Other students can guess the word. Using a multiple-meaning word identified by the teacher, each student writes a sentence on a 3×5 card. The

about	cook	house	paper	stay
as	cry	how	picture	stop
at	cut	in	place	story
away	dance	it	play	tail
back	do	just	pot	take
ball	down	kind	rain	time
basket	duck	leave	rake	to
bear	end	let	ride	too
bed	fall	like	right	tree
big	fast	live	roll	up
book	fish	long	room	use
by	fly	look	run	wait
call	for	make	saw	walk
can	game	may	school	want
care	get	mean	see	way
clean	give	nose	sentence	will
coat	go	on	show	word
cold	have	out	sit	work
color	head	over	so	yellow
come	help	paint	sound	

Figure 5.10. Basic list of 99 multiple-meaning words. Having students make a "mental picture" for each sentence will also greatly enhance their ability to discriminate the meanings. From "Multiple-Meaning Words for Primary Students and How to Teach Them" by E. Searls and L. Klesius, 1984, *Reading Psychology, 5,* p. 58. Copyright 1984 by Hemisphere Publishing. Reprinted with permission.

cards can then be sorted and put in envelopes on which are written different meanings of the word. Children can write stories incorporating as many different meanings of a target group of words as possible. (p. 62)

Variations of some of the mnemonic strategies also could be attempted. These should probably be used only for meanings that are particularly troublesome for an individual student.

In all the activities discussed thus far, the students' background of information, their abstracting ability, and their vocabularies are used and stretched. These are integral components of the verbal factor tapped by the WISC-III.

Teaching takes time, and for students for whom language facility is weak, time is at a premium. School psychologists and remedial teachers must therefore be continually vigilant for new methods that might be more effective for special education students.

It is interesting to speculate why the mnemonic strategies appear to be superior. The procedures I have described all have one thing in common; that

is, they make heavy use of *visualization.* The importance of visualization is described by Bell (1991):

Visualization is a primary factor basic to the processes involved in language comprehension, language expression and critical thinking. It is the sensory information that connects us to language and thought. However, many individuals—both children and adults—have weakness in creating mental images and thereby have weak reading comprehension, weak oral language comprehension, weak verbal skills, and poor critical thinking. (p. vi)

In her book, *Visualizing and Verbalizing,* Bell (1991) provides a step-by-step process for visualization that builds facility in the areas of weakness cited. The procedure is sequential, takes nothing for granted, and has provided excellent clinical results. Workshops in the technique are also available.

Thus, if phonemic processing is the key to deciphering and visualization is the key to comprehension, then the task of special educators is to develop proficiency in these areas. We live in exciting times. I personally am very excited about these newfound "keys" to literacy. I now believe it is possible to remediate many forms of reading disabilities through effective use of these keys. I also believe we are poised to prevent them from occurring in the first place.

WISC-III Factor Splits

Factor splits on WISC-III profiles involve Level II interpretation. These splits are very common in referred students.

Figure 5.12 shows an 11-year-old student's WISC-III profile that illustrates factor splits. Sara obtained the following WISC-III results:

Verbal IQ: 102

Performance IQ: 98

Full Scale IQ: 100 ± 6

Although there is no significant discrepancy (11 points or more) between the Verbal and Performance IQs and the Full Scale IQ indicates average ability, to end the interpretation at this point would be a great disservice to Sara.

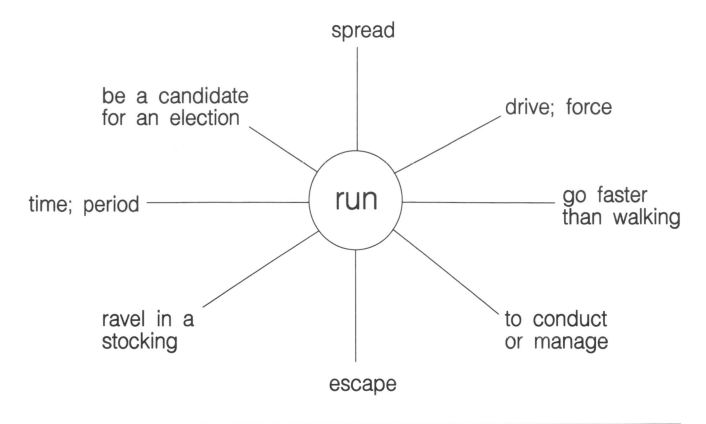

Figure 5.11. Semantic map of a multiple-meaning word. From ''Multiple-Meaning Words for Primary Students and How to Teach Them'' by E. Searls and L. Klesius, 1984, *Reading Psychology, 5,* p. 60. Copyright 1984 by Hemisphere Publishing. Reprinted with permission.

The variability in Sara's subtest and factor scores indicates her strengths and weaknesses. Factors I and II are about evenly developed (even so, the weakness on the Comprehension subtest within Factor I must be accounted for). This pattern is consistent with the similar Verbal and Performance IQs, and is to be expected. However, the Freedom from Distractibility factor is very much lower than either of the other two. Whenever the Factor III average is 3 points lower than the average of either Factor I or Factor II, then it is interpretable psychometrically, and should be considered educationally significant (Kaufman, 1979).

I find this pattern repeatedly in referred students. It is somewhat of a misnomer to call this factor Freedom from Distractibility, however, because distractibility may not be the reason a student scores low on it. The low score may also indicate a developmental delay in any of the following: selective attention, impulsivity, poor facility with numbers, a simultaneous–successive information processing discrepancy, and poor short-term mem-

ory. It may also suggest poor ability for phonemic manipulation. Careful observation, more testing, and/or discussion with the student's teacher and parents are important to confirm or deny the hypotheses suggested.

I will now examine each of these hypotheses in terms of the educational strategies they suggest.

Distractibility. If one can determine that a student's primary problem *is* distractibility, a number of intervention strategies could be employed. Some of the ones I have found particularly useful are the "Good Behavior Game Plus Merit," described in Chapter 3, and the self-monitoring technique described in Appendix 2C.

Drug and/or diet therapy often is advocated for distractible students. Although there is a limited place for drug therapy with hyperactive/distractible students, I do not feel it should be a treatment advocated by school psychologists. I do not advocate drug therapy as an approach, primarily because drug therapy does *not* improve learning, even though it may have a dramatic, positive effect on

Name _Sara_ _____ Sex _____

School _____ Grade _____

Examiner _____ Handedness _____

WISC-III™
Wechsler Intelligence Scale for Children – Third Edition

Subtests	Raw Scores	Scaled Scores				
Picture Completion	22	11		11		
Information	17	10	10			
Coding	32	5				5
Similarities	23	14	14			
Picture Arrangement	32	10		10		
Arithmetic	14	6			6	
Block Design	50	13		13		
Vocabulary	43	15	15			
Object Assembly	27	9		9		
Comprehension	18	7	7			
(Symbol Search)	N/A	(N/A)				N/A
(Digit Span)	10	(6)			6	
(Mazes)	N/A	(N/A)				
Sum of Scaled Scores		52	48	46	43	12	—
		Verbal	Perfor.	VC	PO	FD	PS

Full Scale Score **100**

OPTIONAL

	Year	Month	Day
Date Tested			
Date of Birth			
Age	11	6	29

	Score	IQ/Index	%ile	95% Confidence Interval
Verbal	52	102	55	96 – 108
Performance	48	98	45	90 – 106
Full Scale	100	100	50	94 – 106
VC	46	108	70	101 – 114
PO	43	105	63	96 – 113
FD	12	78	7	72 – 90
PS				–

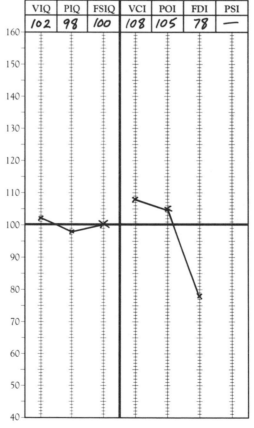

Subtest Scores

	Verbal						Performance					
	Inf	Sim	Ari	Voc	Com	DS	PC	Cd	PA	BD	OA	SS	Mz
	10	14	6	15	7	6	11	5	10	13	9	/	/

IQ Scores			Index Scores (Optional)			
VIQ	PIQ	FSIQ	VCI	POI	FDI	PSI
102	98	100	108	105	78	—

Figure 5.12. Sara's profile.

the distractible behavior. Also, such therapy makes the student think, "I can function *only* when I'm on medication. *I'm better* when I'm on medication." The results of many research studies indicate that the common drugs such as Ritalin® and Cylert® do not enhance student learning. If they do, the actions are drug specific; that is, if a student does better on Mazes while on Ritalin, the improved performance will not generalize to when the student is off the drug. The bottom line is that students must learn to deal with their distractibility, which is a difficult, long-term process.

Treatment of distractibility through diet therapy is also difficult on a practical level, but worth pursuing, especially as some individuals seem to be very sensitive to certain foods and/or additives. Any form of diet therapy should be administered under medical auspices only.

Vitamin therapy also is touted as a treatment for hyperactive/distractible youngsters. Unfortunately, most of the reports and claims are anecdotal in nature, and very little well-controlled research confirms or denies potential benefits or harms. The authors of one double-blind study stated,

> We conclude that large doses of water-soluble vitamins—niacinamide, pyridoxine, ascorbic acid, and calcium pantothenate—have no beneficial effect for children with ADD [attention deficit disorder]. Furthermore, many children had a significant elevation of serum transaminase levels during the vitamin administration and many withdrew from the study because of gastrointestinal complaints, indicating that megadoses of these vitamins are potentially toxic and could cause severe hepatic injury. Because of their ineffectiveness and possible serious side effects, megavitamins should not be utilized in the management of children with ADD. (Haslam, Dalby, & Rademaker, 1984, p. 110)[2]

Developmental delay in selective attention. The terms *distractibility* and *attention span* are often used interchangeably. Attention can be described as the ability to focus awareness selectively. In many special education students, such ability seems to be lacking, for whatever reason. I have found

Ross' (1976) explanation of the development of selective attention to be very helpful at times. Figure 5.13 illustrates Ross' three developmental phases of selective attention.

In the overexclusive phase, the child sees the trees, one might say, but not the forest. Attention is focused on one salient feature of the object, and the child excludes the rest. Some students seem overwhelmed, for example, by the multisensory impact of a rich environment. Perhaps they focus on only one (often irrelevant) feature of the task at hand. In the overinclusive phase, the opposite happens: The child attends to many aspects of the stimulus. This happens to all children, but, in those for whom the phase lasts longer than normal, the label "distractible" applies, according to Ross. Finally, the child (around age 12, on the average) enters the selective-attention phase. He or she is able to focus attention on the appropriate feature of the stimulus necessary to the task at hand. This involves also being able to suppress or inhibit what is irrelevant and unnecessary.

Children, particularly those with learning disabilities, who are slow to enter this phase, were described by Ross as follows:

> It may be that the learning-disabled child, and particularly the disabled reader, is again slow in acquiring this skill (selective attention). Such a child might still be using the overinclusive mode of attention when his or her peers are already functioning at the level of selective attention. Such children would respond to all manner of irrelevant stimuli, making them appear impulsive, distractible, and hyperactive. (p. 55)

The major remedial implication that arises from this perspective is that students who are having difficulty attending to a task must be taught to attend to the relevant features of the task at hand. One way to do this is by increasing the salience of the stimulus:

> If one wishes to teach a child to differentiate between *b* and *d*, for example (or various sight words), it is preferable to present these letter pairs in a variety of sizes and degrees of brightness, as well as in different parts of the writing surface, than to repeat the presentation of the same pair over and over again. (Ross, 1976, p. 58)

---

2. I find the label "attention deficit disorder" of limited value in the school system. It is a clinical term (and often leads directly to drug treatment), it implies a defect in the student, and it does not specify in any way the *nature* (etiology) of the so-called attention disorder.

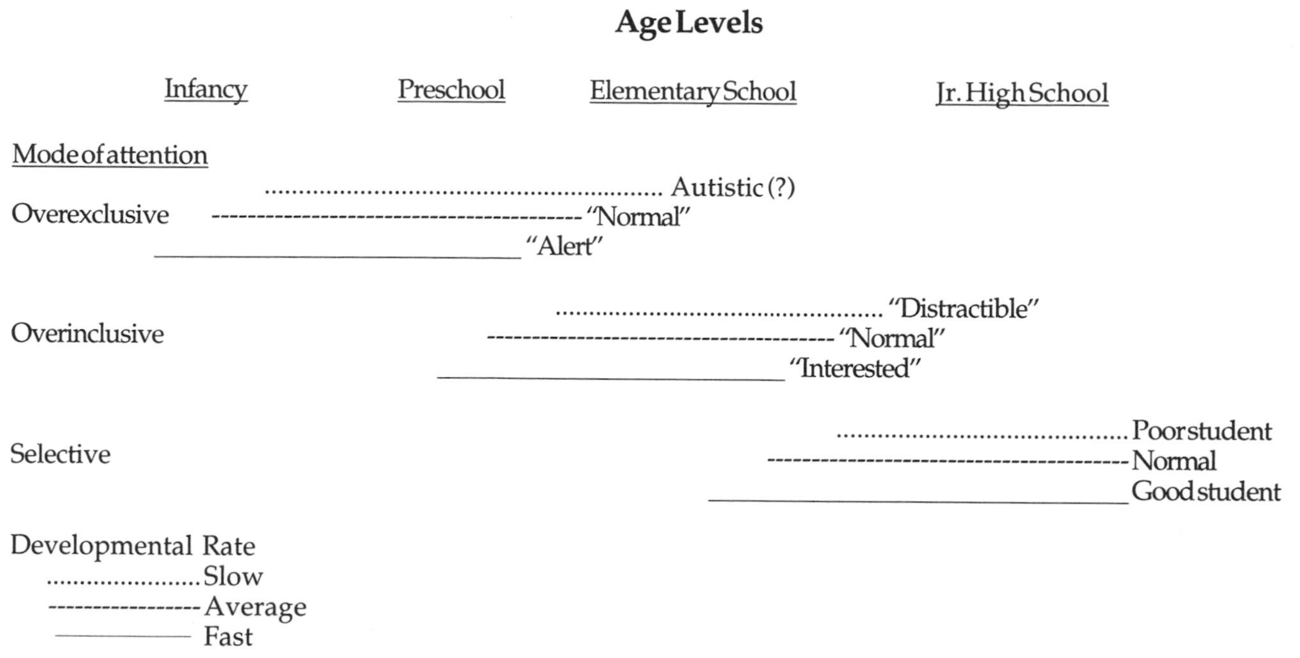

Age Levels

Infancy   Preschool   Elementary School   Jr. High School

Mode of attention

Overexclusive
.... Autistic (?)
-- "Normal"
_____ "Alert"

Overinclusive
.... "Distractible"
------------------------------------- "Normal"
_____ "Interested"

Selective
.... Poor student
-------------------------------------- Normal
_____ Good student

Developmental Rate
.... Slow
------------------ Average
_____ Fast

Figure 5.13. The effect of individual differences in the development of selective attention at various age levels. From *Psychological Aspects of Learning Disabilities and Reading Disorders* (p. 55) by A. O. Ross, 1976, New York: McGraw-Hill. Copyright 1976 by McGraw-Hill. Reprinted with permission.

Repetition, in other words, is not enough. Novelty and assisting the child by helping him or her direct overinclusive attention to salient features, is important.

Impulsivity. Impulsivity is closely related to distractibility. Students who score poorly on the Freedom from Distractibility subtests may do so because they consistently rush through their work, giving whatever comes to mind as an answer, with little reflective thinking evident. Their response style on Picture Completion and Mazes can supplement this hypothesis. Impulsive students tend to be fast on these subtests, and may or may not be accurate. Their speed actually helps them on many of the easier items, and they may even end up with elevated scores on these subtests. Their speed also may hinder them so that they end up with lowered scores.

What is important, in my opinion, is *response style,* not the scaled scores themselves. For example, on the Picture Completion items, it is relatively easy to determine how long the student scans each picture. During Mazes, the student will rush up blind alleys. On Arithmetic, he or she will quickly say,

"I don't know," or make rapid but inaccurate calculations. On Coding, such students have a tendency to begin the task before the administrator completes the instructions. The same is true for Digit Span. Such a response style may mean that the student has very poorly developed plans, or strategies for "stopping, looking, and thinking through," before beginning a task. In fact, forcing such students to spend some time (5 seconds has been found to be the optimal amount) reflecting before they answer can raise the subtest scores on the WISC-R. (A similar study has not yet been replicated on the WISC-III, but there seems little doubt that the results would be identical.) Walker (1981) used only four of the WISC-R subtests (Information, Vocabulary, Picture Arrangement, and Block Design) to determine this; surprisingly, Walker found that the 5-second forced delay was effective for the Verbal, but not the Performance, subtests. Forced delay did not raise the scores of the already reflective students, only the impulsive ones.

When a student is perceived by the examiner as displaying a high degree of impulsivity throughout the testing, the examiner must state on the protocol that the Full Scale IQ is an underestimate of the student's cognitive ability. School psychologists can also supplement their diagnosis of the student's "conceptual tempo" by using Kagan's (1966) *Matching Familiar Figures Test*.

For such students, a number of cognitive self-control techniques have some research support as being effective. The basic steps in *any* self-instructional procedure involve

1. Modeling appropriate strategies for the task and describing it simultaneously to the student

2. Having the student perform the task as the teacher verbalizes it

3. Having the student "think out loud" as he performs the task

4. Having the student whisper (subvocalize) the appropriate self-statements

5. Having the student silently rehearse the appropriate self-statements (adapted from Meichenbaum & Goodman, 1971)

The student can also be taught some coping self-statements to use when an error is made, and some self-monitoring procedures to evaluate how he or she is doing. Any procedure that helps students become aware of their own thinking processes, whether it be in reading comprehension tasks or in doing a maze, can be described as metacognitive in nature.

In my experience, these self-control techniques are best implemented when the student understands the purpose of the method, agrees to its implementation, and is involved in the original planning of its use. I have recommended the use of these procedures in both regular and special classes. Follow-up is important, as is some initial training of the teachers involved. (Whenever possible, this training should be performed by the school psychologist.) In general, I have found these techniques to be quite useful in dealing with distractible students. An extremely useful reference for use with younger students is Shapiro's (1981) *Games to Grow On—Activities to Help Children Learn Self-Control*.

Poor facility with numbers. Because Arithmetic and Digit Span both involve numbers, it is possible that poor facility with numbers, rather than any other reason—such as, short-term memory

difficulty—lies behind the student's low scores on the subtests. However, it is not all that easy to separate these reasons, because limits on short-term memory are also associated with arithmetic processing. Such "confounding" of variables makes the job of diagnosis much more difficult.

In a study of the link between memory span, Piagetian tasks, and arithmetic tasks, Halford (1978) found a correspondence between Piagetian stages and digit span. Preoperational performance requires a memory span of two items; concrete operational performance requires a span of four; and the formal-operations level requires a span of eight. In other words, age-related changes in the ability to do complex arithmetic is determined to some extent by the limitations of the short-term memory span. Many students in special education, when tested on Digit Span, seem to have spans that are below those expected for their chronological age; this makes it difficult for them to remember information presented orally.

Different types of special education populations seem to make slightly different kinds of computational errors in their arithmetic operations, as shown in Table 5.4. In the study from which this table was taken, Frost (1982) suggested that the *affective* component is very important in terms of remediating the arithmetic difficulties of the severely learning disabled group. These students had "coded" some very negative feelings, especially toward subtraction, which proved to be a stumbling block to mastering basic facts. Frost hypothesized that subtraction created the worst feelings because the students subconsciously disliked the idea of "taking away." Frost devised an ingenious remedial program using Cuisenaire rods that were decorated to resemble robots, families, and ethnic groups. Teachers were trained to use the materials with an emphasis on tapping into the students' feelings of "rescuing," "overcoming," and "helping." The students learned that the operation of taking away in arithmetic could be used to "rescue" someone in distress. Thus, the negative affect associated with subtraction was turned into something positive. This intriguing approach produced significant growth in arithmetic skill areas for students. Unfortunately, the arithmetic program itself remains unpublished to date.

Self-instructional training can also be useful as a remedial strategy for students if poor facility with

TABLE 5.4. Error Types: Comparison of Percent Total Error for Regular, Educable Mentally Handicapped (EMH), and Learning Disabled (LD) Student Groups

Error Type	Regular students (Englehardt, 1977) N=198	EMH student (Janke, 1980) N=370	LD students (Safran, 1980) N=37
Basic facts	32	37	28
Grouping	19	5	33
Inappropriate inversion	17	3	7
Incorrect operation	4	24	15
Defective algorithm	16	21	2
Incomplete algorithm	6	4	6
Identity of 0 and 1	1	1	2
Zero	5	5	7

From *The Arithmetic Achievement of Learning Disabled Students: A Training Study* (p. 232) by R. Frost, 1982, unpublished doctoral dissertation, The University of Calgary. Reprinted with permission of the author.

numbers is a problem for them. The basic steps outlined previously can be adapted quite easily to arithmetic problems.

Anxiety. If anxiety is a primary factor in poor performance on the Freedom from Distractibility Index, the school psychologist could suggest a number of helpful strategies, depending on the source of the anxiety. The general strategies of stress reduction I described in Chapter 3, particularly relaxation training (see Appendix 3E), can be very helpful. A program that ran successfully for several years in the San Diego Unified School District, is called *Teaching Children Self-Control* (Wilson, Hall, & Watson, 1979). The program consists of training in deep relaxation and general problem solving. Structured lessons were developed, and manuals prepared, for Grades 1 through 3 and 7 through 9.

Because anxiety also constricts short-term memory, the examiner must decide whether short-term memory difficulty or anxiety is foremost. Frequently, a combination of the two creates problems.

Simultaneous and successive information processing. For students who are significantly stronger on Digits Forward than on Digits Backward on the WISC-III Digit Span subtest ("significant" means a difference of 3 or more on the student's span), the hypothesis of a strength or weakness in simultaneous or successive information processing should be examined. The Performance Scale of the WISC-III can be used to cross-check the hypothesis as follows:

Simultaneous

- Picture Completion
- Block Design
- Object Assembly

Successive

- Picture Arrangement
- Coding
- Mazes

If the averages of the three subtests on the two dimensions differ by 3 points or more, then a significant strength or weakness is psychometrically interpretable. If the student also seems to proceed in a "holistic" fashion on Block Design, working rapidly from the gestalt, he or she may be a simultaneous processor. If the student seems to work in a very methodical, logical fashion, rotating the blocks until the correct design is formed, then the student may be more of a successive processor. It is, therefore, quite difficult at times to use the subtest scaled scores as the basis for diagnosis. Keen observation on the part of the examiner is necessary.

Kaufman and Kaufman (1984) admitted the same problem with the *Kaufman Assessment Battery for Children* (K-ABC). Because it is possible to solve what is primarily a successive task in a simultaneous fashion, or vice versa, the scores cannot be used as the sole basis for diagnosis. To help in the determination, the school psychologist could administer the K-ABC (which is designed to help determine whether a student is significantly stronger or weaker in one or the other of the processing styles) and/or a battery devised by Naglieri and Das (1988).

I find the simultaneous/successive distinction useful for some students. It seems to me, however, that both types of processing are involved in all learning, just as both halves of the brain are always involved in learning. Kaufman and Kaufman (1984) wrote that students who are stronger in one of the styles still require instruction in the other style. Other professionals I have talked to insist that all learning is successive in nature, and that it simply is not possible to do any simultaneous processing.

Whatever one's theoretical stance, I find merit in the idea that some students appear to be more comfortable with certain kinds of teaching/learning styles, and that an awareness of the individual differences among students can help a teacher. It may not even be that the student performs better academically when taught consistently with the favored style, but the student may find learning much more enjoyable.

Because the simultaneous/successive split can be a learning style, it fits into Level III interpretation. I therefore return to the distinction and some of its educational implications in the next chapter.

Short-term memory. The Digit Span subtest is the only WISC-III subtest that measures auditory short-term memory. In my opinion, low scores on Digit Span represent a weak memory "trace" and indicate that the individual simply forgot what was said. The same thing can occur with visual memory, when an individual forgets information that is presented visually. Therefore, I always look closely to see whether the span of the student is significantly below that of his or her peers.

Next, I look at the kinds of errors that the student makes on the Digit Span subtest. For example, if the sequence of numbers presented was 6-1-5-8 and the student says, "6-5-1-8," then the span is not the problem for the student. This student has made a reversal (sequencing) error, but has in fact remembered all the numbers. If another student says "6-1-8," then one of the numbers was completely forgotten. That error, in my opinion, is stronger evidence of a weakness in auditory short-term memory, because one of the numbers and a

"slot" completely disappeared. Both students fail the trial and receive the same score, but the kinds of errors they make are quite different.

Next, I examine the student's Arithmetic subtest. Did I have to repeat a given question for the student to answer it (again, evidence of short-term memory difficulty)? The student might have answered correctly, and might even have a scaled score that is average for his or her age, but if my notes say that nearly all the questions had to be repeated, then facility with numbers may not be the problem. Difficulty with auditory short-term memory is more likely.

Memory, from an information-processing viewpoint, can be divided into three components: encoding, storage, and retrieval. Encoding is the initial acquisition of information. Storage is the length of time the information is available (which may be brief [short-term] or delayed [long-term]). Retrieval can occur by recognition, by cued recall, or by free recall (Parill-Burnstein, 1981). Generally, memory ability increases with age, perhaps because knowledge in general increases with age. (Because the knowledge base expands, incoming information is more meaningful and the student remembers it better.) In information-processing theory, memory is not a single entity, but is closely tied to the development of other cognitive strategies, which also increase with age. These strategies include rehearsal (basic and complex), elaboration (basic and complex), organization, and comprehension monitoring.

Students with learning disabilities have a number of problems with these areas. For example, they do not recall as much relevant information as does a group without learning problems. In addition, before the age of 8, children with learning disabilities do not spontaneously rehearse material that is presented. Parill-Burnstein (1981) summarized the results of several memory studies on learning-disabled groups as follows:

> Children with learning disabilities recalled and recognized fewer items when compared to those without learning problems when auditory or verbal stimuli were employed. Problems discriminating and attending selectively to relevant stimulus features impaired performance. In addition, these children generated fewer correct responses, resampled disconfirmed responses following negative feedback, and used fewer rehearsal strategies spontane-

ously. This latter finding was interpreted from the lack of primacy effects obtained with eight-year-old children with learning disabilities. (p. 109)

Remedial implications. A number of remedial strategies for memory can be recommended by the school psychologist, depending on the individual student:

1. Chunking and rehearsal can be encouraged in acquiring sight words and other academic activities.

2. Sorting by categories is an important teaching and learning strategy (see Appendix 5A). A variation of the suggestions in Appendix 5A is to have the student sort a series into categories (Parill-Burnstein, 1981, p. 110). Then, take away the words and have the student recall the items (free recall). If the student has difficulty, the teacher can make it easier by providing the student with the categories (cued recall). If the student still has difficulty, then present the words again and ask the student to group the words according to the categories provided by the teacher (recognition). These procedures can be added to the word sort activities at any point.

3. The student could be encouraged to use a semantic cue to help encoding (Parill-Burnstein, 1981, p. 110). For example, if the words to be learned are *cowboy* and *horse*, then the student could be asked to relate the two in a sentence, such as "The cowboy rides a horse." Then, ask the student to recall the word pair without any cues (free recall). If the student has difficulty, present one of the pairs (cued recall).

4. Another elaborative strategy is mental imagery. This technique was discussed in relation to reading comprehension and recall in Appendix 2D. The strategy also can be used in learning so-called sight words. An important variation is the keyword approach discussed earlier. The keyword approach also eliminates the primacy effect, because all items are recalled equally well. Perhaps learning disabled groups have particular difficulty with semantic encoding, which is why the more visual encoding of the keyword approach works better for them.

5. Complex elaboration can also be encouraged, where appropriate. This kind of elaboration involves connecting new information to old in some way, such as by
   a. Creating analogies
   b. Developing images
   c. Considering implications
   d. Paraphrasing with an emphasis on the relationship between the two ideas or words.

Metamemory. Part of the remedial process is to involve the student in some way in helping himself or herself. The student has to become aware of when to use a particular memory strategy. This is called metamemory. One such awareness strategy involves the student's own knowledge of his or her span. For example, when nursery school and kindergarten children are asked to predict how many pictures they will remember of a series presented to them, the gap between the prediction and the actual recall is enormous. This gap narrows with age, however, so that by the time the student is in fourth grade, the predictions are as accurate as those of adults, which suggests a developmental metamemory process.

Metamemory does have a practical application. For example, ask the student to predict how many words he or she will remember when a series of sight words is presented. Then present the words and see how close the student comes to the prediction. Award points for close predictions. This procedure is apt to be quite motivating for some students. It may help to tell the student something like, "The average student your age can remember _____ words."

It is also important, when working with individual students, that they receive some feedback regarding their use of a procedure. For example, in teaching the student how to use rehearsal, *strategy plus metamemory training* will be more effective than strategy training alone. This can be accomplished by appropriate feedback, such as

"You did so much better when you whispered those words over and over. I guess whispering helped you remember the words better." Similar feedback should be given when training students in the use of any other memory strategy.

Phonemic manipulation. In Chapter 4, I mentioned the possibilities regarding remediation and prevention of reading problems by increasing students' awareness of and ability to manipulate the basic phonemes of language. The ability to discriminate and manipulate phonemes can be directly assessed using the *Lindamood Auditory Conceptualization Test* (Lindamood & Lindamood, 1979). This test is a useful adjunct to WISC-III testing, particularly when Digit Span is depressed.

Digit Span seems to be related to phonemic processing, although the relationship is by no means a direct one. Cohen, Fil, Netley, and Clarke (1984) made the link as follows:

> Cohen and Netley (1981) have pursued the serial aspect of phonetic processing, suggesting that the poor reading and poor serial [short-term memory] abilities of reading-disabled children are the result of a deficiency in their ability to process serial strings of speech sounds which these authors call phonological patterns (p. 220)

When the school psychologist feels that poor phonemic processing is a hypothesis that should be investigated, then the Lindamood test is the test of choice. There are other, less formal methods for assessing this particular skill, but the Lindamood is the most fully developed at this time.

Remediation of this skill is not restricted to the *Auditory Discrimination in Depth* (ADD) program (Lindamood & Lindamood, 1975), as discussed earlier. There are at least four other ways of training this skill (see Williams, 1984). However, the ADD program is my program of choice (with a caution that teachers require in-depth training first).

Processing speed index. When the WISC-III was revised from the WISC-R, a new subtest called Symbol Search was introduced. For this subtest, the student must make a decision about whether a target symbol (a visual one) appears in a search group. There are two different levels of Symbol Search depending on age. For ages 6 to 7, Symbol Search, Part A, is used; for ages 8 to 16, Symbol Search, Part B, is used. The test is timed, and the student responds with a pencil by slashing either the "yes" or the "no" in the "Yes/No" box.

The subtest correlates highly with Coding and, in fact, Coding and Symbol Search are the two subtests that form the Processing Speed Index, the fourth factor on the WISC-III. Because the factor is clearly more visual than anything else, it can serve to diagnose whether a student has more difficulty with visual than auditory processing. If there is a significant difference between the Freedom from Distractibility Index and the Processing Speed Index, the school psychologist can perform further assessment as required and make appropriate educational recommendations. Suggestions outlined in Appendix 5B might be particularly useful.

GIFTED STUDENTS AND THE WISC-III

School psychologists are frequently asked to assist in the selection of students in upper ability levels. As school divisions increase their program services to the upper ends of "exceptionality," this demand will increase. An important tool in this identification is the WISC-III. As with other areas, however, the WISC-III should not be the only assessment instrument administered.

For the present discussion, I will use Renzulli's (1978) definition of giftedness, a state that

> consists of an interaction among three basic clusters of human traits—these clusters being above-average general abilities, high levels of task commitment, and high levels of creativity. Gifted and talented children are those possessing or capable of developing this composite set of traits and applying them to any potentially valuable area of human performance. (p. 261).

Of the three components mentioned by Renzulli, the WISC-III measures only the first—general abilities. Both task commitment and creativity need to be assessed by other methods, although the examiner might get some feel for the student's task commitment by observing his or her test behavior. Some students who score in the top 5% on the WISC-III may lack the task commitment to do well academically. Such students might be called gifted underachievers. They pose unique problems for school psychologists and other school personnel who must deal with them. I will discuss a general plan for dealing with such students in the next section.

Feldhusen and Wyman (1980) stated the basic school needs of gifted students as follows:

1. Maximum achievement of basic skills and concepts.

2. Learning activities at an appropriate level and pace.

3. Experience in creative thinking and problem solving.

4. Development of convergent thinking and problem solving.

5. Stimulation of imagery, imagination, and spatial abilities.

6. Stimulation to pursue higher-level goals and aspirations.

7. Development of self-awareness and self-acceptance.

8. Development of independence, self-direction, and discipline in learning.

9. Experience in relating to other gifted/talented students.

10. A large fund of information about diverse topics.

11. Exposure to a variety of fields of study, arts, professions, and occupations.

12. Access and stimulation to reading. (p. 15)

Someone reading through this list might be struck by the fact that these needs are no different from those for any child, which is true, to a point. What needs to be taken into account is the general ability of each student. Maximum achievement of basic skills and concepts, for example, is as much a need for the student with a trainable mental handicap as it is for a gifted student; however, these two students require qualitatively different kinds of stimulation.

I believe the needs of the vast majority of gifted students can be met at the local school level by using Renzulli's (1977) Enrichment Triad Model, shown in Figure 5.14, as a framework. The various activities within the model can be described as follows:

- *Type I*—These are activities to which all students should be exposed within the regular classroom program. They include the range of good, basic teaching, and extend to interest centers, field trips and visits, guest speakers, library research, and so on.

- *Type II*—These activities are especially suitable for the top 15% to 20% of the student population, and include special skills training. Training can be best accomplished by a joint regular classroom and partial pull-out enrichment program coordinated by the school's gifted program teacher. The training activities would include critical thinking, divergent–convergent thinking, creative problem solving, deductive and inductive reasoning, and so on.

- *Type III*—These activities are best accomplished through a part-time program within the regular school day. Type III enrichment usually means an independent research study done on an area of interest to the student. Perhaps about half the time that the top 5% of the student population spends in such programs should be devoted to the pursuit of a Type III activity.

A systematic, reasonably accurate selection process is therefore necessary to identify the top 5% of a school's population. Clearly, if Renzulli's definition of giftedness is used, an IQ test should be only part of the process.

The delivery of service to gifted students also should include a number of components. Some of these, such as Individualized Education Programs (IEPs) for identified students, are common to all of special education. Other components, such as curriculum compacting, are more specific to enrichment programs. Readers should consult Cox, Daniel, and Boston (1985) for more details about educational programming in this area.

In my opinion, Renzulli's (1977) model and the three-step identification process could be modified to identify learning disabled students more accurately. Unfortunately, most school districts work only on a referral basis. As a result, many school

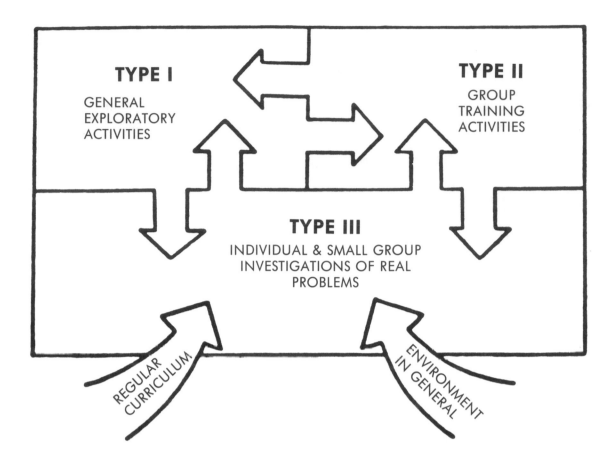

Figure 5.14. The Enrichment Triad Model. From *The Enrichment Triad Model: A Guide for Developing Defensible Programs for the Gifted and Talented* (p. 14) by J. Renzulli, 1977, Mansfield Center, CT: Creative Learning Press. Copyright 1977 by Creative Learning Press. Reprinted with permission.

psychologists simply test and rubber stamp a student as learning disabled. I believe many students who have IQ scores of 100 or higher and who show a discrepancy between achievement and ability are never diagnosed, whereas those students who are simply slow learners are given special service because school districts place students who are below grade level into special education classes. A student with an IQ of 80 is *bound* to be below grade level. The proper questions that need to be asked are (a) Is there a *discrepancy* between the student's ability and achievement? and (b) Is this discrepancy a *significant* one? These questions can be answered with greater psychometric precision and sophistication than once was possible (see, e.g., Reynolds, 1984–1985). With improved identification techniques, school psychologists would be better able to discriminate those students who require a Type

II remedial program from those who require only modification within the classroom (Type I remediation) or who require some special skills training (Type II remediation).

Gifted Underachievers

This group, also sometimes called the gifted learning disabled, poses special problems for the school psychologist. I have found the guidelines presented by Fine and Pitts (1980) to be particularly helpful for this kind of problem. They described the gifted underachiever as a "kind of intellectual delinquent who withdraws from goals, activities, and social participation" (p. 51). Further descriptors of such students and some of their dynamics include the following (adapted from Fine & Pitts, 1980):

1. *Low self-esteem,* including an accompanying unwillingness to take risks. Social isolation is also present. These students may show a great interest in a hobby such as rock collecting. Adults may interpret this as meaning that the students find school boring; however, it maintains the students' social isolation.

2. *Deficient academic skills.* Usually, these students are truly behind academically; however, because they are recognized as very bright, they are seen by teachers as not trying. Because these students often have a "won't/can't" attitude, they often have a resultant deficit in academics.

3. *Passive–aggressive behavior,* with frequent attempts to "get back" at other students and teachers by nonachievement. This causes extreme anger and frustration for both parents and teachers.

4. *Motor delays or deficiencies.* Many of these students would rather talk than play. In fact, their verbal strengths are greatly reinforced at home and school. As a result, these students may avoid paper-and-pencil or gross-motor tasks.

5. *"Adultizing"* the child. Because of these students' verbal strengths, parents and teachers begin treating these children on an adult level (where the children do well). Thus, the children are constantly deflected from the real issue, which is the continual avoidance of academic tasks.

6. *Attribution of blame.* These students typically blame others by intellectualizing and rationalizing any wrongdoing on their own part. "Verbal reasoning" with these students is therefore unlikely to be effective.

7. *Family conflict.* Sometimes such students *cause* severe family conflicts, and sometimes these students are the *scapegoats* in families that unknowingly act out their own conflicts via or "around" these students. The dynamics of family interaction around school assignments are such that the parents wind up spending much time and energy tracking down assignments that the student conveniently "forgets." Much concern and anger are present. The assignments are usually done quickly, once the students put their energy into it.

8. *Parent–school conflicts.* Each side usually blames the other for not motivating the child. This conflict can be very severe and sustained for years.

9. *Interpersonal attitudes.* These students seem to work from an "I'm OK—You're not OK" stance. This component is something that teachers see continually. These students ridicule others and put them down constantly. By provoking others, they invite rejection, but of course deny any responsibility when others then reject them. Parents often perceive that their children are being "picked on" by other students, thus inadvertently maintaining the rejection by reinforcing these students' beliefs that "It's not my fault."

Case example. To illustrate the problem of gifted underachievers, I will describe the case of Thomas in detail. Thomas was originally referred to me while in first grade. The concerns stated by the school at that time were as follows: "Thomas exhibits antisocial behavior both in the classroom and on the playground; this pattern has existed since playschool. Thomas appears to be bright to the point of brilliance."

I began by administering the WISC-III, the *Human Figure Drawing Test* (Koppitz, 1968), and the *Kinetic Family Drawing Test* (Burns & Kaufman, 1972; Reznikoff & Reznikoff, 1956). The WISC-III results are shown in Figure 5.15.

Other than Thomas's high score on Block Design (95th percentile), there were no other indicators of giftedness. The projective drawings were also very "clean" (i.e., free of emotional indicators). Thomas's behavior in the testing situation was impulsive. He "tested *my* limits" frequently, and tried to gain control; however, he was easily manageable. His responses on the Comprehension subtest reflected a lack of social sensitivity.

Name *Thomas* Sex ______

School ______ Grade ______

Examiner ______ Handedness ______

WISC-III™
Wechsler Intelligence Scale for Children–Third Edition

Subtests	Raw Scores	Verbal	Perfor.	VC	PO	FD	PS
Picture Completion	12		10		10		
Information	8	11		11			
Coding	42		11				11
Similarities	8	9		9			
Picture Arrangement	10		9		9		
Arithmetic	10	8				8	
Block Design	31		15		15		
Vocabulary	14	10		10			
Object Assembly	17		11		11		
Comprehension	6	6		6			
(Symbol Search)	N/A		(N/A)				N/A
(Digit Span)	10	(10)				10	
(Mazes)	N/A		(N/A)				
Sum of Scaled Scores		44	56	36	45	18	/

Full Scale Score: 100 (VC, PO, FD, PS: OPTIONAL)

	Year	Month	Day
Date Tested			
Date of Birth			
Age	6	8	14

	Score	IQ/ Index	%ile	___% Confidence Interval
Verbal	44	93	32	87 - 100
Performance	56	108	70	99 - 115
Full Scale	100	100	50	94 - 106
VC	36	95	37	89 - 102
PO	45	109	73	100 - 116
FD	18	96	39	87 - 106
PS	/			-

Subtest Scores

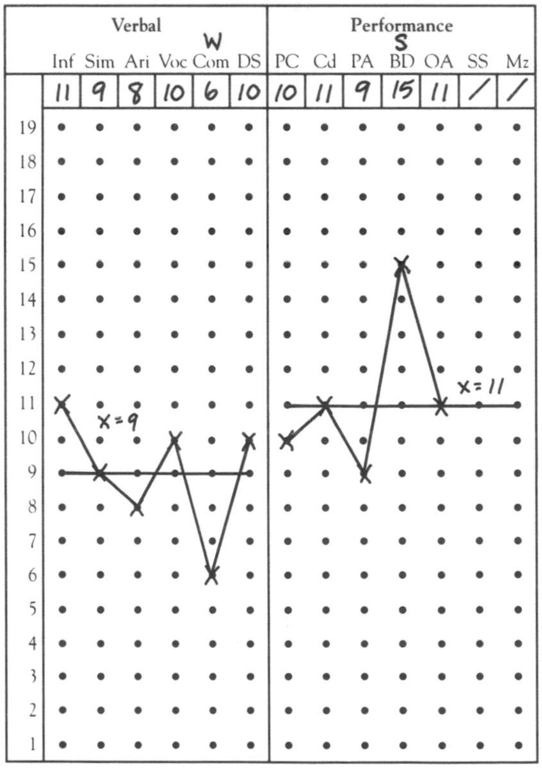
Verbal
Performance
W
S
Inf Sim Ari Voc Com DS PC Cd PA BD OA SS Mz
11 9 8 10 6 10 10 11 9 15 11 / /
x=9
x=11

IQ Scores / Index Scores (Optional)

VIQ	PIQ	FSIQ	VCI	POI	FDI	PSI
93	108	100	95	109	96	

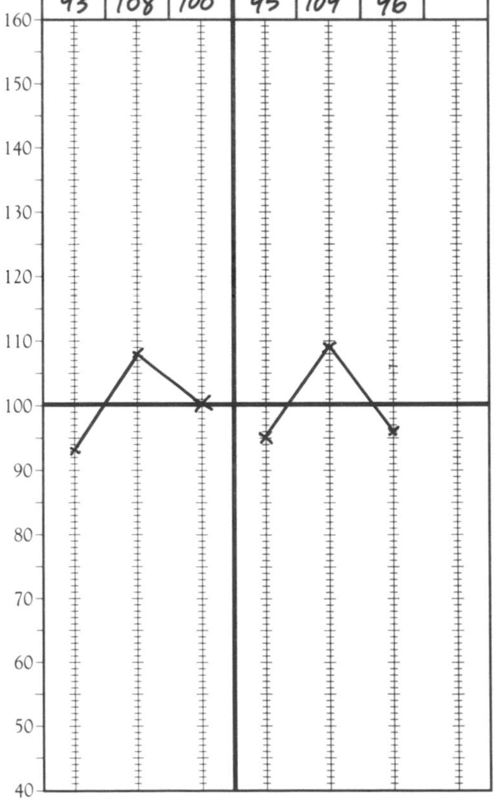

THE PSYCHOLOGICAL CORPORATION®
HARCOURT BRACE JOVANOVICH, INC.
7 8 9 10 11 12 A B C D E
09–980004

Figure 5.15. Thomas's first profile.

I discussed these results with Thomas's parents. In the interview, they pointed out Thomas's unusual interest in medical books and his curiosity. They felt his behavior problems in school were caused by boredom. However, the WISC-III results did not support that he was particularly bright. (What makes diagnosis more difficult is that very bright students exhibit much more variability on retests of individual cognitive assessments than do less bright students.) Because of Thomas's behavior problems, family counseling was recommended, but unfortunately was not acted upon by the parents. Thomas's social problems continued in school, but were manageable enough until fourth grade, when I received another referral on him. This time, he was referred primarily because of a "short attention span" and the "inability to complete many simple tasks." By this time, Thomas's father was *livid* with the school. He considered his son brilliant, and blamed the school entirely for all of Thomas's social problems. Thomas was still interested in medical books, and had extended his interest to a number of other scientific areas; however, he got a "D" in science on his report card, which was incomprehensible to the parents, and understandably so. In a one-to-one situation with an adult, and on a topic of interest to him, Thomas would work quite well. Even then, he was distractible, but the parents did not interpret his behavior as distractibility, but only as further evidence of his brilliance. The father would frequently phone the school and hurl a torrent of abuse on the principal. The situation had deteriorated to a crisis level.

This time, the referral went to the district reading specialist, who performed a thorough academic assessment, and then cross-referred Thomas to me. I decided to readminister the WISC-III (wondering whether I would find anything this time to confirm the parental insistence on Thomas's brilliance) and do a classroom observation.

The WISC-III profile, represented in Figure 5.16, was indeed very different this time. The factor splitting was interesting:

- Verbal Comprehension: 98th percentile
- Perceptual Organization: 93rd percentile
- Freedom from Distractibility: 39th percentile

The reading specialist asked Thomas to write a story. His "story" was about "making a battery."

It was written beautifully and completed in about 15 minutes. The vocabulary was consistent with his high verbal ability. No difficulty was noted on the writing task in terms of attention span or distractibility. Thomas's written work on this occasion was as good as any student's in the school's gifted program, showing that he could, at times, perform at a high level. He also scored very high on some subtests of the *Peabody Individual Achievement Test–Revised* (PIAT-R) (Markwardt, 1989) but showed genuine weaknesses on reading comprehension and planning ability in terms of organizing his thoughts on paper on another writing task. On a second testing occasion, the reading specialist found Thomas much more distractible, even though the story he was writing was in the science area.

These results, overall, presented a very different picture from that in the first grade. Also, Thomas did reasonably well in a one-to-one setting this time, as long as the activity was of high interest to him (even so, his performance was variable).

His behavior in a classroom setting was another story. I observed him, and found him very fidgety and restless. He seemed continually in motion, but never actually out of his seat. He made inappropriate noises. When the teacher gave him a look of disapproval, he looked at me to see how I would react. (This kind of attention-seeking behavior was very typical for Thomas, I learned from the teacher—it was not simply because I was there.) At one point, a student next to him dropped her pen top. It rolled under Thomas's desk. She picked it up. Thomas let go a string of ridicule because the girl would now get "germs." He went on and on about it. When the poor girl finally said, "No, I won't," Thomas let forth an encyclopedic explanation that in no uncertain terms proved that he was right and she was an idiot. It was very easy to see from this incident how Thomas invited rejection from his peers; he was certainly operating from an "I'm OK—You're not OK" attitude. Interestingly, when I described this to his parents, they laughed and did not really see a problem.

How does one go about trying to assist in straightening out such a mess? The following steps were followed in Thomas's case, with modifications appropriate for his situation. These guidelines for intervention are based on suggestions made by Fine and Pitts (1980).

Name _Thomas_   Sex _____

School _____ Grade _____

Examiner _____ Handedness _____

WISC-III™
Wechsler Intelligence Scale for Children – Third Edition

Subtests	Raw Scores	Scaled Scores				
Picture Completion	24		16		16	
Information	20	17		17		
Coding	28		7			7
Similarities	26	18		18		
Picture Arrangement	27		11		11	
Arithmetic	13	7			7	
Block Design	50		16		16	
Vocabulary	33	15		15		
Object Assembly	29		12		12	
Comprehension	18	11		11		
(Symbol Search)	N/A		(N/A)			N/A
(Digit Span)	13	(11)			11	
(Mazes)	22		(15)			
Sum of Scaled Scores		68	62	61	55	18	—
		Verbal	Perfor.	VC	PO	FD	PS

Full Scale Score: **130**

OPTIONAL

	Year	Month	Day
Date Tested			
Date of Birth			
Age	9	3	

	Score	IQ/Index	%ile	95% Confidence Interval
Verbal	68	122	93	115 – 127
Performance	62	116	86	107 – 123
Full Scale	130	121	92	115 – 126
VC	61	130	98	121 – 135
PO	55	123	94	112 – 129
FD	18	96	39	87 – 106
PS				–

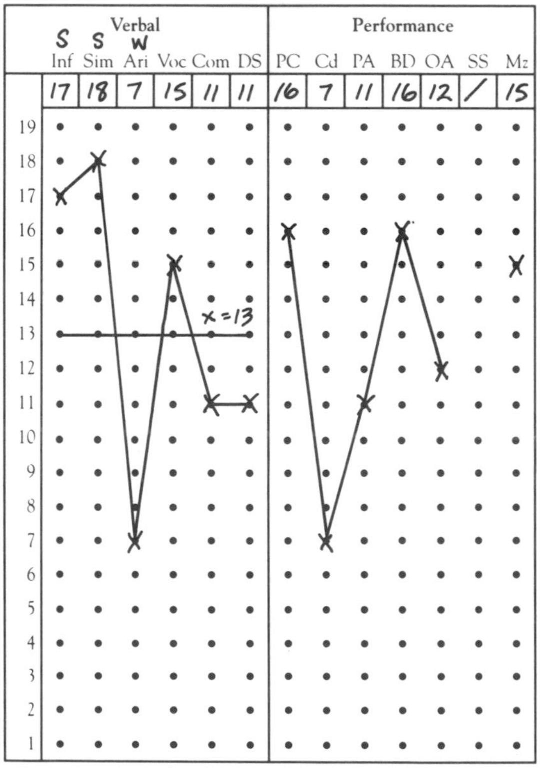

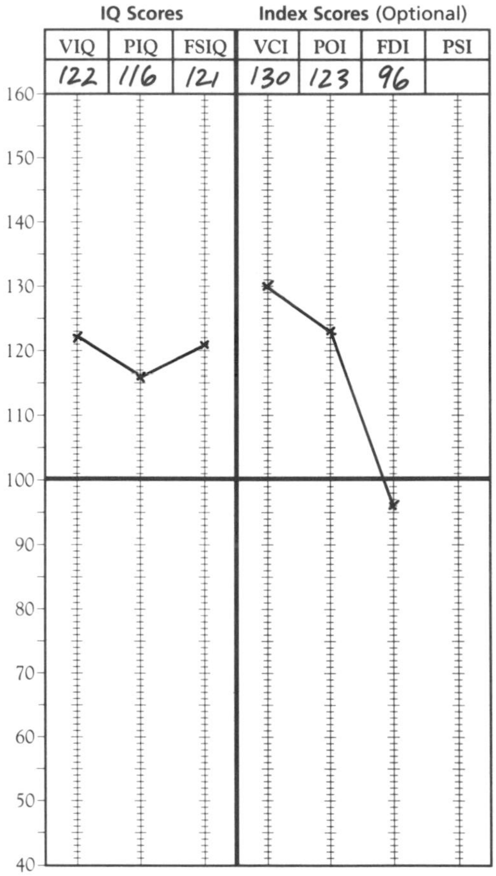

Subtest Scores

	Verbal						Performance						
	S Inf	S Sim	W Ari	Voc	Com	DS	PC	Cd	PA	BD	OA	SS	Mz
	17	18	7	15	11	11	16	7	11	16	12	/	15

x = 13

IQ Scores   Index Scores (Optional)

VIQ	PIQ	FSIQ	VCI	POI	FDI	PSI
122	116	121	130	123	96	

09–980004

Figure 5.16. Thomas's second profile.

1. Involve the parents in a "high confrontation/ high-accountability" program. Involve the parents deeply in a program where goals are clearly established and where they are involved in planning the courses of action to be taken. The "accountability" part included follow-up conferences, modification of original plans, keeping of good records, and establishing someone as a case manager. All of this needs to be done in a nonpunitive, matter-of-fact way. In Thomas's case, a long conference was held, and the issues placed "on the table" by both the parents and the school. We discussed a number of options and courses of action. One thing that had to happen was for the parents to see Thomas in action in a classroom, because their view of him was exclusively in a one-to-one home setting. The parents volunteered to come into the classroom twice a week. The first week they did so, Thomas was, as usual, very distractible, and did not complete his work in class. I believe this was a real eye-opener for his parents.

2. Family dynamics cannot be ignored. If the student is included in the planning, then it is quite likely that the underlying manner in which he is able to manipulate will surface. Thomas was included in the first meeting only toward the end. He agreed to the plan of action and was very pleased that his parents would be in the classroom, because now "they could help me with my work." (This reaction was despite the fact that it had been explained that they would be there like any other parent volunteer to help with the whole class.) The major goal was to help the parents see that Thomas was more than "bored" in school. This, I believe, they began to see to some extent. The father, in particular, was very unrealistic, however. He wanted Thomas to be marked and tested on the work he completed, not what was assigned, for example. Thus, if Thomas did 3 of 15 arithmetic questions and got

them all correct, the teacher was to assign a mark of 100% (this strategy *does* have value in some situations, of course).

3. Follow-up conferences are vital. Fine and Pitts suggested once-a-week conferences at first. The procedure did improve communication between the parents and the school. The major focus of the conferences and daily assignments was simply to help Thomas get them done. If he began to show some consistency, the school was prepared to let him join in some enrichment activities.

4. Fine and Pitts also cautioned about "sabotage" by either parents or teachers in such cases. They stated,

> The literature has made it abundantly clear that the underachieving gifted child is often more than just a child bored with a mundane school experience. Also the pattern of underachievement can become pervasive and diminish not only the child's school satisfaction but have a serious and negative impact on peer–social relationships and the child's place within the family. (p. 55)

Despite modification of written expectations and considerable help with organizational skills, Thomas still had difficulty. A major issue in this case was his disorganized behavior and poor reading comprehension. When Thomas was given treatment in the visualizing/verbalizing process, many of these symptoms were greatly alleviated. For the next 2 years, Thomas was placed in a private school for students with learning disabilities where reinforcement and extension of organizational skills were structured. Additionally, the school had an excellent social skills program. Thomas benefitted enormously and has now been reintegrated into a regular classroom where he is doing very well.

Profile Analysis of Very High IQ Students

In this section, I briefly outline a method of profile analysis developed by Reynolds and Clark (1986) which school psychologists may find very useful for some profiles. Reynolds and Clark made the valid point that it is very difficult to find intraindividual strengths and weaknesses (using Kaufman's, 1979, method) when all subtests are in the very high range. For example, if the mean of the subtests is 18, then how can a significant strength be determined?

The authors recommended a seven-step procedure, which I present as an abbreviated five-step technique.

1. First, administer and calculate all standard WISC-III scores in the usual fashion. Formulate any relevant hypotheses. Next, determine the *age equivalent* for each WISC-III subtest (these can be found in the test manual, p. 259) that most closely corresponds to the student's raw scores.

2. Calculate the *median* age equivalent for the subtests. Eliminate from this calculation any subtests on which the student exceeded the mean performance of the oldest group.

3. Now, treat the median age equivalent as the chronological age for the purpose of *recalculating* the subtest scaled scores. For example, if the student was 10 years old, and you found the median test age to be 13 years, you would enter the 13-year-old table in the WISC-III manual.

4. Recalculate subtest scaled scores and the major IQ scores. Reynolds and Clark stated that such recalculated IQ scores should not deviate much from the range of about 94 to 106. If they do, then recheck your calculations, as there is likely to be a clerical error.

5. Finally, proceed with profile analysis as suggested by Kaufman. Remember,

however, that *interindividual* comparisons cannot be made using this process—only ipsative ones (*intraindividual*) ones.

Readers should make every attempt to become more familiar with the kinds of profiles and problems exhibited by the gifted students with learning disabilities. According to Schiff, Kaufman, and Kaufman (1981), the emotional problems exhibited by such students are helpful indicators.

> Many of these uneven gifted youngsters exhibited talents in art, music, poetry, electronics, business, and the sciences. . . .
>
> Despite these talents, and average or above-average performance in math and reading achievement, the group of children tended to be emotionally upset and disorganized. All expressed a sense of unhappiness, and many felt they did not fit in anywhere. They often complained of being isolated, or scapegoated; images of being corroded, out of control, monster-like, or dumb prevailed. Virtually all had some idea that they could not make their brain, body, or both do what they wanted each to do. They often reported organizing difficulties in simple mathematical calculations, spelling, and handwriting. They reported extremely upsetting feelings with physical education and gross-motor activities, and they often perceived themselves powerless in a fearsome and attacking world. Many sought angry revenge against teachers or children who made fun of them or picked them last in games. The emotional complications of the group as a whole included inadequate impulse control, defective self-concept, narcissistic hypersensitivity, and poorly developed integrative functions. . . . (p. 403)

These descriptions match closely the kinds of experiences I have had with such students over the years. Such students are very challenging indeed. School psychologists should never overlook the fact, however, that remediation of basic learning processes might be needed as a *first* step.

CHAPTER

6

WISC-III Interpretation: Levels III and IV

LEVEL III—SUBTEST STRENGTHS AND WEAKNESSES

Level III interpretation of the WISC-III involves examining individual subtest strengths and weaknesses. Because the focus is on the individual, intra-individual strengths and weaknesses are of primary concern at this level. This interpretation is often fascinating, because many patterns of cognitive abilities are possible.

I begin this section with a discussion of the difference between interpreting patterns for *diagnostic* purposes and for *educational* purposes. Plenty of evidence indicates that the different patterns on the WISC-III I have discussed thus far—such as Verbal–Performance discrepancies, factor splits, and ACID profiles—cannot be used to diagnose a student as learning disabled, educationally disadvantaged, or whatever. Such patterns are also present, often in significant proportions, in the normal population. Many students with no academic problems exhibit significant score scatter, for example. Conversely, some students with academic problems show no scatter. Therefore, it is impossible to diagnose a condition from a WISC-III score or set of scores.

The WISC-III can, however, have educational implications for some students, for example, if a student with or without academic difficulties who shows a split of scores on the WISC-III indicating

a strong field-dependent cognitive style. I believe that profile analysis in such cases is valuable in suggesting educational strategies. Again, however, the WISC-III, by itself, will not be as valuable as information from a variety of sources. Recommendations for any one student are likely to be better when a team approach is used. In this way, the benefits of a number of lines of expertise can converge and serve the student's best interests.

The distinction between what is diagnostically significant and what is educationally significant is important. As I have said repeatedly throughout this book, one cannot diagnose a student based on a WISC-III profile, but to ignore what lies in a particular profile in terms of educational hypotheses will have the effect of "freezing" all WISC-III interpretations at Level I.

This point of view is espoused by some researchers. Kavale and Forness (1984), for example, wrote,

> Despite long-standing cautions, suggestions about grouping WISC subtests into new clusterings have been advanced repeatedly. However, the present findings offer no empirical support for the existence of such groupings. On the contrary, nonsignificant findings show the WISC profiles as possessing no external validity for LD diagnosis. Kaufman suggests that the search for WISC profiles requires good detective work employing "ingenuity, clinical sense,

115

and thorough grounding in psychological theory and research to reveal the dynamics of a child's scaled-score profile." In reality, the problem faced by the WISC detective appears to be the lack of any case to be solved. Thus, the LD group was found to exhibit neither sufficient variability nor singular uniqueness requiring any detective work. . . .

The present findings should not be construed as negative, however. Although WISC profile and scatter analysis is not defensible for diagnosing LD, the WISC remains a valuable tool for global IQ assessment and should be restricted to this purpose. (p. 150)

Kavale and Forness' reasoning is this: Learning disabled groups and normal groups do not differ on WISC profiles. Therefore, the profiles cannot be used to diagnose learning disabilities (and, by extension, any other condition). I agree, even though many clinicians do use the profile for diagnosis. Kavale and Forness also suggested that, when a student *does* have a profile of strengths and weaknesses, clinicians should ignore it; there is nothing to explore and no more detective work to be done. I do not agree with this statement. To leave interpretation at Level I for students whose WISC-III profiles show certain clusters, is ludicrous. Kavale and Forness apparently assumed that diagnosis is the only purpose. They also assumed a very static assessment process (i.e., that, somehow, the differences between a learning disabled student and a normal student will be evident in the standardized numbers themselves). As every school psychologist knows, a student's behavior on some subtests provides many valuable clues, even though the scaled score may fall in the average range. For example, a student may score a 10 on Mazes, but still be very impulsive in his or her approach. The WISC-III must be used in a very dynamic way. It is from the overall impressions (the "detective work") and, of course, from the numbers themselves, that recommendations of an educational nature can be made.

To begin Level III interpretation (assuming that all Level I and II hypotheses have been explored), I recommend Kaufman's (1979) approach. The examiner calculates a Verbal average (using all six subtests and rounding the scaled score average to the nearest whole number). The same is done for the Performance Scale. Any Verbal or Performance subtest that deviates 3 points or more from its respective mean is considered a significant strength or weakness *for that student.*

In Figure 6.1, for example, Denise's Verbal average is 7, which is significantly weaker than the population average to begin with. Within that scale, however, the information subtest is significantly weaker than others, whereas the Vocabulary subtest is significantly stronger.

The next step is to see if any of the significantly strong or weak subtests cluster in some meaningful way. One can consult Kaufman's (1979) work directly for a more detailed explanation of the process and implications, and an overview of some of the hypotheses suggested by this kind of detective work. In Denise's case, Information, Arithmetic, and Digit Span—the Verbal subtests on which she scored lowest—all have memory components, so memory aspects might be further explored in regard to this student. Much of what is uncovered in this way about a student can best be discussed in terms of learning styles.

THE WISC-III AND LEARNING STYLES

According to Dunn (1984), learning style is "the way in which each person absorbs and retains information and/or skills; regardless of how that process is described, it is dramatically different in each person" (p. 12). Learning style and cognitive style are often used interchangeably, but the former is the umbrella term; learning style can include affective and physiological states, as well as strictly cognitive ones. The diagram of Dunn's learning style model is shown in Figure 6.2.

I find the model in Figure 6.2 interesting, but exceedingly complex. In fact, 2,304 different combinations are possible from the model! How can the school psychologist or teacher possibly become familiar with the various implications of each combination? More importantly, would it really make a significant difference to the student's achievement? Unfortunately, instead of providing answers to these questions, researchers have created controversy instead. For example, Dunn (1984) wrote,

In every case [of the research studies she cites] students who were matched with methods, resources,

Name _Denise_ _____ Sex _____

School _____ Grade _____

Examiner _____ Handedness _____

WISC-III™
Wechsler Intelligence Scale for Children–Third Edition

Subtests	Raw Scores	Scaled Scores					
Picture Completion	18		7		7		
Information	11	4		4			
Coding	38		6				6
Similarities	17	9		9			
Picture Arrangement	10		2		2		
Arithmetic	14	5				5	
Block Design	42		9		9		
Vocabulary	37	11		11			
Object Assembly	26		8		8		
Comprehension	19	7		7			
(Symbol Search)	N/A		(N/A)				N/A
(Digit Span)	10	(6)				6	
(Mazes)	15		(6)				
Sum of Scaled Scores		36	32	31	26	11	
		Verbal	Perfor.	VC	PO	FD	PS

Full Scale Score **68** OPTIONAL

	Year	Month	Day
Date Tested			
Date of Birth			
Age	12	0	8

	Score	IQ/Index	%ile	95% Confidence Interval
Verbal	36	84	14	79 – 91
Performance	32	78	7	72 – 88
Full Scale	68	79	8	74 – 85
VC	31	88	21	82 – 95
PO	26	80	9	74 – 90
FD	11	75	5	69 – 87
PS				–

IQ Scores

VIQ	PIQ	FSIQ
84	78	79

Index Scores (Optional)

VCI	POI	FDI	PSI
88	80	75	/

Subtest Scores

Verbal						Performance					
Inf	Sim	Ari	Voc	Com	DS	PC	Cd	PA	BD	OA	SS	Mz
4	9	5	11	7	6	7	6	2	9	8	/	6

Figure 6.1. Denise's profile.

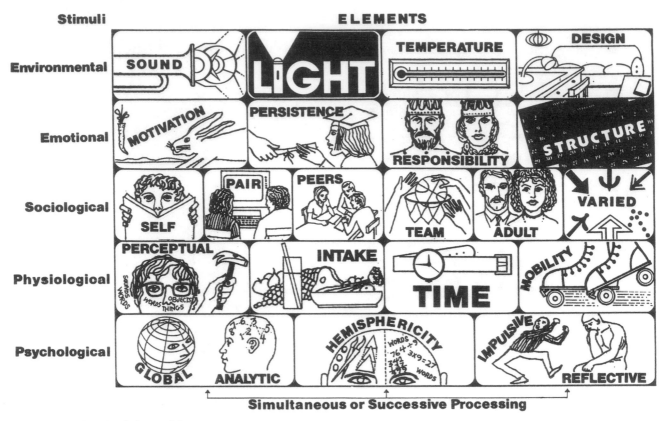

Learning Styles Model
Designed by Dr. Rita Dunn and Dr. Kenneth Dunn

Figure 6.2. Diagnosing learning styles. From "Learning Style: State of the Science" by R. Dunn, 1984, *Theory into Practice, 23,* p. 11. Copyright 1984 by Ohio State University College of Education. Reprinted with permission.

or environments that complemented their reported strong preferences achieved statistically higher; they achieved statistically less well when they were mismatched with their preferences. (pp. 12–13)

Doyle and Rutherford (1984) gave the opposite view:

Advocates of matching models often claim that their methods increase student achievement. The weight of the evidence does not, however, support such claims. In a massive review of research on attribute–treatment interactions, Cronbach and Snow found few consistent results for programs matching instructional treatments to learning styles. With respect to learner preferences, for example, they concluded that "basing instructional adapta-

tions on student preferences does not improve learning and may be detrimental." Other reviews and studies report similar results. Peterson found weak effects for achievement, although she did identify effects of matching on noncognitive variables such as self-esteem and motivation. Kampwirth and Bates reviewed 22 studies on the effects of matching modality preferences with teaching methods. Only two studies reported significant effects on achievement. The remaining 20 studies found either no significant interaction effects or support for the effectiveness of teaching to the nonpreferred modality. (p. 22)

What is the school psychologist or classroom teacher to make of such conclusions? (Certainly, the first recommendation is to proceed with caution!) There are no black-and-white answers. Consideration must be given to the individual student. In my experience, the learning style rationale has been one way to at least turn around a teacher's or parent's attitude. For example, if a student finds that studying with music in the background helps, while a parent insists on quiet and is in conflict with the student over it, then a learning style explanation may help reduce the conflict and lead to improved academics or homework habits. In this case, improved learning has as much to do with attitude changes (in support of Kampwirth and Bates, cited in the foregoing excerpt from Doyle and Rutherford) as it does with learning style per se. However, some evidence indicates that some students do indeed perform better in noisy versus quiet environments. I have found in my consulting work that carefully thought-out recommendations based on a learning style analysis can and do improve the situation for a student. Sometimes, however, it is not academic improvement, per se, that improves. Improvement may occur in less tangible, more difficult-to-quantify ways.

Doyle and Rutherford (1984, p. 22) provided the following considerations to keep in mind about learning styles:

1. There is no single dimension of learners that unambiguously dictates an instructional prescription. Thus, accommodating cognitive style, which is likely to influence motivation primarily, does not necessarily account for other critical variables in learning, such as ability and prior knowledge. Indeed, concentrating exclusively on a single dimension could even be harmful for learning because other aspects of instruction are neglected. Moreover, there is no compelling evidence that matching instruction to learning style is always beneficial. In fact some studies suggest that a mismatch is best under particular circumstances.

2. There are higher-level interactions between learner characteristics and instructional treatments. Thus, the effect of learning style on achievement is likely to be affected by the nature of the learning task, the relationship between teacher and student, the time of the year, and other local conditions. It is difficult, therefore, to predict a simple linear connec-

tion between learning style and instructional dimensions.

3. Most students can adapt to a variety of instructional modes, even if they are not preferred. The central issue is whether the instruction provided is of sufficiently high quality, in terms of such dimensions as task clarity, feedback, and opportunities for practice, to facilitate learning.

4. In a classroom, uniform instructional treatments are often superior to differentiated treatments because they are compatible with the teacher's skills and are easier to manage. In addition, whole-class instruction is not necessarily "uniform" at a process level. Teachers often present information in a variety of formats (discussion, lecture, questions) and adjust to the attributes of learners during individual contacts. Thus, opportunities are provided for different learners to gain access to instruction.

In other words, teaching style needs to be considered too—particularly, *effective* teaching techniques. What is effective may be different for different students. For example, if we take Dunn's "emotional" stimulus category, and look under "Structure" (Figure 6.2), we find good evidence that lower ability students respond better to structured versus unstructured tasks. High-ability students learn well under either condition. Structure means, in this case, direct teaching, explicit guidance, and immediate feedback, with plenty of opportunities for practice. This kind of learning/teaching–style match is certainly at a practical level for the classroom. It seems to me, then, that the important questions regarding learning style are "*What* learning style are we talking about?" and "How does it apply in *this* student's case?"

Most theorists state that learning styles are quite pervasive and stable over time. Such dimensions as field dependence/independence, for example, which is a well-researched cognitive style, seem to be quite stable over time for individuals. Therefore, although certain WISC-III patterns may suggest learning styles, these hypotheses should be explored with teacher input, behavioral observations, and supplementary tests when necessary.

Some learning styles seem to have better research-based support than others. I cannot deal with all possible learning styles in this chapter, so I have selected the following: modality preference, field dependence/independence, simultaneous–successive processing, conceptual tempo, right–left brain processing, and Letteri's approach.

Modality Preference

The modality preference approach to learning style was developed in the early days of remedial education. Students were classified as visual, auditory, or tactile–kinesthetic learners based on their preferred mode of information input. A number of reading programs were developed, stressing one or more of the modalities. Little formal research was available at the time to determine whether any one method was superior to another and for what learners. There is still a dearth of research on the subject.

The Verbal Scale of the WISC-III could be interpreted as auditory–vocal, because all items require the student to listen and respond orally. The Performance Scale is primarily auditory–visual/manual, because input is both auditory (verbal instructions) and visual (pictures, blocks, puzzles, etc.), whereas output is mainly manual (pointing, manipulating items, doing paper-and-pencil tasks, etc.). Therefore, a Verbal–Performance discrepancy on the WISC-III could be interpreted, for example, as a strength or weakness, in auditory or visual learning, depending on the direction of the difference.

I find such an interpretation useful in some individual cases. Most often, the underlying verbal or performance strengths should be the dominant interpretive hypothesis.

The modality interpretations have a number of significant problems. A primary difficulty is that only about 10% of students show a clear-cut preference for one modality over another. Second, very few reliable instruments are available to measure such preferences. Finally, there is a confounding with other, likely more important, variables.

For example, Thorpe and Borden (1985) taught learning disabled students sight words using a VA (visual auditory) approach (the teacher read the word, and the students repeated it, said the sound of each syllable, and said the word again) or a VAKT (visual, auditory, kinesthetic, tactile) approach (the teacher said the word, and the students separated it, traced the letter with their index finger while saying the sounds, underlined the word, and said it again). After five words were completed this way, students said the words again, traced each letter over with their pencils, and underlined the word while repeating it. The VAKT approach produced better results in terms of both on-task behavior and number of words correctly read. However, when praise was added to either the VA or the VAKT method, results improved dramatically for both methods, with a slight advantage to the VA method! Not only was praise a very significant addition to the modality teaching, but it seemed to have as much effect as the modality approach itself.

Larivee (1981) reviewed a number of studies done on method-by-modality studies for beginning-reading instruction, and concluded,

> Differentiating instruction according to modality preference does not appear to facilitate learning to read or the acquisition of specific beginning reading skills. . . . One might infer that adapting the instructional mode to the learner's preferred modality is not important for teaching beginning reading and/or that the tests used to assess modal preferences do not in fact determine a preference, but rather reflect the child's experience with the particular type of task measured. (p. 188)

My conclusion regarding modality training is that, if such an explanation and training are to be used at all, a multisensory approach is best because it is simply more interesting, and therefore helps students attend. Having all senses engaged involves the student more.

Although the divisions are somewhat arbitrary, the following classifications might be helpful:

- Visual: chalkboard, overhead, dittos, posters, charts, maps, video, films, filmstrips

- Auditory: lecture, questioning, discussion, audiotapes, music, listening centers

- Kinesthetic: tracing, drawing, role playing, experiments, printing/writing, drama

Any teacher using a variety of such teaching activities and aids is likely to meet any modality needs of students.

Field Dependence/Independence

The construct of field dependence/independence arose from Witkin's work with World War II pilots. Witkin noticed that some pilots were much more capable than others of orienting themselves to upright positions during complex flying maneuvers. Witkin and his co-workers then developed some rather elaborate testing mechanisms, including tilting chairs and rooms to help them discriminate those individuals who were more adept at repositioning themselves.

After the war, Witkin continued his research, and coined the terms field dependent (FD) and field independent (FI) (Witkin & Goodenough, 1977). He found that the ability to experience the environment in global (FD) or more analytic (FI) ways was a pervasive and essentially stable characteristic of individuals—a cognitive style, if you will. The style pervaded many aspects of the individual's functioning in the environment, not merely in orienting to an upright position. The FD/FI construct is considered an important variable; in fact, it may be the most well documented of the cognitive styles. It is a variable that needs to be considered with a number of individual students.

In general, FIs tend to perceive individual items in their environments as separate from the background context, whereas FDs are much more influenced by the backgrounds and see less differentiation and more fusion with the environment. (Perhaps many of the so-called perceptual problems that students have are simply manifestations of a more FD cognitive style.)

The WISC-III Performance Scale can be used to suggest an FD or FI orientation. Scores on Picture Completion, Block Design, and Object Assembly can be added and averaged. If their average differs from the other three Performance subtests by 3 points or more, then an FD or FI hypothesis can be considered. Higher scores on these three subtests suggest the FI orientation. The Verbal Scale has not been analyzed in this way; however, because FDs have a more general differentiation in their environment, we would expect high-level, more abstract, quality responses on the Verbal items. The examiner can confirm or deny the FD/FI hypothesis by using such tests as the *Embedded Figures Test* (Witkin, 1971), *Group Embedded Figures Test* (Witkin, Oltman, & Raskin, 1971), or *Children's*

Embedded Figures Test (Karp & Konstadt, 1971). Note, however, that Picture Completion, Block Design, and Object Assembly are involved in the simultaneous/successive dichotomy, and are related to Bannatyne's (1974) spatial category. The examiner needs to decide which hypothesis is dominant for each student.

People with FI orientations, as the name suggests, tend to see their world from an internal point of view, and to impose their own structure and organization upon it. FDs, on the other hand, tend to see the world from an external point of view, one from which they can employ the already existing structure as their own. FDs tend to be much more adept at interpersonal relationships.

Figure 6.3 shows a WISC-III profile that suggests an FD orientation. Juan's scores on Picture Completion, Block Design, and Object Assembly are significantly lower than his scores on Picture Arrangement, Coding, Symbol Search, and Mazes. In addition, even though the Vocabulary and Similarities subtest scores were in the average range, the quality of responses was not good. Juan earned 2 points on many of the Vocabulary items by naming several attributes, rather than using one good synonym.

In terms of learning and education, a number of studies suggest the following learning differences between FD and FI students:

> The FD/FI differentiation extends into many areas of human activity, including learning and education. Ruble and Nakamura, for example, suggest that FD children are more able than FI children to solve problems containing social cues. In the area of concept formation, a differentiation is also noted. Witkin et al. cite several studies that suggest that FD learners tend to focus on salient cues when developing concepts. FI learners, on the other hand, tend to objectively sample from the full array of available cues in order to form concepts. Goodenough suggests that motivation is also an area of differentiation. Field dependents tend to be more attentive to intrinsic motivators and self-defined goals. Field dependents tend to be more responsive to extrinsic motivation and goals. (Rasinski, 1984, p. 306)

In terms of reading, specifically, the research suggests that FIs are generally better readers than FDs.

Name _Juan_ _____ Sex _____

School _____ Grade _____

Examiner _____ Handedness _____

WISC-III™
Wechsler Intelligence Scale for Children – Third Edition

Subtests	Raw Scores	Scaled Scores				
Picture Completion	15		7		7	
Information	14	9		9		
Coding	46		10			10
Similarities	14	9		9		
Picture Arrangement	33		11		11	
Arithmetic	14	6			6	
Block Design	19		5	5		
Vocabulary	29	10		10		
Object Assembly	15		5	5		
Comprehension	18	8		8		
(Symbol Search)	23		(10)			10
(Digit Span)	9	(6)			6	
(Mazes)	21		(11)			
Sum of Scaled Scores		42	38	36	28	12	20
		Verbal	Perfor.	VC	PO	FD	PS
		Full Scale Score		OPTIONAL			

	Year	Month	Day
Date Tested			
Date of Birth			
Age	10	10	29

	Score	IQ/ Index	%ile	95 % Confidence Interval
Verbal	42	91	27	85 - 98
Performance	38	84	14	77 - 93
Full Scale	80	87	19	82 - 93
VC	36	95	37	89 - 102
PO	28	83	13	76 - 93
FD	12	78	7	72 - 90
PS	20	101	53	91 - 111

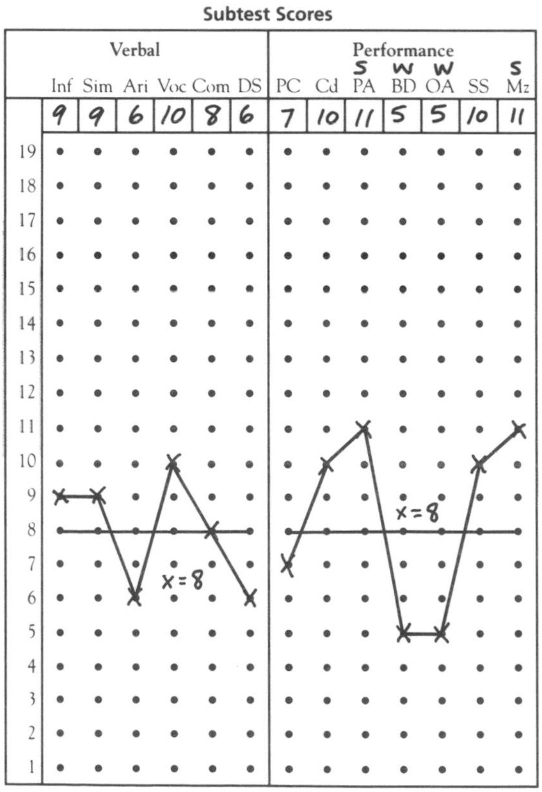

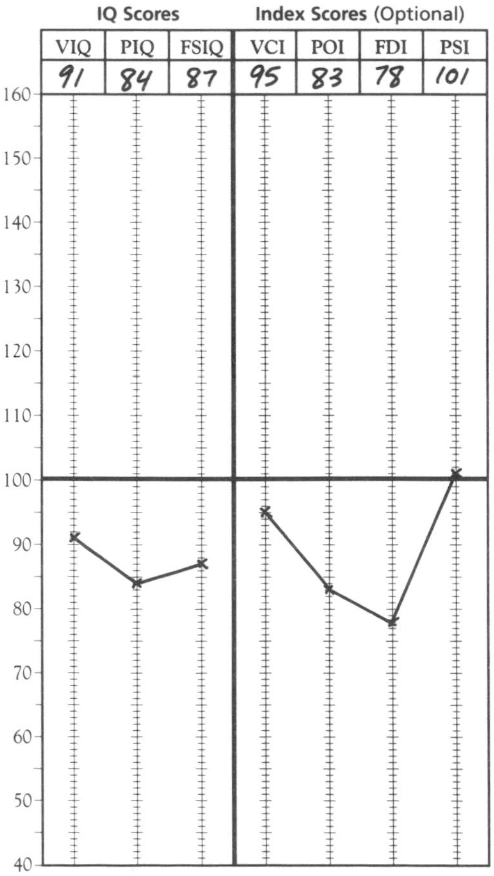

IQ Scores

VIQ	PIQ	FSIQ
91	84	87

Index Scores (Optional)

VCI	POI	FDI	PSI
95	83	78	101

THE PSYCHOLOGICAL CORPORATION®
HARCOURT BRACE JOVANOVICH, INC.

7 8 9 10 11 12 A B C D E

Subtest Scores

09–980004

Figure 6.3. Juan's profile.

Students with learning disabilities are typically FD (Rasinski, 1984).

What accounts for the difference in reading ability between FD and FI students? Some studies have related the psycholinguistic reading model (PL) discussed in Chapter 4 to the FD/FI construct. Mature reading involves word knowledge, word decoding, and comprehension. The mature reader seems to use both top–down and bottom–up processes interactively. The evidence in general seems to suggest better reading at all levels by FIs. Evidence also suggests that the FD reader uses a more bottom–up approach, whereas the FI reader uses more top–down processing. In terms of reading vocabulary, word boundaries are learned more effectively by FIs, a result we might expect from theory, since FIs are better able to disembed items from the background—a process that is certainly necessary in differentiating words from the surrounding lines of print while reading. FD readers pay more attention to the surface features of the word, and are misled by primary word cues when secondary meanings are more appropriate. As an example, an FD reader might choose "knock" for the meaning of "know" in a multiple-choice situation, because "knock" is a surface feature distractor.

When oral reading miscues are used to determine word recognition strategy, it has been found that

> Field independents made more grammatically acceptable miscues, demonstrated stronger grammatical relationship patterns and had better re-tellings of the text than field dependents. Both groups used graphophonic cues in reading; however, the field independents used semantic and syntactic cues to a greater extent. The field dependents responded to the text in a passive and observant manner rather than applying what they knew and integrating it with the text. They seemed more concerned with the surface structure of the text and less with meaningful predictive strategies. This accords with Goodenough's conclusion that field dependents, in general, tend to take a "spectator" approach to learning, while independents assume a more "participant" or hypothesis-making role. This also suggests that field dependents may have a greater reliance upon bottom–up, text-driven strategies for word recognition and accessing word knowledge. Field independents, however, employ more interactive strategies. Complementary findings were reported in a study that looked at the silent text readings of ninth-graders using analysis of a cloze procedure task. This investigation found that the patterns of miscues varied the greatest by cognitive style with frustration level texts. At this level the FI students demonstrated, through miscue analysis, a greater control over meaning (semantic acceptability of errors) and syntax (syntactic acceptability of errors), than the FD students. Similarly, Rounds found that field independent second-grade students were more able to gain from grammatical awareness training than dependents. The FI children apparently had greater proficiency in disembedding or abstracting relevant grammatical generalizations and structures than the FD children. (Rasinski, 1984, p. 309)

In summary, the FIs tend to have superior word knowledge in reading. FIs seem to use more effective cognitive strategies and are better able to predict and use top–down processing to guide their reading. FDs are easily misled by surface features and do not allow meaning acquisition to guide their reading as forcefully as do FIs. Therefore, one might expect that reading comprehension will also be a problem for FDs.

This prediction is supported by a number of research studies (cited in Rasinski, 1984) showing better reading comprehension for FIs. Some of the identified reasons for this are as follows:

1. FIs impose a structure onto the passage and therefore organize the material much more readily than do FDs.

2. FIs comprehend high-importance information in passages more effectively than do FDs.

3. FIs can more easily provide unambiguous interpretations of ambiguous material then can FDs. This is an important finding. It seems that the ability to effectively organize verbal sets is related to the ability to do likewise with nonverbal sets. In other words, the student who shows an FI pattern on the Performance Scale of the WISC-III is likely to handle verbal language effectively as well.

4. FIs have more effective working memory, it seems, than do FDs. Thus,

in reading tasks where complex ideas require the storage of more propositions, the FDs are likely to suffer, and comprehension will drop.

In addition, FDs are not as successful as FIs in using their background knowledge when reading passages. This applies to schema activation in particular. In other words, FIs may have no more background knowledge on a subject than do FDs, but they can apply it more effectively when reading.

Helping field-dependent students become better readers: Suggestions and strategies. The school psychologist often makes recommendations to teachers for instructional purposes. In terms of the FD/FI construct, the following principles can be shared with teachers and remedial reading specialists:

1. Become more aware of which students are probably FD and which are FI. Many students fall somewhere in the middle, but it is likely that many of the poorer readers are FDs. The WISC-III Picture Completion, Block Design, and Object Assembly cluster, as already mentioned, can suggest the hypothesis, but further testing may be necessary.

2. Once identified, grouping for instruction is very important. Rasinski (1984) offered the following considerations:

> The research literature shows quite clearly that field dependents tend to be poorer readers than independents. Consequently, these students will tend to be found in the lower reading groups in their classrooms. The work of Allington and Collins suggests that type of reading instruction provided students in lower reading groups is markedly different than that provided [to] the higher groups. Specifically, when contrasted to high reading groups, the low group readers do less reading, read more orally than silently, get interrupted more often by the teacher for errors made in reading, and are given a greater instructional focus on decoding as opposed to comprehension. These observed practices are in almost complete contradiction to what the research reviewed here points to. The FD/FI research shows that field dependent readers attend too closely to the salient, surface-level cues in texts and that they pay relatively less attention to meaning. The logical implications of this suggest that FD readers should be given help in paying more attention to meaning and less attention to code as they read. They

should be helped in using the less obvious meaning and contextual cues to aid word recognition and vocabulary improvement. They should be encouraged to make meaningful predictions about words in texts. Further, predictions about the meaning of whole texts should be encouraged. Directed Reading Thinking Activities (DRTA) would be highly appropriate here. Scott and his associates recommend too that field dependent students should not be required to read orally in the classroom, since this places high priority on accuracy over meaning for them. For the same reason, teacher interruptions to correct reading errors, especially those errors that do not affect meaning, should be de-emphasized. (p. 315)

The suggestions given in the foregoing passage dovetail very nicely with the psycholinguistic model, and are consistent with the language-immersion approach to reading. However, one must be very careful, because what applies to a group does not necessarily apply to an individual. Individual students might, for example, require in-depth "pre-phonics training" to assist them with decoding even if they have an FD orientation.

3. Help the FD student become a more active reader. The technique of reciprocal teaching may be quite effective for this purpose (Palincsar & Brown, 1984).

4. Help the student develop strategies for organizing text. An advance organizer, for example, has been shown to be useful for both FD and FI students in terms of improving reading comprehension. However, a significant interaction occurs between type of treatment and cognitive style. FD students who are given advance organizers together with prompts within the lesson that draw attention to the organizer, are likely to make the most impressive gains (Satterly & Telfer, 1979). The gains are such that FD students who are given these additional organizers within the text and prompted to use them can increase their reading scores to match the FI students' normal performance. (This is also a good example of a teaching strategy that helps the student perform higher in his or her zone of potential difference.) Another way of imposing more organization on text is the use of imagery (see Appendix 2D). If FD students are taught how to make a mental picture of a story, this will help them in their comprehension—more so than merely listening or even using pictures that accompany the

text. Other organizational strategies, such as instruction in note taking and the SQ3R (*S*urvey, *Q*uestion, *R*ead, *R*ecite, *R*eview) method (Robinson, 1970), also could be helpful.

5. Because FD students have well-developed interpersonal skills, capitalize on this strength as much as possible by using and encouraging

- Reading partners and teams (emphasize cooperation; deemphasize competition)
- Reading clubs
- Book discussion groups
- Collaborative language arts assignments
- Book conferences

Books with people and social situations as the primary content should be appealing to FD students.

6. When students are reading texts, draw their attention to the headings and subheadings. Have them pay attention to key concepts and words, and remind the students of them as they read along.

Simultaneous/Successive Information Processing Styles

I have already introduced the distinction between simultaneous and successive information processing in conjunction with the Freedom from Distractibility index. If a student shows a split on the appropriate Performance subtests, then the hypothesis should be considered. Cross-checks include a split of 3 digits or more on Digits Forward versus Digits Backward (in terms of *span*) and behavioral observations. For example, some students seem to solve the Block Design and Object Assembly items in a very sequential manner—perhaps even assembling parts of the whole before attaching them into a coherent unit—whereas other students seem to see the whole design or object immediately, and assemble it top–down. The profile in Figure 6.4 illustrates a split on the Performance scale in favor of simultaneous processing.

What is simultaneous and what is successive information processing? Kaufman and Kaufman, authors of the *Kaufman Assessment Battery for Children*, which was designed to differentiate students based on these two processing styles, wrote,

A problem requiring sequential processing emphasizes the consecutive, one-after-the-other order in which small amounts of information must be arranged. Sequential processing is logical and analytic; it usually employs language and chronological order, since both depend on arrangements in time. When you listen to a lecture, scribbling notes as the speaker moves from point to point, you are acquiring information sequentially. Later, when you read over your notes in light of the completed lecture, you'll probably use simultaneous processing to integrate and synthesize all the items of information you've jotted down.

A problem requiring simultaneous processing emphasizes complete units, wholes, integrated pieces of information that all must be considered before a problem can be solved or a conclusion reached. Simultaneous processing is holistic and synthetic; it usually employs visual images and spatial arrangements, since perceiving many details at once involves seeing or imagining the entire problem or situation. When you stand appreciatively before a painting, perhaps admiring the overall artistic balance or responding to the mood conveyed by the total scene, you are "processing" simultaneously, perceiving the picture all at once. However, if you concentrate on various details of the picture, moving from one aspect to another systematically, you are analyzing it in a more sequential way. (Kaufman & Kaufman, 1984, p. 4)

The distinction stems from the Russian psychologist Luria, and has been developed more fully in North America by Das and by Kaufman. According to Kaufman and Kaufman (1984), the following are general teaching guidelines for each learning style:

For the sequential learner:

1. Present material step by step, gradually approaching the overall concept or skill. Lead up to the big question with a series of smaller ones. Break the task into parts.

2. Get the child to verbalize what is to be learned. When you teach a new word, have the child say it, aloud or silently. Emphasize verbal cues, directions, and memory strategies.

3. Teach and rehearse the steps required to do a problem or complete a task. Continue to refer back to the details or steps

Name _Joyce_   Sex _____

School _____ Grade _____

Examiner _____ Handedness _____

WISC-III™
Wechsler Intelligence Scale for Children – Third Edition

Subtests	Raw Scores	Scaled Scores					
Picture Completion	16		5		5		
Information	12	4		4			
Coding	50		8				8
Similarities	22	11		11			
Picture Arrangement	35		9		9		
Arithmetic	17	7				7	
Block Design	25		4		4		
Vocabulary	34	9		9			
Object Assembly	22		5		5		
Comprehension	24	9		9			
(Symbol Search)	26		(9)				9
(Digit Span)	12	(7)				7	
(Mazes)	20		(8)				
Sum of Scaled Scores		40	31	33	23	14	17
		Verbal	Perfor.	VC	PO	FD	PS
		Full Scale Score 71		OPTIONAL			

	Year	Month	Day
Date Tested			
Date of Birth			
Age	13	6	26

	Score	IQ/Index	%ile	95 % Confidence Interval	
Verbal	40	89	23	83	– 96
Performance	31	77	6	71	– 87
Full Scale	71	81	10	76	– 87
VC	33	91	27	85	– 98
PO	23	76	5	70	– 87
FD	14	84	14	77	– 95
PS	17	93	32	84	– 104

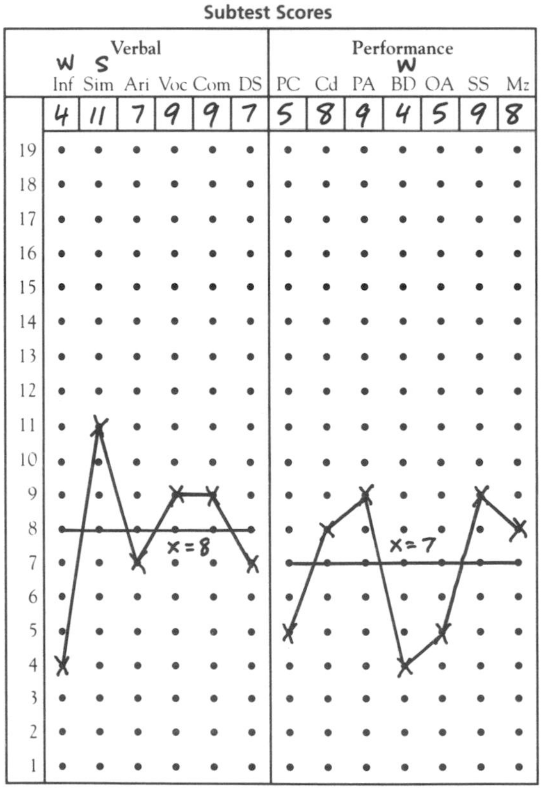

Subtest Scores

	Verbal						Performance						
	W S								W				
	Inf	Sim	Ari	Voc	Com	DS	PC	Cd	PA	BD	OA	SS	Mz
	4	11	7	9	9	7	5	8	9	4	5	9	8

x = 8

x = 7

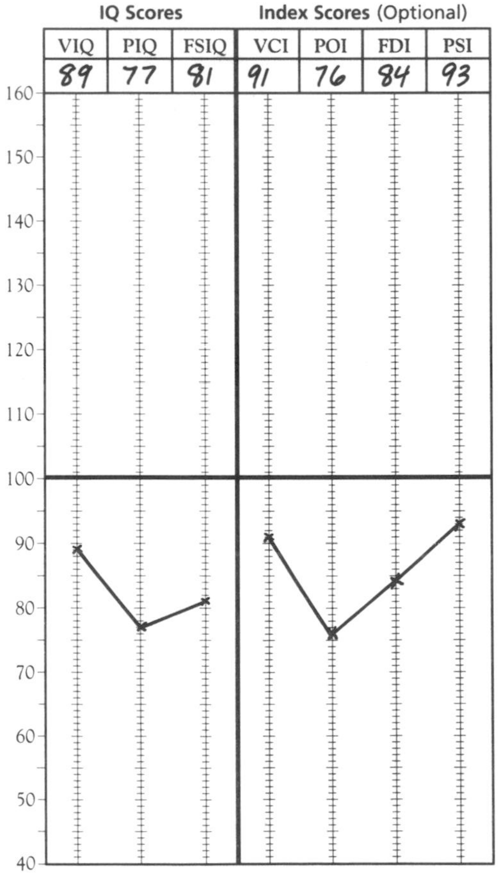

IQ Scores   Index Scores (Optional)

VIQ	PIQ	FSIQ	VCI	POI	FDI	PSI
89	77	81	91	76	84	93

Copyright © 1991, 1986, 1974, 1971 by The Psychological Corporation
Standardization edition copyright © 1989 by The Psychological Corporation
Copyright 1949 by The Psychological Corporation
Copyright renewed 1976 by The Psychological Corporation
All rights reserved. Printed in the United States of America.

THE PSYCHOLOGICAL CORPORATION®
HARCOURT BRACE JOVANOVICH, INC.

7 8 9 10 11 12 A B C D E

09–980004

Figure 6.4. Joyce's profile.

already mentioned or mastered. Offer a logical structure or procedure by appealing to the child's verbal/temporal orientation.

For example, the sequential learner may look at one or two details of a picture, but miss the visual image as a whole. To help such a student toward an overall appreciation of the picture, start with the parts and work up to the whole. Rather than beginning with, "What does the picture show?" or "How does the picture make you feel?" first ask about details:

—"What is the little boy in the corner doing?"
—"Where is the dog?"
—"What colors are used in the sky?"
—"What is the cow looking at?"

Lead up to questions about the overall interpretation or appreciation:

—"How do all these details give you cues about what is happening in this picture?"
—"How does this picture make you feel?"

The sequential learner prefers a step-by-step teaching approach, one that may emphasize the gradual accumulation of details.

For the simultaneous learner:

1. Present the overall concept or question before asking the child to solve the problem. Continue to refer back to the task, question, or desired outcome.

2. Get the child to visualize what is to be learned. When you teach a new word, have the child write it and picture it mentally, see it on the page in the mind's eye. Emphasize visual cues, directions, and memory strategies.

3. Make tasks concrete wherever possible by providing manipulative materials, pictures, models, diagrams, graphs. Offer a sense of the whole by appealing to the child's visual/spatial orientation.

The simultaneous learner may react to a picture as a whole, but may miss details. To help such a student notice the parts that contribute to the total visual image, begin by establishing an overall interpretation or reaction:

—"What does the picture show?"
—"How does the picture make you feel?"

Then, consider the details:

—"What is the expression on the woman's face?"
—"What is the little boy in the corner doing?"
—"What colors are used in the sky?"

Relate the details to the student's initial interpretation:

—"How do these details explain why the picture made you feel the way it did?"

The simultaneous learner responds best to a holistic teaching approach that focuses on groups of details or images, and stresses the overall meaning or configuration of the task. (p. 3)

I frequently find the simultaneous/successive distinction useful, but it seems to me that most learning requires the integration of the two styles. Kaufman and Kaufman (1984) admitted this:

It seems clear that very little learning calls exclusively for one process. We are constantly switching from one to the other, depending on the task before us. Many school-related activities, such as reading and arithmetic, require the integration of both processes. Still, many of us have a favorite learning style, one that we feel most comfortable with when we're confronted with an unfamiliar problem or new information. Our students, particularly those with special learning difficulties, may also have preferred styles. They can begin to feel more successful in school if new tasks are presented to them in ways that are congenial to their mental processing strengths. (p. 4)

Because the simultaneous/successive distinction is relatively new, little research support shows that teaching to a student's preferred style will truly help the student academically. This lack of research is shared by many of the cognitive styles, however, as I have already discussed. School psychologists and teachers who use a learning-styles approach must always ask themselves, "If I teach exclusively toward the student's preferred style, will I harm him by not exposing him to the nonpreferred style?" In general, teachers are probably better off using a variety of strategies and approaches, including both simultaneous and successive techniques, while making some adjustments for individual students when a clear-cut preference in one style is known.

Although primarily the Performance Scale provides data on the simultaneous/successive split, some of the WISC-R Verbal Scale subtests have also been researched using the Luria–Das model (Naglieri, Kamphaus, & Kaufman, 1983). Unfortunately, not all the subtests were used in this study (Information, Vocabulary, Comprehension, and Arithmetic were omitted because of the influence of school achievement on them). For the *normal standardization sample* of the WISC-R (school psychologists can feel confident these also apply to the WISC-III), here is how the subtests "regrouped" on the two dimensions:

Simultaneous Subtests
Picture Completion
Picture Arrangement
Block Design
Object Assembly
Mazes
(Similarities)

Successive Subtests
Digit Span
(Similarities)
Coding

Note that Similarities loads on both dimensions (although it loads more heavily on the simultaneous factor).

The picture changes quite dramatically, however, when subgroups of special education students are sampled. In Naglieri et al.'s (1983) study, separate groups of students with mental handicaps and students referred for learning and behavior problems were used. The authors concluded,

> Whereas the emergence of factors for the WISC-R resembling the Luria/Das successive/simultaneous dichotomy for three groups of children is the main result of this investigation, there is another finding of almost equal value. The factor solutions for the two exceptional populations were highly similar to each other, but both differed from the results for

normal youngsters as follows: (a) Similarities had a clear-cut simultaneous component for normals, but was strongly successive for the exceptional groups, especially the retarded; (b) Picture Arrangement was a simultaneous task for normals, but was clearly successive for the two exceptional groups; and (c) Coding was a successive task for normal children, but not for either exceptional population. (p. 28)

The authors speculated about why this is the case:

> One possible explanation is that normal and exceptional children attack the same problems using different modes of processing. If we assume that normal children use the preferred or more efficient processing style, then it is conceivable that retarded youngsters or children referred for learning problems are using inefficient strategies. (p. 31)

It would seem, then, that simultaneous and successive processing styles are used differently in solving problems by different groups of students. In particular, very poor performance on Similarities, Digit Span, and Picture Arrangement seems to speak for severe problems in successive processing, particularly in exceptional populations.

The educational implications are stated as follows:

> The teaching of more appropriate problem-solving strategies may well be a logical addition to remedial programs for children with learning problems. Similarly, recommendations for prescriptive teaching follow logically from the Luria/Das model. Instruction may be geared toward capitalizing on a child's particular strength (whether it be simultaneous or successive) in processing information, thereby circumventing the problems associated with the weaker mode. For example, consider the child who has not performed well in reading and shows evidence of a successive processing deficit coupled with a strength in simultaneous processing. This is the type of child who may benefit from a sight word instructional approach which emphasizes the holistic nature of word recognition rather than the analysis of discrete phonetic units and their proper ordering. Obviously, such speculation requires careful empirical investigation before these notions should be implemented. (Naglieri et al., 1983, p. 31)

In fact, some studies have indicated that direct training in the processes of simultaneous and successive strategies has a positive effect on reading (Das, Leong, & Williams, 1978). Adding such training to the resource teacher's repertoire, then, seems desirable. An excellent article by Gunnison (1984) gives more detail on developing educational interventions from this model.

In summary, then, the simultaneous/successive model is another area to explore when the Perceptual Organization factor is high and the Freedom from Distractibility factor is low on the WISC-III, because these two factors closely fit this dichotomy.

Conceptual Tempo and Planning Ability

Conceptual tempo. *Conceptual tempo* refers to a speed–accuracy problem-solving approach. I discussed this in detail in the previous chapter. It is most often measured by the *Matching Familiar Figures Test* (MFFT), developed by Kagan (1965). (On the WISC-III, the approach is determined by a behavioral observation made by the examiner.) Students who do the MFFT quickly and make many errors are on the impulsive side insofar as cognitive tempo goes, whereas those who are slow but accurate are called reflective. In any random sample of students, about one-third fall into the impulsive end of the scale. The planning and scanning strategies of such students are often unsystematic, random, and global. Most often, such students do not "stop and think," which can cause problems in three ways:

1. The student may not comprehend the problem sufficiently to recall relevant past experience.

2. The student may have the previous experience relevant to the problem, but fail to recall the item.

3. The student may not be in the habit of relying on past experience to guide present behavior. (adapted from Meichenbaum, 1977)

If students are impulsive, they are failing to inhibit an immediate response. They are acting without fully analyzing the options. This may result from a reluctance or inability to

1. Engage in search-and-scan activities

2. Generate response alternatives

3. Delay actions until consequences are evaluated (adapted from Kendall & Finch, 1976)

On the WISC-III, the examiner might note many instances of impulsivity, from such behaviors as grabbing the stopwatch the instant the student enters the examining room; to rapid, inaccurate scanning on Picture Completion; to rapid, haphazard planning on Mazes; to quickly saying, "I don't know," to any questions for which no answer immediately comes to mind. This kind of behavior leads to an underestimate of the student's potential.

Where behavior and teacher comments warrant a hypothesis of impulsivity, appropriate educational activities need to be recommended. The whole field of cognitive–behavior modification comes to bear here. Impulsive students typically do not plan well. Therefore, remedial attempts need to focus on helping the student to stop and think. Talking out loud, self-instruction, self-control, and modeling are some of the techniques by which this can be accomplished.

Planning ability. Closely related to conceptual tempo is planning ability. The inability to plan and organize is a pervasive characteristic of learning disabled and low-achieving students, and can be viewed as part of a student's style or approach to problem solving.

On the WISC-R (and on the WISC-III), low scores on Picture Arrangement and Mazes may reflect poor planning ability (Kaufman, 1979). However, I find this term a little too global. Moreover, many students I have tested do not have significant strengths or weaknesses on these two subtests in terms of the actual scaled scores, yet are very poor at planning in a classroom situation. In fact, some of them seem to achieve quite high scaled scores on Mazes, especially, but nevertheless display erratic planning skills on other WISC-III tasks or in the classroom.

What, then, is "planning"? Kops and Belmont (1985) devised an interesting experiment to help isolate which features of planning were difficult for a group of second-grade low achievers (LA) and average (or better) achievers (AA). Twenty LAs were paired with 20 AAs in terms of age, *Peabody Picture Vocabulary Test* (Dunn, 1959) and *Draw A Person* (Koppitz, 1968) scores, sex, and social class. Each student had to perform five classroom-like tasks and two standardized tasks—Mazes from the *Wechsler Preschool and Primary Scale of Intelligence* (Wechsler, 1967) and the *Trail Making Test*. Overall, the LAs scored significantly worse on the five classroom tasks in terms of the (a) number of trips taken to complete the tasks, (b) number of correct items brought on the first trip, and (c) time taken to complete the task. The LAs scored significantly *higher* on Mazes, however, but significantly worse on the *Trail Making Test*. To give you some idea of the task requirements in the study, the instructions for Task I were as follows:

> Task I: (Showing picture display board.) "These are some of the materials we would need if we were to make a cake today: a pan, mixing bowl, mixing spoon, measuring cup, and cake mix (pointing to each item on the display board). You will find all of these around the room. Can you find them? Bring them back and place them over here (pointing to a place on the examiner's table) in exactly the same order as these" (indicating the picture display board). (p. 9)

Kops and Belmont discussed the poorer results of the LAs in terms of planning with reference to

1. Planning and set
2. Planning and spatial organization
3. Planning and language
4. Planning and memory
5. Planning and attention

I discuss these findings briefly because I believe they have implications for teaching.

Planning and set. Kops and Belmont (1985) gave the following interpretation of the differential performance of the two groups in terms of set:

> Children of both groups appeared to begin the tasks by attempting to recall all of the items. The average school achievers showed better recall ability than the low achievers as shown by their bring-

ing both more correct items and fewer incorrect ones on the first trip. Crucial for success, however, was the children's subsequent performance, after their return with items on the first trip, since the task was still incomplete. On failing to bring all the necessary items at one time, most average achievers directly consulted the pictures on the display board to remind themselves of missing items. This can be seen as a shift in strategy (plan) from a set for total recall to a set for incorporating the pictures as an integral part of the task.

> The low achievers appeared unable to entertain an alternative method (to change set) and tended to be bound to the original, more demanding strategy (to remember all of the items and use the pictures only as a "crutch"). (p. 12)

Many school psychologists are familiar with the term *perseveration*, or an inability to switch sets. Some of this kind of behavior is displayed on the WISC-III. It seems to me that the inability to switch sets is a metacognitive one, so that pairing a student who has difficulty switching sets with one who does not would be an effective remedial strategy in terms of peer modeling. If that proved ineffective, then more direct teaching and thinking out loud by the teacher or a peer, coupled with a visualization strategy, could prove helpful.

Planning and spatial organization. On Mazes, the LAs did better. The authors interpreted this as a possible strength in solving visual, nonverbal tasks, in contrast to the language-related, school-type tasks involved in the study. They also felt the AAs had developed more careful work habits, which they applied even when they resulted in less efficient (in terms of speed) performance. Kops and Belmont did not feel impulsivity made the difference, in this instance.

Planning and language. Trail making is a language-related spatial task. On this task, the LAs took longer to complete the task, and received lower scores. While doing this task, the authors noted, the LA students talked aloud more frequently, and asked more questions about what was to be done. Relating this to language and planning, Kops and Belmont wrote,

> Meichenbaum and Goodman found that the expression of overt language developmentally precedes the use of covert language in problem solving, a developmental sequence postulated earlier by

Vygotsky and developed further by Luria. Low achievers could be said to be at a lower language developmental level than are average achievers. Such deficient or lagging language development could be a critical factor in the poorer organizational skills shown by the low school achievers. This is of particular importance if one accepts the view developed by Vygotsky that by school entrance age, language has taken on a dominant role in initiating, directing, regulating, and organizing cognitive functions and behavior. (p. 13)

Planning and memory. Low achievers evidenced poorer memory on the school-like tasks, in that they brought fewer correct items and more incorrect ones on the first trip of each task; however,

> It may not be poor memory alone that was the basis of poorer performance by the low achievers, but, rather, less flexibility in reorganizing the tasks. . . . The low achievers' continued attempt to recall all of the items may have created an additional burden leading to poorer organization (or partial disorganization), thus producing memory "failure," which was a critical variable illustrated by an average student who unhesitatingly and quickly from the beginning brought one item at a time as she consulted the display board each time to determine which item was to be sought next.
>
> However, on the Trail Making Test it is probable that slower and poorer recall of the sequence of numbers and letters was central to the low achievers' performance. (p. 13)

Planning and attention. Planning, in part, also means being able to direct one's attention appropriately to the task at hand and is described by Kops and Belmont as follows:

> Directed attention . . . concerns the controlled, sequential shifting of focus from one task element to the next until the task is completed. For this, the child must be able to (a) develop an end goal, (b) develop related subgoals, and (c) maintain these simultaneously in relation to each other as each subgoal is achieved. The child must be able to redirect attention in an orderly fashion, searching first for selected objects and when found to discard it (them) as a focus while shifting attention to the remaining objects as a new focus and so on, all with context to achieving the end goal. (p. 13)

Low-achieving students do not have an independent attentional deficit, according to Kops and Belmont, but rather a

> failure to develop a more effective strategy which led to less well-organized direction and redirection of attention. Yet, where their approach was more adequate to the task (Mazes) the low achievers selected, organized, and sequenced the relevant elements more effectively than did the average achievers. (p. 13)

The authors concluded, with reference to planning and attention, that

> The low achieving children were able to maintain goal direction, decide on a course of action, and monitor and check their performance sufficiently well to complete the tasks. However, they tended not to redefine or alter their original course to improve efficiency. (p. 14)

In light of all the foregoing, Kops and Belmont concluded,

> that planning and organizing is not a unitary set of skills but is, instead, developed in relation to specific cognitive functions. If so, the issue of understanding low achievement is more complicated than now envisioned, and requires careful delineation of the particular demands of given tasks and the related cognitive and strategic competencies required of the child. (p. 14)

The major implication of their study in terms of teaching is that

> It requires that we search both for specific cognitive inadequacies underlying poor learning and for related deficient or inadequate methods used in organizing, retrieving, and using knowledge. This duality of skills requires increased attention to the creation of teaching methods which help the child to link specific material to be learned with methods for organizing, storing, and using knowledge. (p. 14)

As you can see, this kind of analysis is far more helpful than a global diagnosis of attention deficit disorder. The implications for the school psychologist seem to be consistent with the kinds of strategies advocated in this book (see Fry & Lupart, 1986, for more educational strategies for helping students to organize, sort, and retrieve knowledge). In particular, in terms of planning, teacher modeling by thinking out loud, followed by the student doing the same, is an important strategy. However, the thinking out loud strategy should be coupled with visual imagery processing and needs to be adjusted to the specific task demands being made on the student at the time. These demands will vary from classroom to classroom, as well as from task to task.

Right- and Left-Brain Processes

Considerable neurological work has been done in the last 15 years to create a simplistic notion of right- and left-hemisphere specialization. When I say "simplistic," I mean that many people—educators included—now think that the left hemisphere does *x* and the right hemisphere does *y* in some sort of autonomous way. Although certain activities are specialized or favored by one hemisphere, the brain works in an integrated fashion all the time. All learning involves both hemispheres, although the activity of one hemisphere for certain tasks may be higher. Nevertheless, the hemispheres always act in concert. According to the Bilateral Cooperative Reading Model (Chapter 4), the right and left tracks (which are associated with the right and left hemispheres at the higher processing levels) must work in a cooperative, integrated fashion for efficient learning of reading.

Two subtests on the WISC-III Performance Scale seem to involve primarily right-hemisphere functioning: Picture Completion and Object Assembly (Kaufman, 1979). The other subtests involve primarily integrated functioning. Occasionally, a WISC-III profile, such as the one shown in Figure 6.5, shows a split that seems educationally relevant.

As shown in the figure, William did exceptionally well on the integrated subtests:

Right Brain	Integrated
Picture Completion = 6	Picture Arrangement = 12
Object Assembly = 7	Coding = 15
	Block Design = 14
	Mazes = 19
Average = 7	Average = 15
(Percentile 16)	(Percentile 95)

Additionally, William's Verbal Conceptualization index is solidly in the average range.

It is possible to teach reading comprehension using some integrated strategies, provided they are integrated with visualizing and verbalizing (see Appendix 2D). I review three strategies I find appealing from Walker (1985).

Strategy 1—Predicting maps. I have said that predicting is an integral and important aspect of mature reading. A prediction map is like a semantic map, only it conceptualizes the internal process of prediction/revision on the chalkboard. Seeing the process charted this way would, I think, appeal to both hemispheres, so to speak. Sources of information from both the student (reader-based inferences) and the text (text-based inferences) are integrated. The process, when drawn out, might look like the one shown in Figure 6.6.

Walker (1985) described the process as follows:

Initially, the teacher takes an active role by mapping her own constructive process of comprehending as the story is read. The predictions, important textual information, and personal interpretations are mapped interchangeably in the flow chart with the teacher modeling how the comprehending process is restructured during the reading of a story. In using the map, teacher questioning focuses on what the reader is understanding about the text and the sources of information he is using to form his model of meaning. She suggests that he can revise or expand his prediction according to what he has read and what he already knows about what he has read. As the process proceeds, the student becomes actively involved in building his model of meaning and comparing it with the author's intended meaning.

In this technique, the information is displayed in a visuo–spatial orientation and offers the reader more flexibility of options, revisions, and additions during the reading of a story. . . . This engages his divergent, yet simultaneous processing of verbal information and displays his information in a spatial organization which is similar to his thinking style. (p. 138)

Strategy 2—Story dramatizing, emphasizing predicting. For this activity, the teacher needs to choose a good picture storybook. As a prereading activity, the teacher discusses the story with the class, drawing in the students' background knowledge as with any reading lesson. Then the teacher

Name *William* _____ Sex _____

School _____ Grade _____

Examiner _____ Handedness _____

WISC-III™
Wechsler Intelligence Scale for Children – Third Edition

Subtests	Raw Scores	Scaled Scores			
Picture Completion	13		6		6
Information	13	9		9	
Coding	53		15		15
Similarities	15	11		11	
Picture Arrangement	32		12	12	
Arithmetic	14	7			7
Block Design	45		14	14	
Vocabulary	28	11		11	
Object Assembly	16		7	7	
Comprehension	21	12		12	
(Symbol Search)	26		(14)		14
(Digit Span)	12	(9)		9	
(Mazes)	27		(19)		
Sum of Scaled Scores		50 54	43	39	16 29
		Verbal Perfor.	VC	PO	FD PS
		Full Scale Score 104		OPTIONAL	

	Year	Month	Day
Date Tested			
Date of Birth			
Age	9	11	24

	Score	IQ/Index	%ile	95 % Confidence Interval
Verbal	50	100	50	94 – 106
Performance	54	106	66	97 – 113
Full Scale	104	103	58	97 – 109
VC	43	104	61	97 – 111
PO	39	99	47	91 – 107
FD	16	90	25	82 – 101
PS	29	124	95	111 – 130

IQ Scores

VIQ	PIQ	FSIQ
100	106	103

Index Scores (Optional)

VCI	POI	FDI	PSI
104	99	90	124

Subtest Scores

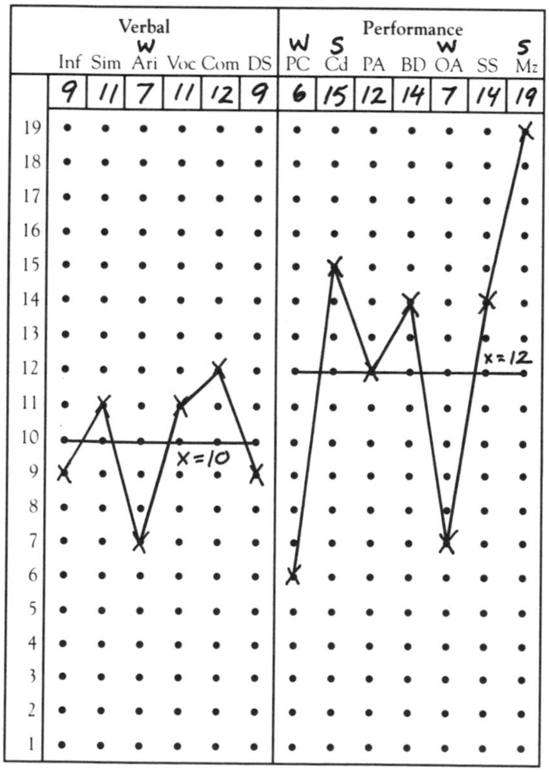

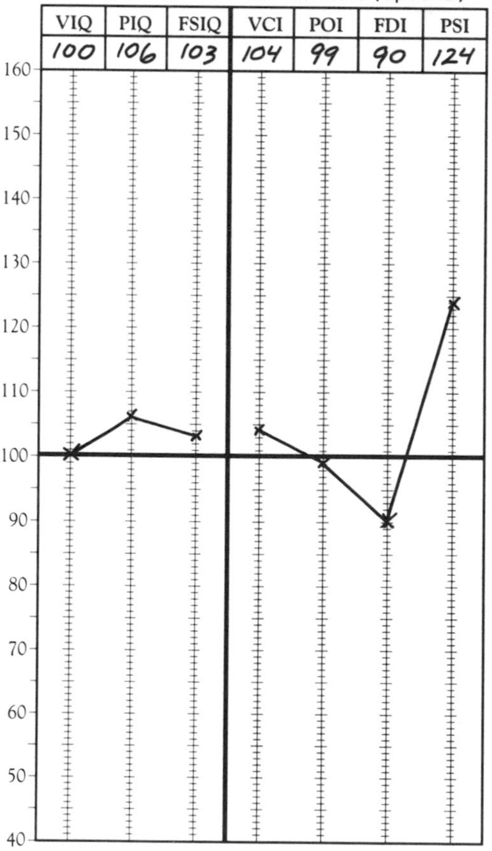

	Verbal						Performance						
	Inf	Sim	W Ari	Voc	Com	DS	W PC	S Cd	PA	BD	W OA	SS	S Mz
	9	11	7	11	12	9	6	15	12	14	7	14	19

Ψ® THE PSYCHOLOGICAL CORPORATION®
HARCOURT BRACE JOVANOVICH, INC.

09-980004

Figure 6.5. William's profile.

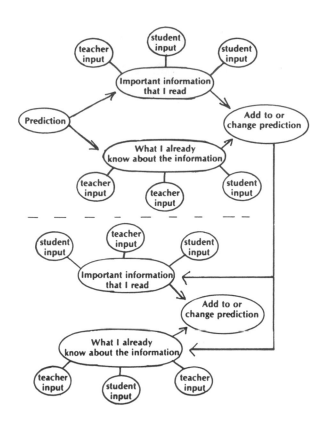

Figure 6.6. Prediction mapping. From ''Right-Brained Strategies for Teaching Comprehension'' by B. Walker, 1985, *Academic Therapy, 21,* p. 137. Copyright 1985 by Academic Therapy Publications. Reprinted with permission.

begins reading the story until students have enough information about the characters and story line to act out (dramatize) a predicted ending:

> The drama begins at the point of interruption, and the students actually dramatize their predictions in a roleplaying experience as various students present story characters. In the process of dramatization, predictions are revised through the roleplaying of the story drama. After the drama, the students write an ending for the story. Finally, the story is read, predictions are confirmed and revised, and the drama analyzed for personal interpretations of the story line as an influential dimension when building a model of meaning. (Walker, 1985, p. 138)

Strategy 3—Guided imagery. This technique requires the teacher to choose a story, and take the students through a guided "mental jour-

ney" designed to evoke their own internal images about the story. Specifically, Walker (1985) wrote,

> The story is read in a calm, serene voice using many pauses so the imagery of the journey can flow through the conscious mind of the student. Usually, the students' eyes are closed and the lights are dimmed. The guided journey is left open-ended so that the students can complete the experience in their imaginations. After the journey is complete, students write how they resolved the problem. . . . As a result of writing how they solved the problem in their imaginations, the students read the story with increased involvement in order to compare the author's version with their own. (p. 139)

Perhaps this strategy is the most right brained of all, although the distinction, as I have noted, is somewhat artificial. Most of these activities involve both hemispheres.

Based on William's WISC-III profile presented in Figure 6.5, the three strategies just listed seem very appropriate, as they would use his strength in the integrated brain functioning areas. An interesting question is *why* the student is so much weaker on Picture Completion and Object Assembly. Kaufman (1979) wrote,

> The right hemisphere seems to be more mature than the left at birth, both physiologically and functionally, and is also a more pervasive force in the very early stages of life. An infant perceives and learns nonverbally, sensorily, and spatially to a large extent during the first year of life, styles of learning that are congruent with the processing mode of the right cerebral hemisphere. Although less mature than the right brain, the left brain is more adaptable at birth and has the capacity of subsuming complex and analytic functions. The greater adaptability of the left hemisphere may conceivably render it unusually vulnerable to the impact of cultural deprivation. Hence disadvantaged children may have a right-brain leaning, at last in part, because of the resilience of the right hemisphere in the face of deprived environmental conditions. (p. 160)

William, however, exhibits the opposite pattern—an integrated, rather than a right-hemisphere, leaning. Did this student not rely on the right hemisphere during infancy? That explanation seems unlikely. Is there a subtle, neurological right-hemisphere deficit? Without neurological testing, it is not possible to even begin to answer this question, and further testing was not done in William's case.

The importance of the right hemisphere to reading, however, is said to be as follows: "The right hemisphere may be indispensable to reading when children are learning to recognize letters and words as gestalts. The left hemisphere meanwhile may convert these symbols into phonological units and into meaning" (Kaufman, 1979, p. 162). This explanation seems to apply to William. He had to have a special program within his first-grade classroom that emphasized sight word acquisition, on which he was very weak from the start. Once William learned the word, his teacher noted, he seemed to remember it. He continued to struggle with reading, however. The WISC-III profile in Figure 6.5 was administered when William was in fourth grade. He was in the school's resource room program at the time. His resource teacher said that William seems to have difficulty when meeting new words, such as polysyllabic ones. His predicting in reading is sometimes meaningless; also, despite his good verbal ability, he has trouble with some word meanings, such as the meaning of the word *moccasin*. He rarely recognized this word in context; even when he did, he did not know what it meant.

William's resource teacher continues to emphasize meaning and predicting in reading, and finds visualization a good strategy with him. She continues to emphasize the meaning base of words with him. William is making gains in reading, but also continues to require extra assistance, and is still well behind in his reading. Does his "right-brain weakness" make the transfer of symbols into meaning more difficult for him? How would a combined teaching of phonemic processing together with visualization affect his learning rate?

Finally, it is important to state again that the WISC-III profile cannot be used to diagnose brain damage in either hemisphere. If the examiner feels that a pattern and/or the student's behavior is peculiar, and other evidence (e.g., a history of trauma) indicates the possibility, then a neuro-psychological referral should be made.

Letteri's Approach

Charles Letteri (1980) developed a comprehensive and intriguing approach to the field of learning styles. Even though his approach does not use the WISC-III per se, I provide an overview for the reader.

Thus far, I have discussed each cognitive style variable suggested by WISC-III profiles and behavioral observations as single variables. Students can be grouped as simultaneous/successive, impulsive/reflective, and so on. What happens, however, when some of these constructs are combined? In other words, instead of being treated as unidimensional variables, they are treated as a multidimensional composite. That is Letteri's approach. Using it, he showed that characteristic profiles can be used to classify students in terms of academic achievement with a high degree of accuracy. He called the profiles Type 1, Type 2, and Type 3. Letteri (1987) described them as follows:

> The Type 1 cognitive profile, significantly associated with high achievement levels in academic performance as measured by standardized tests, indicates a subject articulated in a majority of the following dimensions: analytical, focuser, narrow, complex, reflective, sharpener, tolerant. [Note: I have not discussed most of these cognitive styles in this book.] The Type 3 cognitive profile, significantly associated with low achievement levels in academic performance as measured by standardized tests, indicates a subject articulated in a majority of the following dimensions: global, nonfocuser, broad, simple, impulsive, leveler, intolerant. The Type 2 cognitive profile, significantly associated with average academic achievement performance, is either a nonarticulated profile, that is not articulated at either extreme of the seven cognitive dimensions, or is a mixed profile indicating an inconsistent pattern or articulation with no majority matching a Type 1 or Type 3 profile. (p. 196)

The remedial implications of this approach are of interest to school psychologists. Letteri (1980) wrote,

> In contrast to current research that attempts to identify learning deficits on the basis of a unidimensional construct, the cognitive profile can accurately identify those specific dimensions of subjects' thinking and learning patterns that contribute significantly to their levels of academic performance. As a result, teachers or other professionals have an accurate statement concerning where the specific deficit

is located and can direct their efforts in a more focused and efficient manner to help ameliorate learning deficits. As a result of continuing research, specific strategies and materials have been developed that are capable of augmenting an individual's cognitive profile, that is, moving an individual's articulation from a Type 2 or Type 3 profile to a Type 1 profile. In doing so, an individual's thinking and learning pattern becomes compatible with academic tasks. Results, thus far, indicate that for subjects included in the experimental augmentation group ($N=10$), as opposed to the control group ($N=20$), augmented profiles did move from a Type 3 profile to a Type 1 profile with a corresponding significant ($p=.01$) change in achievement scores. (p. 198)

I, for one, am looking forward to hearing more from Letteri and his Centre for Cognitive Studies. The implications for education are exciting. He wrote,

The curriculum for school-age children should . . . incorporate this information, so that while we build on children's strengths, we can accurately and specifically designate their weaknesses and employ efficient strategies to change these weaknesses to additional strengths. In doing so, every child can hope to have equal intellectual access to learning materials and environments and not just the equal opportunity to sit in their presence. (p. 198)

Subtest-Specific Strengths and Weaknesses

Kaufman suggested that any subtest that deviates 3 points or more from its respective Verbal or Performance average be considered a significant strength or weakness, depending on the direction. He also recommended that, when subtests are grouped into a cluster, all the subtests that fall into that grouping be at or above the average for that scale. For example, if Picture Completion, Block Design, and Object Assembly suggest a field-dependent interpretation, then each scaled score in that cluster should be below the Performance average or close to it for that student. If the cluster suggests field independence, then the opposite holds. Each of the subtests should be at or above the Performance average for that student. If they are not, then some of the hypotheses suggested by

Sattler (1982) in the list below may be worth checking out.

At Level III, the examiner may want to compare certain WISC-III subtests with each other. Sattler provided examples, which follow. They are meant neither to be exhaustive, nor to do anything more than *suggest* a hypothesis concerning a student. (No studies of which I am aware confirm or deny these hypotheses.) Further observations or testing or sources of information may be necessary to verify or confirm any of them. Furthermore, the educational implications need to be drawn out by the artistry of the examiner. To aid in more hypothesis generation (but with the foregoing cautions in mind), Sattler (1982) suggested the following:

1. Information and Comprehension. This is a comparison of the amount of information retained (Information) and the ability to use information (Comprehension). Information requires factual knowledge, while Comprehension requires both factual knowledge and judgment.
   - I>C: High Information and low Comprehension may suggest that children have general knowledge but are not able to synthesize and use information to solve problems involving the social world.
   - I<C: Low Information and High Comprehension may suggest that children have been limited in their exposure to factual material, but use their limited knowledge to make appropriate judgments.

2. Comprehension and Arithmetic. Both the Comprehension and Arithmetic subtests require reasoning ability or, more specifically, the ability to analyze a given set of material and then to recognize the elements that are needed for the solution of the specified problem.
   - C>A: High Comprehension and Low Arithmetic may suggest that reasoning ability is adequate in social situations but not in situations involving numbers.

3. Arithmetic and Digit Span. Both the Arithmetic and Digit Span subtests require facility with numbers and ability in immediate recall. Comparing the two subtests may provide an index of the relative balance between attention (Digit Span) and concentration (Arithmetic).

- DS>A: High Digit Span and low Arithmetic may suggest that attention is better developed than concentration.

4. Similarities and Comprehension.
   - S>C: High Similarities and low Comprehension may suggest that children have the ability to do abstract thinking but cannot apply their conceptualizing ability to solve problems in the social world.

5. Vocabulary and Similarities. Both Vocabulary and Similarities measure level of abstract thinking and ability to form concepts, but Similarities is a better measure of these abilities.
   - S>V: High Similarities and low Vocabulary may suggest that children have the mental ability to do abstract thinking but have had restricted opportunities to learn new words.

6. Vocabulary, Information, and Comprehension.
   - V,I>C: High Vocabulary and Information coupled with low Comprehension may suggest that the individuals are not able to use fully their verbal facility and general knowledge in life situations; they therefore may have impaired judgment.

7. Digit Span—Forward versus Backward.
   - DS(F)>DS(B): High Digits Forward and low Digits Backward may indicate that the child did not put forth the extra effort needed to master the more difficult task of recalling digits backward in sequence.
   - DS(B)>DS(F): High Digits Backward and low Digits Forward may occur when children see Digits Backward as a challenge rather than as a task which consists of a mere repetition of numbers.

8. Similarities and Digit Span.
   - S>DS: High Similarities and low Digit Span may reflect good conceptualizing ability coupled with poor rote auditory memory for digits. Children with this pattern may do poorly in acquiring reading decoding skills that are highly dependent on memorization of sound–symbol relationships. However, their listening comprehension may be strong.

9. Comprehension and Picture Arrangement. Both the Comprehension and Picture Arrangement subtests contain stimuli that are concerned with social interaction. Scores on the two subtests permit comparison of knowledge of social conventions (Comprehension) with the capacity to anticipate and plan in a social context (Picture Arrangement).
   - PA>C: High Picture Arrangement coupled with low Comprehension may indicate that the individuals are sensitive to interpersonal nuances, but disregard social conventions.
   - C>PA: An adequate Comprehension score coupled with a poor Picture Arrangement score suggests that the children can understand social situations in the abstract, but once they are involved in them they may be unable to decide what they may mean or how to act.

10. Picture Completion and Picture Arrangement. This comparison provides an estimate of attention to detail versus organization of detail. Both tasks involve perception of details, with Picture Arrangement requiring logical ordering of details or sequencing.
    - PC>PA: High Picture Completion and low Picture Arrangement may suggest that perception of details in nonsequencing tasks is better developed than that in tasks requiring sequencing and organization.

11. Picture Completion and Block Design. This comparison involves an estimate of visual perception versus visual–motor–spatial coordination.
    - PC>BD: High Picture Completion and low Block Design may suggest that children have adequate nonspatial visual perceptual ability but have difficulty in spatial visualization.

12. Object Assembly and Picture Arrangement. This comparison provides an estimate of inductive reasoning versus sequencing. Both tasks require synthesis into wholes without a model to follow, with Picture Arrangement involving sequencing in addition.
    - OA>PA: High Object Assembly and low Picture Arrangement may suggest that visual inductive reasoning skills are better developed than visual sequencing skills.

13. Object Assembly and Block Design. This comparison provides an estimate of inductive reasoning (Object Assembly—working from parts to a whole) versus deductive reasoning (Block Design—working from a whole to parts). Both tasks involve perceptual organization and spatial visualization ability.
    - OA>BD: If Object Assembly is higher than Block Design, it may suggest that non-

verbal inductive reasoning skills are better developed than nonverbal deductive reasoning skills.

14. Block Design, Object Assembly, and Coding [I believe we can safely add Symbol Search to this cluster]. The Block Design, Object Assembly, and Coding subtests require visual–motor coordination; that is, they involve motor activity guided by visual organization. A visual direction is involved in the execution of the tasks. The role of visual organization differs in the three subtests. In the Block Design subtest, visual organization is involved in a process consisting of analysis (breaking down the pattern) and synthesis (building the pattern up again out of the blocks). In the Object Assembly subtest, the motor action consists of arranging parts into a meaningful pattern. In the Coding subtest, visual organization is of the same kind that is found in such activities as writing or drawing. Thus, the name "visual organization" does not refer to the same function in every case.

• BD > Co [or Symbol Search]: High Block Design and low Coding may suggest that visual organization skills involving analysis and synthesis are better than those involving visual–motor coordination. (pp. 201–203)

Once the clustering of subtests into the various learning style categories has been sifted through, and the various groupings such as those in the foregoing list have been analyzed, some profiles may have some subtests that are significantly elevated or depressed, and that do not seem to fit into any particular larger grouping. At this point, it may be necessary to give a subtest-specific interpretation. For example, if Similarities and Arithmetic are the only two subtests significantly elevated on a student's Verbal Scale, then these could reflect specific strengths in abstract categorical reasoning and mental computational skills, respectively.

LEVEL IV—PATTERNS WITHIN A SUBTEST

There is not a great deal to say about Level IV interpretation. The examiner should be alert to the student who is internally inconsistent on a subtest. For example, if a student gets the first two items wrong on the Picture Arrangement subtest, then the next two correct, and the next three wrong, the student may have attentional problems or perhaps anxiety about the item content of certain social situations. The same holds true for the other subtests. On Information, as another example, if the student shows an erratic pattern of correct and incorrect responses, and obtains the same scaled score or raw score as another student the same age who simply reaches the ceiling of five incorrect in a row with no previous errors, the former student may have higher "potential." Again, perhaps the student is anxious or lacks knowledge of certain items tapped by the questions. The examiner can look at the item content to see specifically if the student consistently gets certain *kinds* of problems incorrect before categorically stating that he or she has a weakness in background knowledge.

This level of interpretation of the WISC-III is very close to, and perhaps indistinguishable from, Level V interpretation, which I discuss in the next chapter.

CHAPTER 7

WISC-III Interpretation: Level V

Most school psychologists simply do not have time for an item-by-item analysis of WISC-III responses. They should, however, have some background on this kind of analysis and be aware of additional hypotheses such an examination reveals.

An excellent reference for this level of interpretation from which I quote extensively is Shawn Cooper's (1982) book, *The Clinical Use and Interpretation of the Wechsler Intelligence Scale for Children–Revised.* (Almost all of what Cooper wrote applies to the WISC-III.) Cooper performed an exhaustive, question-by-question analysis of every WISC-R item. I cannot go into, nor is there any need for, the same detail as Cooper provided. My intent is to highlight, subtest by subtest, some important Level V considerations for each.

Level V analysis truly changes the WISC-III administration and interpretation from a static to a dynamic nature. This level also illustrates how much WISC-III interpretation is truly the "art of synthesis," based on the examiner's knowledge and experience.

Even though the actual administration of the WISC-III alternates Verbal with Performance subtests, I find it more useful in this chapter to discuss all the Verbal subtests, and then all the Performance ones.

VERBAL SUBTESTS

Information

In Chapter 4, I introduced Cooper's general classification of the WISC-R Information questions into various categories, which I adapted to the WISC-III. This classification is useful in determining the background items with which a student has difficulties. For example, many students I have assessed seem to have difficulty with the time, number, and directionality items (depending on their ages). Knowledge of this difficulty could provide the impetus to offer or suggest to the teacher that such concepts be reinforced for specific students. The same recommendation can be given to parents, some of whom do not directly teach their children the way to use the calendar; the division of the year into months, days, and weeks; and more subtle concepts such as leap year. Because the Information subtest contains items that are directly teachable, this is a reasonable line of approach. The purpose, however, is not to teach to the WISC-III subtest, but to help fill important voids that may exist for a particular student in critical areas of background knowledge.

Additionally, the examiner can observe the student's way of handling the questions. For example, the student who says the items are very easy, according to Cooper, may be bolstering "his own sense of adequacy in anticipation of questions he may be unable to answer" (p. 34). Alternatively, if the student claims not to know the answer to a question, is this a simple statement of fact, or did the student make this statement a little too quickly, indicating a careless or incomplete memory search, or impulsivity? To what extent does this behavior affect the WISC-III score? If many of the student's responses are impulsive, the WISC-III score definitely underestimates the student's ability.

Another frequent response is "We haven't taken that yet" or "My teacher hasn't taught that yet," or some similar statement. This response may indicate the student's avoidance or denial of personal responsibility in learning. Is this a characteristic of the student? Useful supplementary tests to investigate this hypothesis include the *Intellectual Achievement Responsibility Questionnaire* (Crandall, Katkovsky, & Crandall, 1965), or perhaps a locus-of-control measure (Bialer, 1961). Perhaps the student merely shrugs rather than directly saying, "I don't know." Again, the student may be avoiding the admission of a perceived personal inadequacy.

Perhaps the student does say, "I don't know," but feels badly about it. This reaction is generally communicated nonverbally and should be noted on the protocol.

Perhaps the student guesses. Is this good risk-taking on the student's part? If the guesses are unusual or bizarre, what is going on? Is the student trying to impress you? Is the student simply too uncomfortable to admit not knowing certain things?

What is the student's reaction to several failures in a row? To success? To praise? Does the student quickly retreat and show discouragement after several failures? Is there an obvious positive reaction to praise and a negative one to failure? Does this mean the student is unnecessarily externally motivated? If so, Dinkmeyer, McKay, and Dinkmeyer's (1980) distinction between *praise* and *encouragement* may be important for the teacher. A praise statement, such as "That's great" or "You're a good student," may be used excessively by a parent or teacher. The student then becomes "hooked on praise," so to speak, and begins to feel that his or her worthiness *depends on meeting someone else's standards.* Encouragement, on the other hand, is an acknowledgment of effort. It focuses on the stu-

dent's strengths and progress, and it helps the student evaluate his or her own efforts. "I like the way you handled that," "I'm glad you're happy with your work," and "Your drawing makes me feel happy; how do you feel about it?" are phrases that show acceptance and are apt to internally motivate the student. I do not mean that praise should never be used. It is important, in my experience, that students know when standards *are* being met. Some students, however, are excessively competitive; encouraging statements may help temper some of their excess zeal. Such statements are also very useful with students who do not experience much academic success. For these students, encouraging effort and helping them recognize the gains they are making, are very important.

Cooper also suggested that, for each WISC-R subtest, certain responses may indicate psychopathology, anxiety, or defensiveness. Although specific responses on the WISC-R may indicate disturbances in cognitive processing or affect, once again, by themselves, they cannot be used to diagnose any particular condition. Examiners need to be very cautious in giving a teacher any feedback about a student's possible "abnormal" responses. If the examiner suspects psychopathology, then an appropriate clinical referral needs to be made.

With that important caveat, Cooper suggested that the content of some students' responses may indicate very distorted ideas, concepts, or beliefs. Examiners need to be very cautious, however, with their own values and how those values may influence interpretations.

Very confused responses that seemingly have nothing to do with the questions also may indicate disordered thought. Again, cautious probing is necessary to determine what, exactly, the student meant. Many responses are seemingly bizarre on the surface, but may make perfect sense after the student explains the responses.

Additional examiner strategies. Cooper made one particularly good suggestion regarding the Information subtest, which is to time the response time—the interval between the question asked and the beginning of the student's answer. This interval can be very important, because some students simply need more processing time to come up with an appropriate answer. The teacher can encourage higher-level cognitive thinking by increasing the "wait-time" between questions. This concept has been well researched and has some important educational implications. For example, in a typical reading lesson, the following occurs:

1. In an average 25-minute reading lesson, a teacher will ask 36 questions, or about one question every 43 seconds.

2. Some 63% to 75% of the questions are text-based, requiring mainly literal recall. The remainder are scriptal based, and require higher level processing on the part of the students. Higher level processing requires more time, however.

3. Once a teacher asks a question, *less than 1 second* of "think-time" is given before the teacher asks another question or another student. This is clearly inadequate. Research shows that waiting 4 to 5 seconds is necessary, and clearly improves student responding.

4. Worse, "high-ability reading groups" receive a better balance of text versus scriptal questions (about 50%/50%), but the average and low groups receive significantly fewer scriptal questions. (based on Gambrell, 1983)

There are also large individual differences in think-time for students. I recall examining many students whose response times were exceedingly slow. This information, together with the research data on wait-time, is clearly important in making recommendations to a teacher about a specific student.

The strategy of timing the student can be used for any of the WISC-III subtests. If there is a discrepancy between think-time for some subtests and that for others, what implications are there for the student in a specific classroom setting?

Similarities

Because of a 2, 1, or zero scoring system on the Similarities subtest, examiners may miss some of the verbal classification possibilities. Students do grow in classification skills with age, and their concepts can be stretched by teaching activities.

Farnham-Diggory (1978) provided a good description of various types of verbal groupings:

1. *Superordinate concept formation.* In these types of responses, the student states a superordinate concept for the two items (e.g., "Orange and peach are the same because they are both fruits"). The superordination may also be itemized by the student (e.g., "A banana you eat, and a peach you eat, too"). This type of superordination is less generalized than the first. (It is a more concrete response and, of course, receives a lower score on the WISC-III.)

2. *Complex formations.* In these types of responses, the student selects one attribute and tries to group the other items using the same attribute. There are five different kinds of complex formations:

   a. *Association complex*—"A bell makes a sound and a drum does, too."

   b. *Key ring complex*—"A bell is silver and sometimes a drum is, too."

   c. *Edge matching complex*—This consists of forming associations between pairs of words that then pile up in linked pairs. These formations are easier to observe when three or more items are to be classified. Because only two stimulus items are on each question of the Similarities subtest, this formation cannot be observed. Suppose, however, that the student had to tell why an apple, peach, and potato are the same. An edge matching response might be, "Apple and peach look alike; potato and peach are round."

   d. *Collection complex*—The student finds an attribute that relates the pair, but does not quite make the link (e.g., "A grape is purple and a pineapple is yellow").

   e. *Multiple grouping complex*—Again, several stimulus words are necessary to observe this type of grouping. The student forms several subgroups, but does not build the bridge among them. Suppose the list consists of banana, peach, meat, and milk. An example of a multiple grouping complex would be, "A banana, peach, and meat, you eat; and milk, you drink."

3. *Thematic groupings.* This kind of grouping is the lowest form of classification. In fact, it is not classification at all. In this case, the student relates two or more items in some idiosyncratic way, usually in the form of a story (e.g., "A boat and a car are the same because you can pull the boat with your car").

Research clearly shows that, as students grow older, their groupings definitely move from complex formations to superordinate ones. However, teaching activities designed to enhance and encourage classification and sorting can be done by the teacher. One excellent strategy is the Word Bank and Word Sort described in Appendix 5A. For example, a teacher can have the students use their banks to find all the color words, feeling words, food words, listening words, and so forth. Such sorts are called *closed sorts.* In an *open sort,* the student is asked to devise his or her own classification scheme (a more difficult task). Students can share their groupings, and the types of formations just listed can be more closely observed by the teacher.

In terms of affective states and the Similarities subtest, the examiner needs to watch for responses such as "they burn you" for Item 2 and "they're enemies" for Item 7. Cooper suggested that the student's handling of the task in such cases is being dominated by aggressive or anxious feelings; however, I think that this hypothesis should be cross-checked by the examiner with other WISC-III items (Item 8 on the Comprehension subtest is particularly good), as well as with spontaneous comments made by the student throughout the testing and observations from significant others in the student's life.

Cooper also suggested that very high scores on Similarities, in contrast to low scores on the other Verbal subtests,

would suggest that the individual is very much able to deal with objects or events as verbal ideas but that the individual has lacked the broader development of his/her intellectual functioning across the wide range of cognitive tasks sampled by the entire Wechsler Intelligence Scale. (p. 72)

Cooper called this an indicator of psychopathology; however, I would be extremely cautious about such a hypothesis. I have seen a number of students with surprisingly elevated Similarities subtests, in contrast to the other Verbal subtests. I prefer the quoted interpretation without the psychopathological implication.

Arithmetic

I have already discussed a number of facets of the Arithmetic subtest, particularly in regard to Level II analysis of Arithmetic as part of the Freedom from Distractibility factor. Because most of the problems on this subtest involve mental manipulation of numbers, the subtest by itself may not correlate very well with actual classroom-based arithmetic operations. However, informally testing the limits would prove useful in some cases. For this subtest, I would suggest the following procedure:

1. If the student fails an item, repeat it. If the student says he or she doesn't know the answer, ask the student to repeat the question (this is to test whether the difficulty is in short-term memory).

2. If the student does not know the answer, give the components and see if the student can perform the calculation(s). Classify the errors, using Sternberg's (1984) analysis, into

    a. Lack of metacomponent awareness (i.e., the student has no idea what operations are to be employed to solve the problem)

    b. Lack of performance awareness (i.e., the student knows what operations are to be used, but makes a mental calculation error, such as adding 10 to 18, and getting 29)

    c. Lack of learning components (i.e., the student has not learned the basics of, say, addition, to begin with)

Sometimes these error classifications become blurred, but the examiner should at least attempt a distinction, because the implications for teaching are different depending on the kind of error the student generally makes.

The following is a rough classification of each item on the Arithmetic subtest, in terms of the operations involved (adapted from Cooper, 1982, pp. 109–114):

1. Basic serial counting with a visual stimulus.
2. Basic serial counting with a visual stimulus.
3. Segmenting a set—visual stimulus present.
4. Same as Item 3, but more complex because a larger set is involved.
5. Subtraction with a visual stimulus present.
6. Transition item—could easily be on the Information subtest. No real math operation involved.
7. Subtraction. (The examiner should watch, on this item and others, to see if the student is using fingers as an aid. Often, students hide their hands under the table!)
8. Addition.
9. Addition with sum < 10.
10. Subtraction.
11. Addition (grouping two equal sets).
12. Subtraction.
13. Addition with sum > 10.
14. Subtraction—two-digit number, less a one-digit number.
15. Multiplication.
16. Subtraction of two-digit numbers.
17. Division.
18. Addition (or multiplication) followed by subtraction.
19. Multiplication.
20. Division.
21. Division with verbal complexity.
22. Fractions (probability).
23. Manipulating fractions.
24. Complex division and multiplication.

Only by working with the regular or special education teacher, however, can the school psychologist translate the particular combination of strengths and weaknesses on each item of the subtest into remedial strategies. Levy (1981) wrote,

> It is clear that the psychologist and classroom educator must attend to the presentation and response requirements of the task. Through holding the mathematical content constant and varying the presentation and response behavioral requirements of the subtest, instructional pathways are identified. The identification of the specific presentation and response combinations, which are associated with strengths and weaknesses in WISC-R Arithmetic subtest performance, possesses obvious instructional implications for both the regular and special education teacher. (p. 86).

Thus, the teacher and school psychologist need to compare and contrast the student's performance on the Arithmetic subtest, on which most items are presented orally, to his or her performance on paper-and-pencil math, for which most items remain visually present to the student.

As with other Verbal subtests, the student's response time for each item can be noted. Individual differences will appear, and inordinately lengthy response times can be noted. It is valuable to a teacher, for example, to know that a student can properly answer the question, but that he or she requires extra processing time.

Testing the limits is important for some students on the WISC-III and on academic tests. An excellent set of probe questions can be found in the manual for the *Diagnostic Achievement Battery–2* (Newcomer, 1990).

Vocabulary

Cooper wrote,

> Glasser and Zimmerman note that Vocabulary is probably the best single measure of general intellectual level, and that it provides an indication of the child's learning ability, fund of information, richness of ideas, kind and quality of language, degree

of abstract thinking, and character of thought processes. It also reflects a child's level of education and environment. The Vocabulary subtest is of value because of the qualitative aspects that may be seen in different individuals' unique definitions of the same item, which may vary in abstractness, detail, or degree of sophistication. Glasser and Zimmerman note that from the clinical point of view, the most important feature of verbal definitions is the insight they can provide into the nature of a child's thought processes, particularly among those children who display poor orientation to reality. (p. 134).

In terms of psychopathology, anxiety, or defensiveness, according to Cooper, the examiner should look to the content of the responses, particularly the kinds of associations the word has for the student. This, he wrote,

can provide information regarding the extent to which the definitions the child offers are conventional, consensually valid, or more individualistic and idiosyncratic; in this sense, the examiner can observe the extent to which the child's definitions are more typical or less typical, more normal or more deviant. (p. 141).

Again, however, diagnosing any form of psychopathology from such responses is not valid. The answers are merely suggestive. In my experience, students commonly give responses suggesting aggressive or hostile feelings. When these responses occur and fit with descriptions from other sources about the student, they may take on greater significance.

The examiner should also watch for any self-derogatory statements the student makes in replying to Verbal subtests, or spontaneously. They should be followed up by the examiner. Self-concept inventories can be useful for providing supplementary information and triggering a good clinical interview with the student. I have found the *Culture-Free Self-Esteem Inventories–2* (Battle, 1992) to be very useful in this respect. These inventories are not time-consuming, and break the global construct of self-esteem into general, academic, parental, and social areas. Percentile scores can be calculated for each area. Discrepancies from one area to another are clearly visible and valuable in terms of providing a direction for a recommended course of treat-

ment. For example, a student who scores very poorly on academically related self-esteem, but high in all other areas, will likely require a different type of support or intervention than a student who scores low in all areas. This inventory also has a built-in social desirability scale. It can be administered to elementary students, through high school and adult levels.

Speech articulation and syntax are other areas the examiner can observe as the student responds to each item. Is the student competent in language use? Is articulation normal? If not, does it merit the attention of a speech therapist? Are the student's responses direct or roundabout? Are many associations involved that are vague? If the student does not have rapid naming ability, this may interfere to some extent with reading and writing.

Examiners also need to note the quality of responses. This is very important in relationship to the school environment. Cooper noted,

Even if the individual achieves, for example, a low average Vocabulary subtest score, but fails a number of definitions or obtains partial credit on a number of words, the examiner would conclude that the individual will have difficulty with a variety of language-based aspects of school learning, including reading, expressive writing, understanding complicated written or spoken instructions, and perhaps even with verbal expression. On the other hand, to the extent that the individual's Vocabulary score is average or above, one would conclude that the individual has a greater comfort in using language for understanding and/or communicating and that the individual is much more likely to be successful in various verbally weighted school subjects, such as reading, expressive writing, or various kinds of classroom discussion. (p. 144)

Comprehension

I find the Comprehension subtest particularly valuable in providing insight into a student's knowledge of some social standards. The early items on the subtest directly test knowledge or awareness of appropriate behavior in social situations.

Additionally, because rather lengthy verbal responses are required, an excellent sample of the student's facility with language is obtained. The student who responds correctly but who requires frequent probing, as the subtest allows, may be more of a nonverbal communicator. This information is very valuable to a teacher who wants to know whether a student can "handle" the language arts curriculum. This type of student can handle the curriculum on a cognitive level much better if additional nonverbal tasks, such as drama, role playing, puppetry, and drawing, are incorporated into the activity. Risk-taking in purely verbal situations, in other words, needs to be encouraged.

I also have found that many aggressive youngsters who are referred because they simply do not seem to know social rules display a good knowledge of what they should do. Their difficulty lies not in lack of awareness of standards, but in complying with them. A useful, inexpensive resource for this problem is the *Getting Along with Others Program* (Jackson, Jackson, & Monroe, 1983). This program or relevant portions of it can easily be incorporated into resource and remedial behavioral programs as needed. It can also be used in certain parts of the regular classroom program (e.g., in the health curriculum), or for an individual or small group of students. Over 17 sessions, students are taught the basics in such skills as following directions, interrupting a conversation, joining a conversation, handling name calling and teasing, and saying "no" to stay out of trouble. Another valuable portion of the program is the five teaching strategies suggested, which can be used by any teacher in a variety of classroom situations. Opportunities for transfer of the skills into home and school environments are provided.

If students score very low on the Comprehension subtest, they may have poorly developed social awareness and/or understanding. These youngsters also can profit from the kinds of skills taught in *Getting Along with Others Program*.

I frequently find myself watching for a student's locus of orientation. For example, the student who consistently answers with such replies as, "Tell my Mom," has not internalized any self-responsibility. This student may be very passive and lack a good sense of an internal locus of control, which is important for both social and academic successes. Responses suggesting an external orientation are more common among younger students (which is normal, in that the growth from externality to internality is age related), so age should be taken into account before seriously entertaining this hypothe-

sis. Locus of control can also be cross-checked using the *Intellectual Achievement Responsibility Questionnaire* (Crandall et al., 1965) or a similar scale.

In general, then, the responses to the Comprehension subtest allow the examiner

> to observe the individual's knowledge of social rules, the clarity or confusion that characterizes his/her expression of this knowledge, the certainty or uncertainty the individual displays in selecting among possible responses, and the differential response the individual may reveal in dealing with neutral or more emotionally arousing questions on this subtest. (Cooper, 1982, p. 180)

Digit Span

Because I have discussed the educationally relevant aspects of Digit Span in other chapters, there is nothing of significance to add here.

PERFORMANCE SUBTESTS

Picture Completion

One strategy I always use on Picture Completion is to time how long the student takes to respond to each item. This is relatively easy, because each item has a time limit of 20 seconds. From the length of time it takes the student to respond and the accuracy of the response, I make an initial judgment regarding the student's cognitive tempo (see Chapter 6). This becomes a working hypothesis that I modify in light of further observed behavior.

The examiner should watch for whether the student says, "I don't know," to an item, or "There's nothing missing." If the response is the former, how quickly does the student say that? If said too quickly, the response may suggest a feeling of inadequacy, together with low task persistence. This quick response is to be distinguished from a realistic "I don't know," which is said after careful scanning, and simply reflects an honest self-appraisal in light of a difficult item. Usually, the tone and manner in which the student says," I don't know," conveys to the examiner which is the more likely hypothesis. Clinical impressions, together with supplementary testing, can suggest very important avenues of remediation. Simple responses such as "I don't know" can convey a wealth of meaning.

Figure 7.1 is a graphic representation of how high and low academic achievers differ in the ways they judge the outcomes of their efforts on a task. If a student is given an arithmetic task, for example, and the student obtains the correct answer, the high achiever will typically attribute success to himself or herself, whereas the low achiever will attribute it to something external, such as luck or the task's being an easy one. Contrariwise, if the high achiever does poorly on a task, then the high achiever attributes it to task difficulty, luck, or poor effort. Hence, he or she is more likely to try harder the next time. The low achiever, by contrast, sees failure more as the lack of ability, leading to self-punishment and negative expectations, and perhaps is more likely

to avoid the task in the future. Involving the student in goal setting and goal assessment, together with changing the learned helplessness response (see Appendix 3D), can be very helpful.

The student who says, "Nothing is missing," is redefining the task slightly and projecting responsibility outside himself or herself. The student who says, "I can't find anything missing," has accepted responsibility.

Cooper made a good point regarding the item content of Picture Completion. Items 4, 6, 7, 12, 22, and 27 all have human contents and "hence may set off specific anxiety in the individual regarding interpersonal relationships or regarding the individual's noticing visual information or cues regarding people" (p. 53). In the previous chapter, I discussed the field dependent/independent distinc-

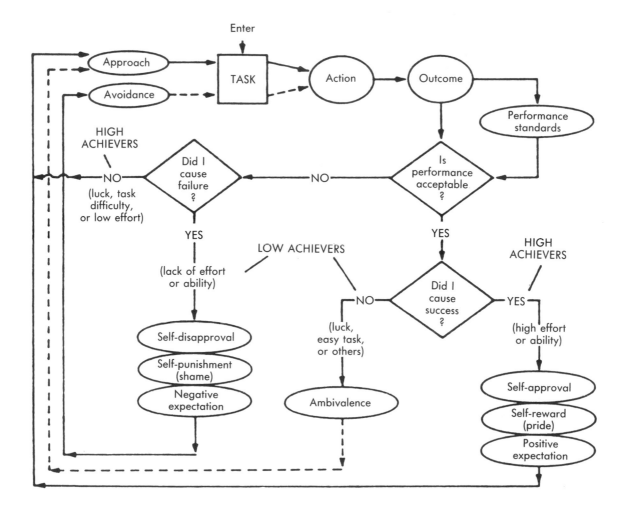

Figure 7.1. An attributional model of achievement motivation. From "Why Jimmy Doesn't Try" by R. Cook, 1983, *Academic Therapy, 19*(2), p. 158. Copyright 1983 by Academic Therapy Publications. Reprinted with permission.

tion. One strength of field-dependent students is usually their people orientation. Looking at how the student performs on the cited items (relative to age, of course), as well as on Items 1 and 5 of Object Assembly, may be helpful in providing suggestions as to a field-dependent or field-independent cognitive style.

Another useful approach to the field-dependent/independent contrast comes from the work of Castaneda and Woltz (1978). These authors treated field independence in much the same way as Witkin, Oltman, Rakin, and Karp (1971), but they claimed field-dependence is more like "field sensitivity." This concept comes from their work with students from other cultures, particularly Hispanic, in which group membership takes on a more important role than in traditional American culture. Field-sensitive students may simply be responding to the greater needs of the group rather than to their individual needs.

Castaneda and Woltz suggested that teachers need to be more aware of where students are on the field-dependent/independent dimension and try to balance their teaching activities to cater to both ends of the spectrum. In particular, they suggested the strategies listed in Figure 7.2. The authors emphasized, and I agree with them, that there is no point in always trying to match a student's learning style with a similar teaching style. Students need exposure to both styles to try to achieve a healthier balance.

Another behavior I watch, as mentioned earlier, is whether the student names the missing items (and how quickly), or whether he or she merely points. I call this rapid naming ability. The student who is poor at rapid naming is likely to have some difficulties with both oral expression and reading.

Picture Arrangement

A behavior for school psychologists to look for on Picture Arrangement is whether the student thinks out loud while performing the tasks. This information is valuable to the teacher, because thinking out loud can help problem solving in some situations. It also gives the examiner some ideas as to the student's level of internal language. A lot of thinking out loud, however, suggests a certain immaturity in the problem-solving process.

Another observation that can be made on this subtest (as on many of the Performance subtests) is whether the student persists beyond the time limits of the item and solves it. If he or she does, such information is valuable to the teacher, in that the student may be able to solve difficult academic tasks if given slightly more time to complete them.

Cooper also suggested that one should observe whether the student displays a very uneven sequence of successes and failures before reaching a ceiling. An uneven sequence "would suggest that the individual's social understanding is disrupted by inattention, anxiety, variable social comprehension or even confusion in dealing with interpersonal stimuli" (p. 88).

Comparing the Picture Arrangement subtest to its Verbal counterpart, the Comprehension subtest, provides some information on whether a student can verbally state what is an appropriate response to certain social situations and/or recognize the logical flow of social events. Sometimes low Comprehension and high Picture Arrangement scores indicate more ability to use visual than verbal cues in the environment. Thus, the student could be described as socially alert, even though he or she cannot express social rules verbally.

Block Design

Block Design is an excellent measure of reasoning with nonverbal input. The task allows the examiner to observe a number of things about the student. One thing I do is draw the design the student makes for each item in the block spaces provided on the protocol. I also note the types of errors made, such as reversals and transpositions. This lets me know whether the student has made a careless or impulsive error, such as a reversal, or simply had no idea how to solve the puzzle. Some students seem to work the entire time in a seemingly random fashion, never using a systematic strategy. Would thinking out loud and the four-step planning process suggested earlier be suitable for such a student?

I also observe whether the student uses one hand, switches hands, or uses both to solve the problem, thereby getting an impression of the student's neurological maturity. I also note how the student reacts as more stress is introduced by way of task complexity, particularly for older students

FI Strategies

- Encourage students to work alone on tasks.
- Provide competitive learning activities.

- Allow students to discover new concepts by themselves; trial and error.
- Emphasize facts and details of lessons.

- Provide learning exercises that require students to deal with concepts abstractly.
- Encourage students to formulate their own novel solutions to problems.
- Provide rewards that emphasize achievement.

- Encourage task orientation in the classroom.

FS Strategies

- Encourage students to work with others on tasks.
- Provide activities that foster cooperation between students.
- Demonstrate new concepts and skills personally to students; allow them to see the teacher do it first.
- Provide an overview of material, discussing major principles and relationships.
- Present concepts in a way that has relevance to the student's own life. Use personalized examples.
- Encourage students to express their feelings and thoughts openly in class.
- Provide personalized rewards, expressing one's own pleasure in the student's work.
- Encourage students to be sensitive to others; attempt to establish a group feeling.

Figure 7.2. Field-independent (FI) and field-sensitive (FS) teaching strategies.

when Item 10 is introduced. Does the student display uncertainty or inadequacy, or does the student react to the more complex task as a challenge with, say, a delightful gleam in the eye? Impulsivity and task persistence can also be observed. Does the student give up quickly or go beyond the time limits?

Some suggestion as to a simultaneous or successive information processing style (see Chapter 6) can also be partially observed on Block Design. Does the student move to a rapid solution by grasping the overall pattern (a more successive approach)? Or does the student successfully integrate some combination of the two?

Cooper noted that some students accept an obviously inaccurate design as correct, even if pressed. They may simply shrug, or say it is correct, thus deflecting responsibility for their performance because they will not acknowledge it in the first place. Such students can be expected to have difficulty in handling correction or constructive criticism, he suggested.

Cooper also noted that high scores on Block Design may reflect high energy and an orientation to things, rather than people. This makes sense in the field-independent, field-dependent style approach, because Block Design loads on the field-independent side. Field-independent students, as

noted earlier, are less sensitive to a people orientation. Is such a style a problem for the student? Is he or she *too* thing-oriented? Would some of the teaching strategies relating to field sensitivity (see Figure 7.2) be helpful in this particular student's situation?

I also note whether the student frequently checks the sides of the blocks. According to Cooper, such a response may indicate an excessive concreteness that would impede general adaptive ability.

There is some relation between Block Design and some academic areas. Geometry, for example, which deals with abstract visual–spatial reasoning and manipulation, seems to involve similar processing as on Block Design. The student who does well on Block Design might also do well in vocationally oriented courses, such as shop and home economics, where manipulation of concrete objects is called for, or, at a higher level, in engineering courses. This does not mean, however, that a high score on Block Design automatically means the school psychologist should recommend vocational or engineering courses! Nor does it mean that a student with a low score on Block Design should be excluded from such courses. However, if a school psychologist has to make, say, a vocational placement recommendation, then the student's strengths and weaknesses need to be taken into account, including, of course, his or her performance on Block Design.

Object Assembly

Object Assembly, like Block Design, requires motor coordination to solve a visual-input problem. Unlike Block Design, Object Assembly involves "meaningful" items in that the student, in all likelihood, has some visual "imagens" for the items. The student must integrate the visual pieces into a meaningful whole. Speed is a factor, especially with older students. Because students who do very well on Object Assembly may be able to channel their intellectual energy "through their hands" to solve such problems, these students also may do well in shop, crafts, and possibly dramatic activities.

Questions asked by the examiner about student behavior on this subtest are similar to those on the Block Design subtest. Does the student persist, or make only feeble attempts? Is the student angry or upset if he or she cannot do a puzzle? Does the student who cannot integrate a piece claim that it "doesn't fit," thereby shifting responsibility away from himself or herself?

Sometimes I turn Object Assembly into a game-like situation by asking the student either to turn around or close eyes as I put out the pieces. I observe the student's reaction. Many students respond favorably, which is a valuable piece of information for the teacher in some cases. Some, however, are very solemn throughout the administration, and they respond to this "game" in an almost affectless way, as they do the other subtests. Such students tend to be quite passive, and are likely to ask what the pieces are supposed to make, for example, rather than guessing themselves. Some students "peek" when they close their eyes, another behavior worth noting.

I also make some note of the kinds of errors the student makes on each item. The most common errors are inversion on Items 2 and 3. The errors may be due to carelessness with fine detail or a lack of self-correction. If impulsivity is contributing to this, many of the self-control procedures cited earlier could be helpful.

Is the student rigid or flexible in solving the puzzles? Does the student try various other rotations when the choice is obviously incorrect, or rigidly try the same approach over and over? The eye-piece on the face often reveals the level of flexibility. Some students try to force the piece, or rotate through every possibility except the correct one.

Does the student use form and line cues when doing the puzzles? Item 3 is the only item with no line cues, so performance on this item can be compared with that on the others. Can the student shift from one cue to the other easily?

The examiner can also observe whether the student seems to use a more simultaneous or successive approach in solving the puzzles.

Coding (and Symbol Search)

Low scores on Coding (and Symbol Search) may suggest poor paper-and-pencil coordination, and could have implications for the student's printing and cursive handwriting ability and/or performance on timed paper-and-pencil tasks in a school setting. Because I presented a number of strategies for writing and spelling in Appendix 5B, I do not deal with academic implications of these subtests here. Instead, I focus on what the examiner can look for in a student doing these tasks.

Frequently, students who perform poorly on Coding and Symbol Search also do poorly on Digit Span. Perhaps it is because their choice of strategy—memorization—is the same and they are not very good at it. However, some students do poorly on Digit Span, but not on Coding and Symbol Search, or vice versa. Perhaps they use some feature of each task to their advantage. Digit Span involves trying to memorize numbers given orally by the examiner. The student who forgets the numbers cannot do the task. On Coding and Symbol Search, however, the student may be able to perform well because the key is always present. Does the student take advantage of this and, therefore, do better on these subtests? If the reverse is true, is it because auditory memory is better for the student than visual memory?

The examiner should note how the student handles the task. A think-out-loud strategy can sometimes be an aid, but may slow the student and hamper his or her efforts after some time, because thinking-out-loud is developmentally less mature than some other strategies.

Sometimes, the student stops after working the first row on the Coding subtest. Did the student not listen or process the instructions? Or is it part of a more pervasive, passive orientation, in which the student requires more adult structure and guidance to complete the task?

Cooper suggested an interesting examiner strategy for Coding, which requires keeping track of how many items the student completes after every 20-second interval. Presumably, if learning is occurring, performance will become more rapid, or at least remain constant, as time progresses. The examiner could see how many items the student performs in each 20-second interval, or compare the first minute to the second. Attention or mood may be behind any variations noted, as can self-correction. A student who stops to correct an error will be severely penalizing himself or herself.

The examiner could also allow the student to complete the entire Coding subtest (noting where he or she was after 2 minutes), and compare the number of items completed over selected time intervals. When the examiner uses this strategy, according to Cooper, he or she should note that the numbers 1, 2, and 3 predominate in the first line, whereas the remaining digits appear in the second line and are more frequent thereafter. The frequency of 1, 2, and 3 in the first line may account for some variability over timed intervals, presumably because the first line is easier for the student simply due to repetition.

I have found that a similar and useful supplementary test is the *Basic Visual–Motor Association Test* (BVMAT) (Battle, 1990). This standardized test uses a task very similar to coding, but involves letterlike shapes rather than numbers and shapes. The manual provides data to show that the BVMAT can be used as an effective and quick screening device where the situation demands, or can be a useful supplement or posttest where the testing integrity of Coding needs to be preserved, or when the retest interval is too short.

As a last word to this section, I will comment on the Symbol Search subtest. Because this subtest has never been used on previous Wechsler tests, there is presently a dearth of both research and experience with it. My feeling is that it may be related to some of the work of R. P. Carver (1992) on reading efficiency and cognitive speed. There is less of a *heavy* paper-and-pencil and visual memory component on Symbol Search than on Coding. Carver relates cognitive efficiency on such tests to his theory of reading comprehension, which he calls *rauding*.

Mazes

Mazes, like Digit Span and Symbol Search, is an optional and supplementary task on the WISC-III. However, I invariably administer Digit Span and either Symbol Search or Mazes.

Impulsive behavior can easily be noted on Mazes. The student may race up blind alleys, cut corners, or wander off the lines in a rush to get the job done. Such a student may indeed even score quite high on the subtest as a consequence, but at the sacrifice of neat work. I have already discussed in detail the educational implications of the planning and impulsivity aspects of the Mazes subtest.

Sometimes, students do exceptionally well on this subtest in contrast to the other subtests. My first question to such students is whether they play a lot of mazelike video games. Very often, they do, which affects my interpretation of the results.

Some students start the maze from the exit and work backward to the middle. Is this type of response a clever strategy or a deliberate circumvention of the stated rules? Examiner judgment based on student reaction to the other WISC-III subtests can help to answer this question. The examiner must correct the student who uses this exit-first procedure.

Does the student show task persistence as the complexity of the mazes increases, or does the student have an "Oh, no, I can't do this" reaction (verbally or nonverbally)? In other words, does the student retreat and surrender in the face of some stress, or mobilize efforts to the challenge?

Cooper contrasted Mazes to some other subtests, in terms of comparing the student's handling of auditory or visual information with personal or impersonal information:

- Mazes vs. Coding—linear, sequential performance involving linguistic symbols (Coding) vs. linear, sequential information which excludes linguistic information (Mazes).

- Mazes vs. Picture Arrangement—dealing with visual, sequential information with social content (Picture Arrangement) vs. visual, sequential information only (Mazes).

- Mazes vs. Digit Span—external, visual, sequential processing (Mazes) vs. internal, auditory, sequential processing (Digit Span).

- Mazes vs. Comprehension—visual, abstract, sequential reasoning (Mazes) vs. person-relevant, verbal, sequential understanding (Comprehension). (pp. 221–222)

In each case, I would look for a scale score point discrepancy of 3 or more points before concluding that any difference is statistically significant. Also, such information is irrelevant unless it can be coupled with a remedial recommendation. Because remedial strategies based on such constructs as visual sequential memory and auditory closure have not proven to be very educationally useful, the preceding contrasts should be employed with caution and used with discretion in certain cases. Sometimes, for instance, it is helpful for a teacher to know the student can do well if a memory constraint is removed, such as if the score on Mazes were significantly higher than that on Digit Span.

TEMPORAL PLOTTING

On the WISC-III, as on the WISC-R, Performance and Verbal subtests are alternated during test administration. When a WISC-III profile is plotted on the face-sheet of the test protocol, however, the subtests are listed under the Verbal and Performance Scales, so the plotted sequence differs from the actual administration sequence.

The purpose of temporal plotting is to determine whether the sequence of subtest presentation is a factor more important than other hypotheses suggested by a traditional analysis. The procedure, which was introduced by DiPasquale (1986), has some interesting ramifications. DiPasquale presented case examples to show that factors such as fatigue and recess breaks may affect the subtest results. This approach has some merit, in my opinion, and should be incorporated into the analysis of a WISC-III profile where it seems appropriate to do so (this does not happen frequently, in my experience). Temporal plotting complements the five-level approach I have suggested in this book. It may suggest further hypotheses and remedial approaches, and provide insights not afforded by the other levels.

To do a temporal plot of the WISC-III, simply devise a face sheet on which the subtests can be plotted in the same order as administered. Then connect the scores and decide, based on the results and the observations of the student during testing, whether there is a temporal effect.

Afterword

As you can appreciate by reading to this point, a remarkable degree of background knowledge, sophistication, clinical judgment, and expertise is necessary to do justice to full WISC-III interpretation. Furthermore, the school psychologist must be able to link hypotheses with remedial strategies in a way that makes sense for the classroom or remedial teacher and parent. In previous chapters, I covered a lot of ground in an attempt to help you uncover some of the hypotheses that are generated in the level-by-level interpretation I have used for the foundation for this book.

I realize that most school psychologists simply do not have the time to pore over each WISC-III protocol with a fine-tooth comb; nor do they necessarily have the time to write brilliant and complete reports. Most good consultation and information transpire verbally in the parent–teacher interviews; however, every school psychologist needs a sound data base with which to begin. It is my sincere hope that *The WISC-III Companion* helps you achieve a greater depth of interpretive understanding, which will assist you in your role as a consultant and helper.

References

Abrams, J. C., & Smolen, W. O. (1973). On stress, failure, and reading disability. *Journal of Reading, 16,* 462–466.

Adams, M. J. (1990). *Beginning to read.* Cambridge: MIT Press.

Adams, M. J. (1991). Why not phonics *and* whole language? In W. Ellis (Ed.), *All language and the creation of literacy.* Baltimore: Orton Dyslexia Society.

Badian, N. A. (1981). Can the WPPSI be of aid in identifying young children at risk for reading disability. *Journal of Learning Disabilities, 17,* 583–587.

Bannatyne, A. (1971). *Language, reading, and learning disabilities.* Springfield, IL: Thomas.

Bannatyne, A. (1974). A note on recategorization of the WISC scaled scores. *Journal of Learning Disabilities, 7,* 272–274.

Barbe, W. B. (1961). *Educator's guide to personalized reading instruction.* Englewood Cliffs, NJ: Prentice-Hall.

Battle, J. (1982). *Enhancing self-esteem and achievement: A handbook for professionals.* Edmonton: James Battle and Associates.

Battle, J. (1990). *Basic visual–motor association test* [BVMAT]. Edmonton: J. Battle and Associates.

Battle, J. (1992). *Culture-free self-esteem inventories for children and adults* (2nd ed.). Austin, TX: PRO-ED.

Bell, N. (1991). *Visualizing and verbalizing.* Paso Robles, CA: Academy of Reading Publications. Also available from Foothills Educational Materials, Calgary, Alberta.

Benson, H. (1975). *The relaxation response.* New York: Morrow.

Bialer, I. (1961). Conceptualization of success and failure in mentally retarded and normal children. *Journal of Personality, 31,* 482–490.

Binet, A., & Simon, T. (1905). Méthodes nouvelles pour le diagnostic du niveau intéllectuel des anormaux. *L'Année Psychologique, 11,* 191–244.

Blaha, J., & Wallbrown, F. (1984). Hierarchical analyses of the WISC and WISC-R: Synthesis and clinical implications. *Journal of Clinical Psychology, 40*(2), 556–571.

Bradley, L., & Bryant, P. (1983). Categorizing sounds and learning to read—A causal connection. *Nature, 301,* 419–421.

Brigance, A. H. (1978). *The Brigance diagnostic inventory of early development.* North Billerica, MA: Curriculum Associates.

Burns, R. C., & Kaufman, S. H. (1972). *Actions, styles and symbols in kinetic family drawings (K-F-D).* New York: Brunner/Mazel.

Carnine, D. (1979). Direct instruction: A successful system for educationally high-risk children. *Journal of Curriculum Studies, 11*(1), 29–45.

Carnine, D., Elkind, D., Hendrickson, A. D., Meichenbaum, D., Sieben, R. L., & Smith, F. (1983). Direct instruction: In search of instructional solutions for educational problems. In *Interdisciplinary voices in learning disabilities.* Austin, TX: PRO-ED.

Carrier, C., Joseph, M., Krey, C., & LaCroix, P. (1983). Supplied visuals and imagery instructions in field independent and field dependent children's recall. *Educational Communications and Technology Journal, 31*(3), 153–160.

Carter, J. L., & Russell, H. L. (1985). Use of EMG biofeedback procedures with learning-disabled children in a clinical and an educational setting. *Journal of Learning Disabilities, 18*(4), 213–216.

Carver, R. P. (1992). What do standardized tests of reading comprehension measure in terms of efficiency, accuracy and rate? *Reading Research Quarterly, 27,* 346–359.

Castaneda, A., & Woltz, D. (1978). *The bicognitive inventory.* Hollister, CA: Cybernetic Learning Systems.

Clark, A. M. (1984). Early experiences and cognitive development. In E. W. Gordon (Ed.), *Review of research in education.* Washington, DC: American Educational Research Association.

Cohen, R., Fil, D., Netley, C., & Clarke, M. (1984). On the generality of the short-term memory/reading ability relationship. *Journal of Learning Disabilities, 17,* 218–221.

Cone, T., & Wilson, L. R. (1981). Quantifying a severe discrepancy: A critical analysis. *Learning Disability Quarterly, 4,* 359–371.

Cook, R. (1983, November). Why Jimmy doesn't try. *Academic Therapy, 19*(2), 155–163.

Cooper, S. (1982). *The clinical use and interpretation of the Wechsler Intelligence Scale for Children–Revised.* Springfield, IL: Thomas.

Cox, J., Daniel, N., & Boston, B. (1985). *Educating able learners: Programs and promising practices.* Austin: University of Texas Press.

Crandall, V., Katkovsky, W., & Crandall, V. (1965). Children's beliefs in their own control of reinforcements in intellectual–academic achievement situations. *Child Development, 36,* 91–109.

Curriculum Guide (EMH). (1980). Edmonton: Alberta Department of Education.

Curriculum Guide (TMH). (1982). Edmonton: Alberta Department of Education.

Darveaux, D. (1984). The good behavior game plus merit: Controlling disruptive behavior and improving student motivation. *School Psychology Review, 13,* 510–514.

Das, J. P., Leong, C. K., & Williams, N. H. (1978). The relationship between learning disability and simultaneous–successive processing. *Journal of Learning Disabilities, 11,* 618–625.

DeBruyn, R., & Larson, J. (1984). *You can handle them all.* Manhattan, KS: The Master Teacher.

Dinkmeyer, D., & McKay, G. (1976). *Systematic training for effective parenting.* Circle Pines, MN: American Guidance Service.

Dinkmeyer, D., McKay, G., & Dinkmeyer, D. (1980). *Systematic training for effective teaching.* Circle Pines, MN: American Guidance Service.

DiPasquale, G. (1986). The temporal plot: Another tool for WISC-R profile interpretation. *Canadian Journal of School Psychology, 2*(1), 55–60.

Dolch, E. W. (1936). A basic sight vocabulary. *The Elementary School Journal, 36,* 456–460.

Downing, J., & Leong, C. K. (1982). *Psychology of reading.* New York: Macmillan.

Doyle, W., & Rutherford, B. (1984). Classroom research on matching learning and teaching styles. *Theory into Practice, 23*(1), 20–25.

Dreikurs, R. (1950). *Fundamentals of Adlerian psychology.* New York: Greenberg.

Duffelmeyer, F. (1985). Teaching word meaning from an experience base. *The Reading Teacher, 30*(1), 6–9.

Dunn, L. M. (1959). *Peabody picture vocabulary test.* Circle Pines, MN: American Guidance Service.

Dunn, R. (1984). Learning style: State of the science. *Theory into Practice, 23*(1), 10–190.

Engelmann, S., & Osborn, J. (1987). *DISTAR Language I.* Chicago: Science Research Associates.

Englert, C. S. (1984, October). Measuring teacher effectiveness from the teacher's point of view. *Focus on Exceptional Children.*

Eysenck, H. J. (Ed.). (1973). *The measurement of intelligence.* Baltimore: Williams & Wilkins.

Fagan, W. T. (1980). Reading and the mentally handicapped. *Mental Retardation for Special Educators.*

Farnham-Diggory, S. (1978). *Learning disabilities.* Cambridge: Harvard University Press.

Feldhusen, J. F., & Wyman, A. R. (1980). Super Saturday: Design and implementation of Purdue's special program for gifted children. *Gifted Child Quarterly, 24,* 15–21.

Feuerstein, R. (1980). *Instrumental enrichment.* Baltimore: University Park Press.

Fine, M., & Pitts, R. (1980). Intervention with underachieving gifted children: Rationale and strategies. *Gifted Child Quarterly, 24*(2), 51–55.

Flesch, R. F. (1949). *The art of writing.* New York: Harper.

Frey, H. (1980). Improving the performance of poor readers through autogenic relaxation training. *Reading Teacher, 33,* 928–932.

Frost, R. (1982). *The arithmetic achievement of learning disabled students: A training study.* Unpublished doctoral dissertation, University of Calgary.

Fry, P., & Lupart, J. (1986). *Cognitive processes in children's learning.* Springfield, IL: Thomas.

Gambrell, L. (1983). The occurrence of think-time during reading comprehension. *Journal of Educational Research, 77*(2), 77–80.

Gardner, R. (1981). Digits Forward and Digits Backward as two separate tests: Normative data on 1567 school children. *Journal of Clinical Child Psychology, 10,* 131–135.

Garton, S., Schoenfelder, P., & Skriba, P. (1979, January). Activities for young word bankers. *The Reading Teacher,* pp. 453–457.

Gentile, L., & McMillan, M. (1987). *Stress and reading difficulties: Research, assessment, intervention.* Newark, DE: International Reading Association.

Gentry, J. R. (1984). Developmental aspects of learning to spell. *Academic Therapy, 20,* 12–16.

Gettinger, M. (1984). Applying learning principles to remedial spelling instruction. *Academic Therapy, 20,* 41–47.

Gettinger, M. (1985). Effects of teacher-directed versus student-directed instruction and cues versus no cues for improving spelling performance. *Journal of Applied Behavior Analysis, 18,* 167–171.

Gillet, J., & Kita, M. (1979, February). Words, kids, and categories. *The Reading Teacher,* pp. 538–542.

Gillet, J. W., & Temple, C. (1982). *Understanding reading problems, assessment and instruction.* Boston: Little, Brown.

Goodman, K. (1973). Strategies for increasing comprehension in reading. In H. M. Robinson (Ed.), *Improving reading in the intermediate years.*

Greenbaum, C. R. (1987). *The spellmaster assessment and teaching system.* Austin, TX: PRO-ED.

Gunnison, J. (1984). Developing educational interventions from assessments involving the K-ABC. *Journal of Special Education, 18,* 325–343.

Halford, G. S. (1978). An approach to the definition of cognitive developmental stages in school mathematics. *British Journal of Educational Psychology, 48,* 298–314.

Hall, R. J. (1984). Orthographic problem solving. *Academic Therapy, 20,* 67–75.

Hallahan, D., & Sapona, R. (1984). Self-monitoring of attention with LD children: Past research and current issues. In J. Torgeson & G. Senf (Eds.), *Annual review of learning disabilities* (pp. 97–101).

Hamachek, D. E. (1975). *Behavior dynamics in teaching, learning, and growth.* Boston: Allyn & Bacon.

Hansen, H. S. (1973). The home literacy environment—A follow-up report. *Elementary English, 50,* 97–98.

Haslam, R. H. A., Dalby, J. T., & Rademaker, A. W. (1984). The effect of megavitamin therapy on children with attention deficit disorders. *Pediatrics, 74,* 103–111.

Herzfeld, G., & Powell, R. (1986). *Coping for kids: A complete stress-control program for students ages 8–18.* West Nyack, NY: Center for Applied Research in Education.

Holmes, B. J. (1985). A critique of programmed WISC-R remediations. *Canadian Journal of School Psychology, 1*(1).

Jackson, N., Jackson, D., & Monroe, C. (1983). *Teaching social effectiveness to children.* Champaign, IL: Research Press.

Jacobson, E. (1938). *Progressive relaxation.* Chicago: University of Chicago Press.

Jastak, S., & Wilkinson, G. S. (1984). *Wide range achievement test–Revised.* Wilmington, DE: Jastak Associates.

Kagan, J. (1965). Reflection–impulsivity and reading ability in primary grade children. *Child Development, 36,* 609–628.

Kagan, J. (1966). Reflection–impulsivity: The generality and dynamics of conceptual tempo. *Journal of Abnormal Psychology, 71,* 17–24.

Karp, S. A., & Konstadt, N. (1971). *Children's embedded figures test.* Palo Alto, CA: Consulting Psychologist's Press.

Kaufman, A. S. (1979). *Intelligent testing with the WISC-R.* New York: Wiley.

Kaufman, A. S. (1992). Evaluation of the WISC-III and WPPSI-R for gifted children. *Roeper Review, 14*(3), 154–158.

Kaufman, A., & Kaufman, N. (1983). *K-ABC: Kaufman assessment battery for children.* Circle Pines, MN: American Guidance Service.

Kaufman, A., & Kaufman, N. (1984). *Training packet for sequential or simultaneous mental processing.* Circle Pines, MN: American Guidance Service.

Kaufman, J., Hallahan, D., Haas, K., Brame, T., & Boren, R. (1978). Imitating children's errors to improve their spelling performance. *Journal of Learning Disabilities, 11*(4), 33–38.

Kavale, K., & Forness, S. (1984). A meta-analysis of the validity of Wechsler scale profiles and recategorizations: Patterns or parodies? *Learning Disability Quarterly, 7,* 136–156.

Kendall, P., & Finch, A. (1976). A cognitive–behavioral treatment for impulse control: A case study. *Journal of Consulting and Clinical Psychology, 44,* 852–857.

Kennedy, L. D., & Halinski, R. S. (1975). Measuring attitudes: An extra dimension. *Journal of Reading, 18,* 518–522.

King, J. R. (1984). Levels of categorization and sight-word acquisition. *Reading Psychology, 5,* 130–131.

Kirk, S. (1972). *Educating exceptional children.* Boston: Houghton-Mifflin.

Koeppen, H. S. (1974). Relaxation training for children. *Elementary School Guidance and Counseling, 9*(1), 14–21.

Koppitz, E. M. (1968). *Psychological evaluation of children's human figure drawings.* New York: Grune & Stratton.

Kops, C., & Belmont, I. (1985). Planning and organizing skills of poor school achievers. *Journal of Learning Disabilities, 18*(1), 9–14.

Kosiewicz, M. M., Hallahan, D. P., Lloyd, J., & Graves, W. (1982). Effects of self-instruction and self-correction procedures on handwriting performance. *Learning Disability Quarterly, 5,* 71–78.

Langer, J. A. (1986). *Children, reading and writing: Structures and strategies.* Norwood, NJ: Ablex.

Lansdown, R. (1974). *Reading, teaching, and learning.* London: Pitman.

Larivee, B. (1981). Modality preference as a model for differentiating beginning reading instruction: A review of the issues. *Learning Disability Quarterly, 4,* 180–188.

Learning Disabilities Association of Canada. (1991). *Learning Disabilities Association of Canada policy manual.* Ottawa, Ontario: Author.

Letteri, C. (1980). Cognitive profile: Basic determinant of academic achievement. *Journal of Educational Research, 73,* 195–198.

Levin, J. R. (1981). On functions of pictures in prose. In F. J. Pirozzolo & M. C. Wittrock (Eds.), *Neuropsychological and cognitive processes in reading.* New York: Academic Press.

Levin, J., Johnson, D., Pittelman, S., Levin, K., Shriber, L., Toms-Bronowski, S., & Hayes, B. (1984). Vocabulary learning strategies. *Reading Psychology, 5,* 1–15.

Levy, W. (1981). How useful is the WISC-R Arithmetic subtest? *Topics in Learning and Learning Disabilities, 1*(3), 81–87.

Lindamood, C., & Lindamood, P. (1979). *The LAC (Lindamood Auditory Conceptualization) Test* (rev. ed.). Allen, TX: DLM Teaching Resources.

Lindamood, P., & Lindamood, C. (1975). *Auditory discrimination in depth.* Allen, TX: DLM Teaching Resources.

Maier, A. (1980). The effect of focusing on the cognitive processes of learning-disabled children. *Journal of Learning Disabilities, 13*(3), 34–38.

Markwardt, F. C. (1989). *Manual for the Peabody individual achievement test–Revised (PIAT-R).* Circle Pines, MN: American Guidance Service.

Mastropieri, M., Scruggs, T., & Levin, J. (1985). Mnemonic strategy instruction with learning disabled adolescents. *Journal of Learning Disabilities, 18*(2), 94–100.

McCall, R., Appelbaum, M., & Hogarty, P. (1973). Developmental changes in mental performance. *Monographs of the Society for Research in Child Development, 38*(serial 150), 1–83.

McCarthy, D. A. (1972). *Manual for the McCarthy scales of children's abilities.* San Antonio, TX: Psychological Corp.

McLeod, J., & Greenough, P. (1980). The importance of sequencing as an aspect of short-term memory in good and poor spellers. *Journal of Learning Disabilities, 13*(5), 27–33.

McNeil, J. (1984). *Reading comprehension: New directions for classroom practice.* Glenview, IL: Scott, Foresman.

Meeker, M. N. (1969). *The structure of intellect.* Columbus, OH: Merrill.

Meichenbaum, D. (1977). *Cognitive behavior modification: An integrative approach.* New York: Plenum.

Meichenbaum, D., & Goodman, J. (1971). Training impulsive children to talk to themselves: A means of developing self-control. *Journal of Abnormal Psychology, 77,* 115–126.

Mishra, S., Ferguson, B., & King, P. (1985). Research with the Wechsler Digit Span subtests: Implications for assessment. *School Psychology Review, 14*(1), 37–47.

Morris, J. M. (1966). *Standards and progress in reading.* Slough, England: National Foundation for Educational Research.

Naglieri, J. A., & Das, J. P. (1988). Planning–arousal–simultaneous–successive (PASS): A model for assessment. *Journal of School Psychology, 26,* 35–48.

Naglieri, J. A., Kamphaus, R., & Kaufman, A. (1983). The Luria–Das simultaneous–successive model applied to the WISC-R. *Journal of Psychoeducational Assessment, 1,* 25–34.

Naisbitt, J. (1982). *Megatrends.* New York: Warner.

National Association of School Psychologists. (1986). *Intervention assistance teams: A model for building-level instructional problem solving.* Stratford, CT: NASP Publication Office.

Newcomer, P. L. (1990). *Diagnostic achievement battery* (2nd ed.). Austin, TX: PRO-ED.

Nicholson, T. (1986). Reading is not a guessing game—The great debate revisited. *Reading Psychology, 7,* 197–210.

Paivio, A. (1990). *Mental representations: A dual coding approach.* New York: Oxford University Press.

Palincsar, A. S., & Brown, A. L. (1984). Reciprocal teaching of comprehension fostering and comprehension monitoring activities. *Cognition and Instruction, 1*(2), 117–175.

Parill-Burnstein, M. (1981). *Problem solving and learning disabilities, an information-processing approach.* New York: Grune & Stratton.

Pearson, P. D. (1976). A psycholinguistic model of reading. *Language Arts, 53,* 309–314.

Pyle, D. (1979). *Intelligence, an introduction.* London: Routledge and Kegan Paul.

Rasinski, T. (1984). Field dependent/independent cognitive style research revisited: Do field dependent readers read differently than field independent readers? *Reading Psychology, 5,* 303–322.

Reichurdt, K. W. (1977). Playing dead or running away—Defense reactions during reading. *Journal of Reading, 20,* 706–711.

Renzulli, J. (1977). *The enrichment triad model: A guide for developing defensible programs for the gifted and talented.* Mansfield Center, CT: Creative Learning Press.

Renzulli, J. (1978). What makes giftedness? Reexamining a definition. *Phi Delta Kappan, 60,* 180–184, 261.

Reynolds, C. (1984–1985). Critical measurement issues in learning disabilities. *The Journal of Special Education, 18,* 451–476.

Reynolds, C., & Clark, J. (1986). Profile analysis of standardized intelligence test performance of very high IQ children. *Psychology in the Schools, 23,* 5–12.

Reznikoff, N. A., & Reznikoff, H. R. (1956). The family drawing test: A comparative study of children's drawings. *Journal of Clinical Psychology, 12,* 167–169.

Robinson, F. P. (1970). *Effective study* (4th ed.). New York: Harper & Row.

Rogers, C. R. (1951). *Client-centered therapy: Its current practice, implications, and theory.* Boston: Houghton-Mifflin.

Ross, A. O. (1976). *Psychological aspects of learning disabilities and reading disorders.* New York: McGraw-Hill.

Sachs, F. G., & Banas, N. (1985). The ENIGMA reading program. *Academic Therapy, 20,* 481–485.

Sadoski, M., Paivio, A., & Goetz, E. (1991). A critique of schema theory in reading and a dual coding alternative. *Reading Research Quarterly, 26,* 463–484.

Samuels, S. J. (1976). Automatic decoding and reading comprehension. *Language Arts, 53,* 323–325.

Satterly, D. J., & Telfer, I. (1979). Cognitive style and advanced organizers in learning and retention. *British Journal of Educational Psychology, 49,* 169–178.

Sattler, J. (1982). *Assessment of children's intelligence and special abilities* (2nd ed.). Boston: Allyn & Bacon.

Schanzer, S., & Wohlman, J. K. (1979). Homework organizer for teachers and students. *Academic Therapy, 14,* 577–579.

Schiff, M., Kaufman, A., & Kaufman, N. (1981). Scatter analysis of WISC-R profiles of learning-disabled children with superior intelligence. *Journal of Learning Disabilities, 14*(7), 400–404.

Schunk, D. (1984). Enhancing self-efficacy and achievement through rewards and goals: Motivational and informational effects. *Journal of Educational Research, 78*(1), 29–34.

Scruggs, T., & Mastropieri, M. (1984, November). Improving memory for facts: The keyword method. *Academic Therapy, 20*(2), 159–161.

Searls, E., & Klesius, J. (1984). Multiple-meaning words for primary students and how to teach them. *Reading Psychology, 5,* 55–63.

Selye, J. (1974). *Stress without distress.* New York: Signet.

Shapiro, L. (1981). *Games to grow on—Activities to help children learn self-control.* Englewood Cliffs, NJ: Prentice-Hall.

Shelton, T., Anastopoulos, A., & Linden, J. (1985). An attribution training program with learning-disabled children. *Journal of Learning Disabilities, 18*(5), 261–265.

Smith, D. E. P. (1969). Increasing task behavior difficulty in a language arts program by providing reinforcement. *Journal of Experimental Child Psychology, 4*(8), 45–62.

Smith, F. (1975). The role of prediction in reading. *Elementary English, 52,* 305–311.

Smith, H. K. (1972). Reading for different purposes. In V. Southgate (Ed.), *Literacy at all levels.* London: Ward Lock.

Smith, M. D., Coleman, J. M., Dokecki, P. R., & Davis, E. E. (1977). Recategorized WISC-R scores of learning disabled children. *Journal of Learning Disabilities, 10,* 444–449.

Sternberg, R. (1984). How to teach intelligence. *Educational Leadership, 42*(1), 38–48.

Sternberg, R. J., & Ketron, J. C. (1982). Selection and implementation of strategies in reasoning by analogy. *Journal of Educational Psychology, 74,* 339–413.

Taylor, I., & Taylor, M. M. (1983). *The psychology of reading.* New York: Academic Press.

Terman, L. M., & Merrill, M. A. (1960). *Stanford–Binet intelligence scale.* Boston: Houghton-Mifflin.

Thorndike, R. L., Hagen, E. P., & Sattler, J. M. (1986). *Guide for administering and scoring the Stanford–Binet intelligence scale: Fourth edition.* Chicago: Riverside.

Thorpe, H., & Borden, K. (1985). The effect of multisensory instruction upon the on-task behaviors and word reading accuracy of learning-disabled children. *Journal of Learning Disabilities, 18*(5), 279–286.

Torgeson, L. M., & Houch, D. G. (1980). Processing deficiencies of learning-disabled children who perform poorly on the Digit Span test. *Journal of Educational Psychology, 72,* 141–160.

Truch, S. (1980). *Teacher burnout and what to do about it.* Novato, CA: Academic Therapy.

Truch, S. (1991). *The missing parts of whole language.* Calgary, Alberta: Foothills Educational Materials.

U.S. Department of Health, Education, and Welfare, Office of the Secretary, Secretary's Committee on Mental Retardation. (1969). *The problem of mental retardation.* Washington, DC: Government Printing Office.

Vernon, P. (1979). *Intelligence, heredity, and environment.* San Francisco: W. H. Freeman.

Walker, B. (1985). Right-brained strategies for teaching comprehension. *Academic Therapy, 21*(2), 133–141.

Walker, N. W. (1981). Modifying impulsive responding to four WISC-R subtests. *Journal of School Psychology, 19*(4), 335–339.

Wallbrown, F. H., Blaha, J., & Vance, B. (1980). A reply to Miller's concerns about WISC-R profile analysis. *Journal of Learning Disabilities, 13*(6), 340–345.

Wechsler, D. (1939). *The measurement of adult intelligence.* Baltimore: Williams & Wilkins.

Wechsler, D. (1944). *The measurement of adult intelligence* (3rd ed.). Baltimore: Williams & Wilkins.

Wechsler, D. (1949). *Manual for the Wechsler intelligence scale for children.* New York: Psychological Corp.

Wechsler, D. (1967). *Manual for the Wechsler preschool and primary scale of intelligence.* San Antonio, TX: Psychological Corp.

Wechsler, D. (1974). *Manual for the Wechsler intelligence scale for children–Revised.* San Antonio, TX: Psychological Corp.

Wechsler, D. (1991). *Wechsler intelligence scale for children–Third edition.* San Antonio, TX: Psychological Corp.

Whiting, S. A., & Jarrico, S. (1980). Spelling patterns of normal readers. *Journal of Learning Disabilities, 13*(1), 45–47.

Whitworth, J. R., & Sutton, D. L. (1978). *The WISC-R compilation.* Novato, CA: Academic Therapy.

Whitworth, J. R., & Sutton, D. L. (1993). *The WISC-III compilation.* Novato, CA: Academic Therapy.

Williams, J. (1984). Phonemic analysis and how it relates to reading. *Journal of Learning Disabilities, 17,* 240–245.

Wilson, C., Hall, D., & Watson, D. (1979). *Teaching children self-control.* San Diego: Department of Education, San Diego County.

Witkin, H. A. (1971). *Embedded figures test.* Palo Alto, CA: Consulting Psychologist's Press.

Witkin, H. A., & Goodenough, D. R. (1977). *Field dependence revisited.* Unpublished research bulletin, Educational Testing Service, Princeton, NJ.

Witkin, H. A., Oltman, P. K., & Raskin, E. (1971). *Group embedded figures test.* Palo Alto, CA: Consulting Psychologist's Press.

Witkin, H. A., Oltman, P., Raskin, E., & Karp, S. (1971). *A manual for the embedded figures test.* Palo Alto, CA: Consulting Psychologist's Press.

Woodcock, R. W. (1973). *Woodcock reading mastery tests.* Circle Pines, MN: American Guidance Service.

Wormeli, C., & Carter, D. E. (1990). *Canada quick individual educational test.* Surrey, British Columbia: Canadian Edumetrics.

The Language-Immersion Environment

I recommend a combination of top–down (i.e., meaning-based) and bottom–up (i.e., data-based) approaches to teaching reading in the regular and remedial classrooms. The top–down, seeking-for-meaning approach is best served by what I call a language-immersion environment, of which the language-experience approach is a part. The student is literally immersed in a total language environment, and his or her language–knowledge–experience base is used as the building block for the next step. The student is not taught skills in isolation in a special room in the corner of the school. Instead, remediation is based on what is meaningful and interesting to the student. The resource room becomes a lively and integral part of the total school environment. Close cooperation with the student's homeroom teacher becomes necessary so that remedial lessons, if possible, are based on homeroom or overall school-based themes. Additionally, the remedial teacher needs to tap into the student's interests and reading attitudes (see Chapter 3 and the accompanying questionnaires in this appendix). The bottom–up approach is best served by in-depth training in phonemic processing, of which the *Auditory Discrimination in Depth* program (Lindamood & Lindamood, 1975) is the best example. It is important that students who have problems with decoding receive remediation in this area *first*. Too much reliance on top–down strategies does not produce good readers.

Remedial reading lessons should, if possible, be designed around the key elements of themes (i.e., once students have some fluency in decoding), and students should be encouraged to predict what will happen in stories. In this way, the search for meaning will be foremost, because these elements are largely top–down. In addition, because many disabled readers are passive learners, an attempt to make them more active participants should be built in, which can be done by stimulating students to think through good questioning. Finally, as much as possible, teachers should try to link what each student already knows to what he or she still needs to know. This means tapping into a student's language and experience base.

This approach means that teachers need to spend a great deal of time preparing their students before doing any actual reading, so as to make full use of their language and experience bases. For example, Karen Clark made the following program suggestions for prereading strategies:

I. Selecting the Instructional Reading Matter

Select a text or passage that is neither too difficult nor too easy for the student(s) and that is consistent with your current theme. Always know what the student's instructional reading level is. If you are using an ungraded text, be sure to do a readability test on it. In addition to examining vocabulary, check the passage for complexity of concepts. The key to this approach is using appropriate reading material.

II. Questioning

The following questioning procedures are designed to (a) stimulate student curiosity about a passage to be read, (b) activate prior content knowledge, and (c) lead the student to anticipate and elaborate upon what is read, or focus attention on specific information.

A. Teacher questioning. Establishing specific reasons for reading a passage is crucial. (You may wish to review the discussion in Chapter 3 again about reading purposes.) Ask yourself what it is that you want your students to know after they read the selection. Once this is determined, purpose-setting questions can be developed to focus student attention on the relevant aspects of the story or text.

By asking questions at various levels of comprehension, teachers will activate prior knowledge. For example, in a story about a coyote, the literal-level questions might be

1. Where was Ben sleeping?

2. What did he hear?

The inferential-level questions might be

1. Why was Ben afraid?

2. How is a coyote like a dog?

3. In what ways do you think they are different?

4. Why did Ben have nothing to fear?

These are not the only questions that might be asked, but they are representative of the kinds of questions that can be asked to prepare the students for the concepts of vocabulary they will encounter when the story is read.

B. Teacher–student reciprocal questioning. The objective of active comprehension is to have students learn to ask their own questions and to guide their own thinking in learning from the text

before, during, and after reading. Student-generated questions can lead to improved comprehension. Generating questions requires deep processing of the text. If you model good questioning behavior, then the student will eventually learn to formulate his or her own questions. This might be done by having the student read the title of the story or look at an illustration. It may be accomplished by having the student progress through a lesson with your guidance, where the student is provided a safe atmosphere in which to ask questions in an effort to understand the story. Gradually, you take less and less of a role in question formulation. As the student begins to ask his or her own questions without your prompting, the student is engaging in active comprehension.

The *request procedure* is one way of having the student learn to formulate questions. Begin with an expanded pre-reading plan (PReP) (the PReP has been adapted by Karen Clark from Judith Langer's, 1986, work). The PReP assists the teacher in

1. Determining the prior knowledge a student possesses about a specific concept, as well as the manner in which this knowledge is organized

2. Becoming aware of the language a student uses to express knowledge about a particular concept

3. Making judgments about how much additional background information must be taught before the student can successfully read the text

4. Developing the vocabulary and syntax with a group

The PReP calls for an extensive group discussion before the students read the text. I return to the example of the boy and the coyote to illustrate the procedure.

Initial associations with the concept. The following might be used:

1. *Association Activity*—You might say something like this to your group: "Tell me anything that comes to your mind when you hear the word *coyote* (or see this picture)." As each student in the group freely associates and tells what

ideas come to mind, the responses can be written on the chalkboard.

During this phase, the students have an opportunity to make associations between a key concept and what they already know. You could draw on the chalkboard a schema, as shown in Figure 2A.1.

2. *Reflections on Initial Associations*—Next, the students should be asked questions, such as "What made you think of the coyote's sharp teeth?" This phase encourages students to become more aware of the associations they have made, to listen to each other's responses, and to become aware of their changing ideas. Through this procedure, they gain the insight that permits them to evaluate the usefulness of these ideas in the reading experience.

3. *Reformulation of Knowledge*—After each student has had an opportunity to think

about and tell his or her ideas concerning the concept, you may read a short story about a coyote to the class, or show a filmstrip, or perhaps merely show a picture of the coyote. Then you return to the first schema of the coyote, and ask if the students would like to add anything to the schema or change anything. Usually, considerably more is added, and sometimes the schema changes because a student wishes to delete an item.

Concept stretching. If the students still do not have a good schema for coyote, you may wish to stretch their concept of *dog* to include *coyote*. What you can encourage them to do, then, is to brainstorm about something they know well to help them relate as many characteristics of the known, to link with the unknown. Perhaps their brainstorming leads to the schema shown in Figure 2A.2. (Again, discuss responses as needed.)

Vocabulary development (see also Chapter 5). At this point, the group might be ready to make

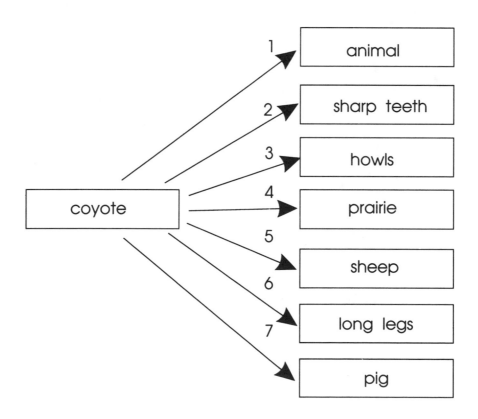

Figure 2A.1. Schema for the concept *coyote*.

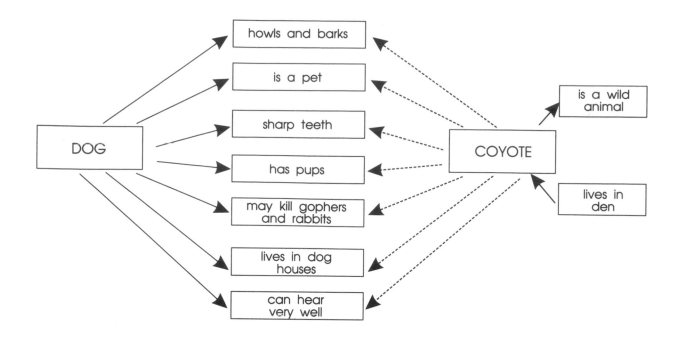

Figure 2A.2. Expanded schema for the concept *coyote*.

some predictions about the vocabulary in the story. As the teacher, you could

1. List key words as predicted by the students. Pronounce each word as it is written on the board.

2. Elicit sentences. Ask the students to use a word from the list and make up a sentence that might be in the story. Record the sentence verbatim and underline the word or words used from the list. Be sure to record the sentences exactly as stated, even if the information is not correct.

3. If necessary have the students dramatize the vocabulary—that can be a lot of fun.

4. Read and verify the sentences. Have the students read the story and see if their predicted sentences are close to the ones in the story.

Notice how the foregoing lesson framework is truly a language-immersion one. The key elements of theme, predictability, and active involvement are

all beautifully woven together into a meaningful tapestry. In this example, there is also a strong emphasis on linking the known to the unknown.

It is also possible to adapt a basal reader to a language-immersion approach. The following steps are suggested for this purpose:

1. Determine all new and important vocabulary in the forthcoming basal story.

2. Identify the important concepts the students must have in order to understand the story.

3. Make up a story built around the list of vocabulary words. Use a theme in keeping with a concept you wish to stretch or expand upon, from the basal story.

4. Read or tell the story to the reading group.

5. After storytelling, have the students discuss the story. If appropriate, provide opportunities for the students to participate in some of the experiences they will

encounter in the story. For example, if the story is about a child's new kite, have the students make kites and fly them. The experience will serve as a basis for language and concept development.

6. Have the students tell the story back to you, as you write it on the board or chart paper. Ask questions to elicit responses that contain the new vocabulary words if these do not come naturally from the students.

7. Have the students read the story in unison several times. Individual sentences or the whole story may be read by several or all of the students.

8. Have the students underline the new vocabulary words in the story one at a time, in response to requests such as the following:
   a. Find the word that describes how Tina felt when she could not find her puppy.
   b. Find the word that means the opposite of *found*.
   c. Find the word that begins with *h* and rhymes with *cold*.

9. The next day, after choral reading of the language-experience story, provide any additional schema development that is required to understand the new basal story, and proceed with directed reading of the story. You will likely find that the students will be pleased to find words they already know and have so recently encountered. Because the new vocabulary is not a burden, the students are free to enjoy and appreciate the new story.

Although the above lesson is an interesting way to challenge students in their prereading thinking, it should not be considered *the* way to remediation. It is most discouraging that some school boards issue "edicts" stating that phonics is not to be taught because it is inconsistent with the whole language philosophy.

The lesson illustrations above are almost exclusively whole language. However, they take for granted that both the decoding and comprehension processes are already intact. When it comes time to actually read the story, the disabled reader who cannot decode will struggle through the passage. If the student uses top–down processes to make a "meaningful" guess, he or she is unlikely to be successful, because many options are possible even with a prediscussion. Worse, the student may get the word correct one day, but the next day, in a new context, he or she will not know the same word. That is because, to be a good reader, the student must be very fluent with the decoding process.

The same can be said with comprehension. In Chapters 4 and 5, I discuss the relevance of dual-coding theory to reading and oral language comprehension. Some students will require intensive stimulation of visual imagery processing *before* the heavy dose of language used in the above lesson will become meaningful.

I am not opposed to whole language lessons once students have achieved a certain level of processing in both decoding and comprehension, so I have included this example. However, it is a mistake to believe that such lessons actually *remediate* those basic processes.

As director of The Reading Foundation in Calgary, I have become highly sensitized to this issue. Every day, we treat children, adolescents, and adults with reading disabilities. Our program aims to restore the basic processes of decoding and/or comprehension. Most of the children and adolescents in our program are already in resource rooms where they are getting heavy doses of lessons similar to the one described above. The unfortunate experience is that this approach is not making a significant difference to these children's reading. Thus, parents are still often reporting a high degree of frustration on their child's part over reading. Once the basic processes are restored, however, such lessons make wonderful extensions of the child's processing.

READING ATTITUDE QUESTIONS

1. When I read, I _____.

2. Reading makes me _____.

3. School is _____.

4. I wish teachers were _____.

5. When someone reads out loud to me _____.

6. Television is _____.

7. To me, books _____.

8. I like to read about _____.

9. On weekends, I _____.

10. I'd rather read than _____.

11. Last night, I read _____.

12. To me, homework _____.

13. When I am in the library _____.

14. Comic books _____.

15. When I take my report card home _____.

16. When I read arithmetic _____.

17. The future looks _____.

18. I think reading is _____.

19. I like to read when _____.

20. I would like to be _____.

21. For me, studying _____.

22. Reading science _____.

23. Reading poems _____.

24. I'd read more if _____.

25. When I read out loud _____.

Student responses to this informal survey can be very interesting at times! Often, such surveys are of value in planning recommendations, IEPs, and so forth.

WHICH BOOK WOULD YOU CHOOSE?

Name_____ Grade_____ School_____ Date_____

If you could choose one book each from four of the following groups, which would you select? Mark your answers 1, 2, 3, or 4, in the order you would choose them (1=first choice; 2=second choice; 3=third choice; 4=fourth choice).

_____ Adventure

_____ Animals

_____ Biography

_____ Fairy Tales

_____ Frontier and Western

_____ History

_____ Mysteries

_____ Myths and Legends

_____ People and Places in Other Lands

_____ Poetry

_____ Prehistoric

_____ Science

_____ Science Fiction

_____ Space

_____ Sports

_____ Stories about Boys and Girls

Teaching Sequencing

Perhaps the WISC-III results and parent and teacher behavioral observations suggest that sequencing is a problem for the student. If it is, the school psychologist's job is to provide recommendations that relate to academics. The following are two complementary methods (the first from Karen Clark) for emphasizing sequencing of time and story events. Be sure to add the imagery process (see Appendix 2D) to these suggestions.

Method 1

This method teaches time concepts of a general nature.

1. You may wish to begin with a clock. Show the students how to read a clock and stress the idea that one hour follows another. (You could incorporate both digital and analog time with older students.)

2. On the chalkboard, draw a circle and divide it into eight sections. Ask the students to think about the events of their daily routine, such as dressing, eating meals, and going to bed. Write these ideas, in sequence, around the circle. Discuss the repeated events of their daily lives.

3. You may wish to help the students construct time lines of their lives, beginning with birth and including important events up to the present.

4. Select an appropriate book from the great wealth of children's literature. For example, Tomie De Paola's *Strega Nona* or Beatrix Potter's *Peter Rabbit* would be appropriate for a child in second or third grade. Read the book to the students, and then discuss the important events. List these events on a time line constructed as a group project.

5. Using discarded books, have the students search for time-related words or phrases. Ask them to locate and underline words and phrases such as *later, soon, tomorrow,* and *in the future.* Discuss the meaning of these words and how they relate to sequencing. For instance, a sentence beginning with *later* would not describe the first event of a series, whereas *in the evening* refers to the end of the day.

6. Have the student look at the illustrations in a story. Ask him or her why snow-covered ground would not be a suitable illustration for a summer story setting. Show the student the illustration from a

picture-story book, such as the old folk tale "The Peddler and His Caps." Have the student tell the story through the ideas reflected. Encourage him or her to use sequence words such as *next, and then, at last,* and *later.* Then read the book to the student to see how accurate the student was in prediction concerning time. When questioning the student, wait for the response, and then ask, "And *then* what happened?" or "And at *last* . . . ?" Use these language cues to help the student answer a question that requires events to be ordered sequentially.

7. Let the student draw his or her own illustrations for stories just read. The pictures should reflect the passage of time. A story such as "The Three Billy Goats Gruff" would be a good one to illustrate.

8. Write four or five sentence strips from the story being read. Mix them up and have the student read them, and then place them in the order in which they occur in the story. If the student is still a nonreader, use pictures from the story, rather than sentences. If the student has marked difficulty with sequencing, then an additional component is to have him or her "think out loud" while performing the task. If not, demonstrate the technique yourself. Encourage the student to try it on his or her own while trying to sequence the pictures or sentences. Once the student shows progress, reduce the thinking out loud to a whisper, and then fade it entirely.

Method 2

This method reinforces sequencing skills in a reading lesson, and can be adapted for any grade level.

1. Use a story from a theme you are currently working on.

2. Write the title on the chalkboard and ask the students to predict the subject matter of the story.

3. Present sentences from the story to the students. You could do this, for example, by placing them on strips. Prepare an envelope for each student that contains five or six sentences. Have the students individually try to put the sentences in order on the basis of what makes sense. If a student is still a nonreader, use pictures rather than sentences.

4. Have students compare and discuss their answers with two other students.

5. Discuss with the entire class the possible sequences, as well as the rationale behind each one. Be sure to emphasize natural-language sequencing words, such as *first, second, next,* and *afterwards,* that occur in the story.

6. Have students read the story from which the sequence statements were selected. While reading, they should be encouraged to compare other sequences with the text and change them as they consider appropriate.

This strategy highlights and strengthens the students' abilities to predict, confirm, and integrate information while reading, but assumes that the students can, for the most part, read (decode). Again, I would stress that adding the visualization–verbalization process will greatly enhance these methods.

Distractibility

Although the material in this appendix relates specifically to Chapter 2, it also has applications with respect to Chapters 3 and 5.

Distractibility is a behavior. As such, it is observable both in the classroom and at home. It is also observable when the student is being tested with an instrument such as the WISC-III. Low scores on the subtests making up the WISC-III Freedom from Distractibility factor (Factor III) may result from distractibility. However, this hypothesis must be verified by sources of information that lie beyond the WISC-III scores themselves.

If distractibility is a major problem for a student, then the "Good Behavior Game Plus Merit" mentioned in Chapter 3 should be considered. That approach involves the whole class, rather than only the distractible student. Behavior management approaches have also proven useful at times. Research on diet management of distractibility and its associated problem, hyperactivity, has been equivocal. As an approach to the problem in the classroom, however, it is unlikely to be helpful. Treatment with drugs, such as Ritalin® and Cylert®, has consistently shown that, although a student's motor activity or overactivity settles down, no concomitant increase in academic achievement occurs. The school psychologist is therefore left with trying to suggest creative ways of managing the student's needs in the classroom environment.

Because distractibility is a behavior, it can be modified by encouraging self-control. Students may be described as being inwardly or outwardly distractible. If they are inwardly distractible, they may give the appearance of attending while, in fact, they are off-task, because they are daydreaming—lost in "inner space," so to speak. If they are outwardly distractible, the teacher usually knows it, because the student gazes at the wall or whatever else captures his or her fleeting attention, is out-of-seat inappropriately, is restless and fidgety, or is interrupting others inappropriately.

Although both types of distractibility are harmful academically, the latter is the more noticeable, and therefore the more likely of the two to be referred to the school psychologist for intervention. In this appendix, I present two methods for dealing with this problem.

Method 1—Developing Concentration Skills in Listening and Reading

This method, drawn from some suggestions by Karen Clark, is useful for younger students with milder degrees of distractibility. It is not really a "method" as such, but some global suggestions for the teacher.

1. Read or tell a story to the student. Ask him or her to retell the story. Follow up with specific questions. Begin with factual questions that stress memory for detail. Then ask questions requiring the student to draw inferences. At the end of the story, ask the student what might happen next.

2. After the student reads or hears a story, show him or her pictures, and have the student put them in the order in which they occurred in the story. (You could also include some of the thinking-out-loud procedures suggested in Appendix 2B for sequencing.)

3. Have the student read directions for making something. Have the student perform the task by following the directions.

4. Teach the student to use verbal and non-verbal cues when listening. For example, when reading a story, change the intonation of your voice as you read various characters' parts. Have the student listen attentively and determine which character you are portraying. Have the student become aware of special cues that indicate sequence, as suggested in Appendix 2B.

5. Facilitate the student's learning of verbal materials by organizing oral instructions in a clear, logical sequence. It is often helpful to write these in point form on the chalkboard. It is also helpful to have the same points typed or written and attached to the student's desk.

6. Give the student passages that contain irrelevant material or nonsensical statements. Ask the student to read through the entire passage and then circle the statements that are inappropriate.

7. When presenting an oral lesson, or when the student must read or write, be sure that no distractions are on the student's desk, and that background noise is at a minimum. As the student gains facility with paying attention, he or she will learn to filter out distractions automatically.

Method 2—The Random ''Beeper''

This procedure (adapted from Hallahan & Sapona, 1984) can be used with a whole class or a single student as young as 7 years old in virtually every subject area.

1. Prepare an audio-cassette tape that contains beeps or tones that occur about every 45 seconds. Nothing else should be on the tape between the beeps. The interval between the beeps can be as short as 10 seconds or as long as 90 seconds. If you are using the procedure with only one student, place the tape recorder on his or her desk. If you are using it with the whole class, place it where everyone can hear it.

2. Explain to the students that, each time they hear the beep, they are to ask themselves, "Was I paying attention?" If the answer is yes, they are to record it under the "Yes" column of a self-recording sheet taped to their desks. If the answer is no, they are to record it in the "No" column. For younger students, happy and sad faces can be substituted for the words.

Your job as the teacher is to define clearly what "paying attention" means; to show the students how to mark the recording sheet; and to ask the students to repeat your instructions to be sure they are clearly understood. It is also important to solicit their cooperation beforehand.

It is better to use this procedure with written, independent work, than during the oral part of a lesson. With larger groups, however, you could try wrist-counters rather than recording sheets. Wrist-counters are minimally disruptive.

If you are concerned that students will "cheat," then create the illusion of surveillance, or include a reinforcement if their "yes" marks agree with yours. You may also wish to build in some reinforcement as a back-up if the number of "yes" marks reaches a specified criterion.

This procedure has been researched and shown to be effective in improving the on-task/off-task behavior of students with learning disabilities.

Finally, keep in mind that much of the distractibility the student displays may be the result of a reading problem. By providing success in either of the two major processes (decoding and/or comprehension) that may be disrupted, the result is often improved attending and diminished distractibility.

Using Imagery to Improve Story Recall and Comprehension

The following simple technique has been shown to bring dramatic improvement in students' recall of stories (Carrier, Joseph, Krey, & LaCroix, 1983; see also Levin, 1981). The percentage of correct answers nearly doubled on both recall and inferential questions over pretest scores. Additionally, the mental imaging technique was more effective than using the actual pictures that accompanied the text.

1. Select the passage you wish your class, small group, or student to read. This passage could be any suitable story consistent with your objectives or one that is part of your regular curriculum. It should be at the reading level of the student(s).

2. Instruct the group or student to form a "picture in their mind" either before or after they read the passage. Sometimes it is also necessary to remind some students to form mental pictures while they are reading the passage. (Of course, you should never introduce the passage without considerable oral discussion beforehand, emphasizing whatever other aspects of language development or reading is important for that group or student.)

3. Provide time (about five minutes) for a discussion of the students' "pictures" after they read the story. Be sure to respond positively to their "pictures" and provide other suitable images of your own that are consistent with the story.

4. If it is appropriate to do, test the students at this point, either verbally or with written questions, that sample both recall and inference.

5. You may need to give your students some practice in forming mental images before this technique can be used on a regular basis in your teaching. Once you are sure they have caught on, then simple instructions to have them use the technique are all that is necessary.

The study from which this is drawn involved students at the sixth-grade level. Research has shown that imagery training does not appear to be effective until the student is 9 or 10 years old. For students younger than that, pictures in the text will help comprehension—provided that the pictures are consistent with or central to the overall message. Teachers of younger students should therefore assist them in deriving information from pictures in the text as an adjunct to reading comprehension (but not decoding).

Contrary to the research claims in the prior paragraph, Bell (1991) found her visualizing–verbalizing technique to be effective at all age levels. Teachers should also keep in mind that some students may require intensive stimulation in imagery processing before the above procedure will be effective for them.

Self-Rating Scales for Teacher Effectiveness

Classroom Management

Respond to each item in terms of the extent to which it describes you:

1 = Not at all descriptive
2 = Descriptive to a small extent
3 = Descriptive to a moderate extent
4 = Descriptive to a large extent
5 = Descriptive to an extremely large extent

Classroom Set-Up and Organization

1.1. I arrange physical space and instructional materials to minimize disruptive movement around my classroom, and to facilitate easy access to high-use materials.	1	2	3	4	5
1.2. I establish and implement minimally disruptive traffic patterns and procedures.	1	2	3	4	5
1.3. I establish and implement procedures for nonacademic class business (tardiness, material use, movement in and out of the room, distributing materials, talk among students, bathroom breaks, etc.).	1	2	3	4	5
1.4. I establish and implement procedures for academic business (seatwork, obtaining help, volunteer behavior in small groups, learning centers, set-up and take-down of lessons, etc.).	1	2	3	4	5

Teaching Rules and Procedures

2.1. I communicate clearly what behavior will be tolerated and what will not.	1	2	3	4	5
2.2. I give behavior reminders and statements of desired behaviors in advance of activity.	1	2	3	4	5

177

2.3. I clearly introduce rules, procedures, and consequences at the beginning of the school year and whenever needed.	1	2	3	4	5
2.4. I state rules and provide discussion of rules and procedures.	1	2	3	4	5
2.5. I present examples and nonexamples of rules and procedures.	1	2	3	4	5
2.6. I require student rehearsal of rules and procedures.	1	2	3	4	5
2.7. I monitor rule compliance and provide feedback.	1	2	3	4	5
2.8. I act upon noncompliance by stopping inappropriate behavior immediately, and require students to practice procedures until they are performed automatically.	1	2	3	4	5

Mainstreaming Rules and Procedures

3.1. I position myself in the room to provide a high degree of visibility (e.g., I can make eye contact with my students).	1	2	3	4	5
3.2. I scan the room constantly, and make eye contact with all my students on an equal basis.	1	2	3	4	5
3.3. I detect disruptive behavior early and cite the rule or procedure in responding to the disruptive behavior.	1	2	3	4	5
3.4. I reinforce appropriate performance through specific praise statements.	1	2	3	4	5
3.5. I administer praise contingently (contingent upon the behavior I want).	1	2	3	4	5
3.6. I include students in the management of their own behavior.	1	2	3	4	5
3.7. I use nonverbal signals to direct students when I am teaching other groups of students.	1	2	3	4	5

Instructional Organization

Respond to each item in terms of the extent to which it describes you:

1 = Not at all descriptive
2 = Descriptive to a small extent
3 = Descriptive to a moderate extent
4 = Descriptive to a large extent
5 = Descriptive to an extremely large extent

Allocated Time

1.1. I maximize time instruction by continually scheduling students in direct instruction (e.g., I interact with 70% or more of the students per hour).	1	2	3	4	5
1.2. I minimize time in noninstructional activities (e.g., I spend 80% or more of class time in instructional activities).	1	2	3	4	5
1.3. I keep transition time between lessons short (e.g., no more than 3 minutes between change of students and activity; no more than 30 seconds when changing activity only).	1	2	3	4	5
1.4. I establish procedures for lessons that signal a clear beginning and end.	1	2	3	4	5
1.5. I gain all students' attention at the beginning of the lesson and maintain student attention during lessons at a 90% level.	1	2	3	4	5

1.6. I prepare students for transitions in advance by stating behavioral expectations and informing students that the lesson is drawing to a close.   1   2   3   4   5

Engaged Time

	1	2	3	4	5
2.1. I maintain students' attention during seatwork at 80% levels or higher.	1	2	3	4	5
2.2. I monitor seatwork of students continuously through eye-scanning.	1	2	3	4	5
2.3. I circulate among students between lessons to assist students and monitor progress.	1	2	3	4	5
2.4. I maintain seatwork accuracy at 90% levels or higher.	1	2	3	4	5
2.5. I tell the rationale for seatwork and communicate the importance of the assignment to students.	1	2	3	4	5
2.6. I provide active forms of seatwork practice clearly related to academic goals.	1	2	3	4	5
2.7. I set seatwork and assignment standards (neatness, accuracy, due-dates, etc.).	1	2	3	4	5
2.8. I use tutoring (e.g., peers, volunteers, aides) and other specialized instructional technology to increase the opportunities for active academic responding during seatwork.	1	2	3	4	5
2.9. I establish procedures for early finishers, students who are stalled, and those seeking help.	1	2	3	4	5
2.10. I schedule time to review seatwork.	1	2	3	4	5
2.11. I require that students correct their work and make up missed or unfinished work.	1	2	3	4	5
2.12. I give informative feedback to students in making written or oral corrections.	1	2	3	4	5

Teaching Presentation

Respond to each item in terms of the extent to which it describes you:

1 = Not at all descriptive
2 = Descriptive to a small extent
3 = Descriptive to a moderate extent
4 = Descriptive to a large extent
5 = Descriptive to an extremely large extent

Lesson Presentation—Introductory Phase

	1	2	3	4	5
1.1. I review prior learning by requiring active student recitation or practice of day's drill.	1	2	3	4	5
1.2. I state the objectives of the lesson and communicate to students what they will be expected to do to demonstrate mastery of a new skill.	1	2	3	4	5
1.3. I provide an overview of the lesson.	1	2	3	4	5
1.4. I relate new concepts to old ones by stating how a new skill is like or different from those the student already knows.	1	2	3	4	5
1.5. I use the student's prior experiences to aid comprehension and understanding.	1	2	3	4	5
1.6. I convey the purpose for learning by stating the rationale.	1	2	3	4	5

Lesson Presentation—Demonstration Phase

2.1. I model behavioral responses for factual learning, and I model the steps of a procedure in procedural learning.	1	2	3	4	5
2.2. I require students to rehearse new behaviors and procedures based on imitation of my modeling.	1	2	3	4	5
2.3. I point out distinctive features of new concepts.	1	2	3	4	5
2.4. I state concept definitions and provide rehearsals.	1	2	3	4	5
2.5. I present many examples and nonexamples of new concepts or generalizations, and explain why they are examples or non-examples.	1	2	3	4	5
2.6. I provide discrimination activities (e.g., series of examples and nonexamples to test student performance and understanding).	1	2	3	4	5
2.7. I ask students to give a rationale or explain decisions in determining why particular instances are examples or nonexamples of the concept.	1	2	3	4	5
2.8. I deliver specific cues and prompts prior to the initiation of student responses, to maintain accuracy above 80%.	1	2	3	4	5
2.9. I ask frequent questions to test understanding and provide opportunities for academic practice.	1	2	3	4	5

Extended Practice and Evaluation

3.1. I repeat practice opportunities until students are not making errors.	1	2	3	4	5
3.2. I use error correction procedures (e.g., prompts or models), rather than tell answers or call on another student.	1	2	3	4	5
3.3. I provide error drill by repeatedly presenting concepts on which students have erred.	1	2	3	4	5
3.4. I follow up on correct responses with contingent and specific praise.	1	2	3	4	5
3.5. I maintain a brisk pace during the lesson.	1	2	3	4	5
3.6. I provide daily, weekly, and monthly reviews.	1	2	3	4	5
3.7. I provide frequent tests to determine students' mastery of academic objectives.	1	2	3	4	5
3.8. I reteach or make instructional decisions on the basis of students' performance on tests.	1	2	3	4	5
3.9. I maintain continuous records and graphs of student progress.	1	2	3	4	5

Adapted from "Measuring Teacher Effectiveness from the Teacher's Point of View" by C. S. Englert, 1984, *Focus on Exceptional Children* (October). Adapted with permission.

Potential Reinforcers

	Like	Don't Like	OK
1. Ten minutes of extra recess.	——	——	——
2. Getting to talk to a group of friends during the last 10 minutes of class.	——	——	——
3. Getting to choose a special seat partner.	——	——	——
4. Winning a "Super Student" badge.	——	——	——
5. Having a note sent home to parents praising my work.	——	——	——
6. Reading comic books for 10 minutes.	——	——	——
7. Helping in the classroom.	——	——	——
8. Helping the caretaker or building supervisor.	——	——	——
9. Helping the principal.	——	——	——
10. Doing helpful chores in the classroom (e.g., cleaning erasers).	——	——	——
11. Decorating the classroom.	——	——	——
12. Making a "class shield" or "coat of arms."	——	——	——
13. Helping with photocopying.	——	——	——
14. Collating and stapling papers.	——	——	——
15. Being the classroom "postman."	——	——	——
16. Earning stickers.	——	——	——
17. Working toward "special days" (e.g., Popcorn Day, Hot Dog Day).	——	——	——
18. Earning time for free reading.	——	——	——

19. Creating games of my own and sharing. _____ _____ _____

20. Listening time (headphones only). _____ _____ _____

21. "Show and Tell" time. _____ _____ _____

22. Helping hand out assignments. _____ _____ _____

23. Earning time with a "class mascot" (e.g., a stuffed animal). _____ _____ _____

24. Being able to bring a pet to school. _____ _____ _____

25. Helping clean the classroom or schoolyard. _____ _____ _____

26. Helping the teacher correct papers. _____ _____ _____

27. Reading the newspaper. _____ _____ _____

28. Doing special problems (e.g., "Monster Math"). _____ _____ _____

29. Learning a magic trick and doing it for the class. _____ _____ _____

30. Having lunch with the teacher. _____ _____ _____

31. Doing research on a project I'm interested in. _____ _____ _____

32. Doing a science experiment. _____ _____ _____

33. Helping in the library. _____ _____ _____

34. Bringing my parents to school for a special interview. _____ _____ _____

35. Building a model. _____ _____ _____

36. Doing some "lip synch." _____ _____ _____

37. Working on a jigsaw puzzle. _____ _____ _____

38. Building with blocks. _____ _____ _____

39. Drawing maps of the town, city, or school. _____ _____ _____

40. Going on a "treasure hunt." _____ _____ _____

41. Cooking something special for the class. _____ _____ _____

42. Field trip. _____ _____ _____

43. Having time to draw. _____ _____ _____

44. Doing "mime" for the class. _____ _____ _____

45. Visiting or reading time with an older person. _____ _____ _____

46. Working with clay or sand. _____ _____ _____

47. Looking at an atlas. _____ _____ _____

48. Making a puppet. _____ _____ _____

49. Planting and caring for a flower. _____ _____ _____

50. Writing letters to special people. _____ _____ _____

Hints for Successful Study at Home

Dear Parent,

There are several ways you can help your child with his or her reading at home. A very important aspect of this help is to build a positive attitude toward reading. This can be done in a number of ways:

1. Become involved with your child when he or she reads. Put your arm around your child. Take an interest in your child's activities. Show your child that you are interested and show approval. Laugh along with the story, and interject your own observations at appropriate moments.

2. Encourage frequent use of your local library. Take your child to the library. You don't necessarily need to own a lot of books at home. Help your child select books appropriate to his or her interests and reading ability. If a book is too difficult for your child to read, but he or she shows interest in it, perhaps that's the one you can read to him or her for that week.

3. Help set a purpose for your child's reading, but be sensitive to your child in this regard. Try not to make it too much of a "teaching situation." If your child is resisting you, don't force the matter; however, if you can do it in a positive atmosphere, have your child read a passage silently several times. Ask your child to read the passage each time for a different purpose:
   a. Ask, "What do you think is the main idea?"
   b. Ask, "What happens first in the story? Second? Third?"
   c. Ask a specific question that focuses on an important detail of the story.
   d. Ask any other specific question about the story.
   e. If the story is a tale, or involves a problem of some sort, ask your child to focus on the following:
      (1) What was the problem?
      (2) How was it solved?
      (3) What is the lesson in the story?
   Your child may have difficulty if all the questions are asked at the end. If so, make the task easier by pointing out to the child what, in each section of the story, to focus on (e.g., "Now,

in this part, watch for . . ."). These questions may be used whether you read the story to your child or the child reads independently. Remember, however, that the atmosphere needs to remain pleasant. If you find yourself arguing with your child over reading assignments, consider using a tutor or an older, helpful student to do these activities instead.

4. Help your child look up words in dictionaries, encyclopedias, and other reference sources. Show your child how a dictionary is organized. If your child is interested, show him or her how to use a thesaurus, as well. If you can afford the investment, a set of encyclopedias is a valuable asset to your home, as long as its use is encouraged, and you participate in that encouragement.

5. If your child has reading problems, then your attitude toward reading is crucial. You must be patient and satisfied with one step at a time, no matter how small that one step may be. Remember how pleased you were when your child took his or her first step. Convey that same pleasure as your child takes each small step toward better reading. Above all, do not show disappointment or convey to your child that he or she is not meeting your demands and expectations. Equally damaging are attitudes of anger, hostility, or indifference. Do not hesitate to seek professional advice if your child's reading problem and/or frustration persists. If your child doesn't like to read, it is almost a sure sign that something is wrong. Seek a second (or third) opinion if your child is still struggling despite getting extra help at school.

Changing Learned Helplessness

Many students with learning difficulties exhibit signs of learned helplessness. Such students do not attribute success (or failure) on a task to their own effort or lack of effort. If they do well, they tend to think it is merely because the test was too easy, or the teacher praised them simply because the teacher was being nice to them. If they do poorly, they generally attribute it to a lack of their own ability rather than to a lack of effort.

Consequently, one characteristic of such students is that they "quit before they even start." They may be very slow to start a project or assignment, or may simply put their heads down, giving a nonverbal sign of defeat. They frequently require teacher prompting to keep going on a task if and when they do start, and are quick to give up when the first obstacle is reached. Frequently, they do not ask for assistance when they should. They may become destructive or withdrawn. They also exhibit little pride in their work, such as not sharing it with the teacher or peers.

A number of researchers have shown that it is possible to change the internal thinking (attributions) a student makes when faced with a difficult task. A relatively short training period has been shown to increase task persistence and change the negative attributions.

The following procedure has been adapted from Shelton, Anastopoulos, and Linden (1985). (Personal communication with T. Shelton provided more details, particularly the sequence of the sentences for each session.)

Time Required

The total time needed is 3 hours spread over 3 weeks. Sessions should be about ½ hour long, twice weekly. To begin, do the training one-on-one. As you become more adept, you will be able to work with small groups by making some adjustments.

Materials Required

1. Tape recorder. For the first two sessions (Week 1), the student is to listen to an appropriate model (a student the same age and sex) who reads a sentence correctly, and again with errors. When the sentence is read correctly, the student says,

    • "I got that right. I tried hard and did a good job."

   When the student makes an error, the student says,

    • "No, I didn't get that quite right, but that's OK. Even if I make a mistake, I can go back and try harder to get it right."

2. Sixteen sentences of about the same length on individual cards or strips. Ten of the sentences should be within the student's reading level. These are designated as E for Easy. The remaining six should have three words above the student's reading level. These are designated D for Difficult. Because students become more familiar with the sentences through the training sessions, you may have to prepare a second set of 16 sentences in the same fashion as the first.

3. A suitable space—together with patience, respect, and care.

Procedure

Session 1. Establish rapport with the student. Explain why you are working together. As much as possible, involve the student in the process. You might say, for instance,

- "You and I are going to work together on a project. I've noticed that when we do things in school, you sometimes put your head down and don't try it, or you seem to give up quickly after you start. Do you notice that about yourself?"

If the student responds "yes," continue; however, if he or she says "no," then do some mild confrontation using more examples. Usually, the student will admit there could be a problem. Then you might say,

- "Well, sometimes part of the difficulty is what we tell ourselves when we do something right or get it wrong. I'm going to have you listen to someone read some sentences to show you what I mean." [Play the recording.]

Ask:

- "Did you notice what the person said when he [she] got it right?" [Have the student repeat it.]

- "And what about when the person got it wrong? What did he [she] say?" [Have the student repeat it, or play the recording again.]

- "Now I'd like to have you give it a try. I'm going to show you some sentences, one at a time, that I'd like you to read out loud. Some of the sentences will be easy and others will be hard, but I want you to read all of them and do the best you can."

Introduce an Easy sentence. The student should get it right. Then say,

- "OK, what should you say to yourself when you get it right?"

Have the student say the appropriate phrase first out loud, then in a whisper, and then silently. This sentence is important, because it follows the natural way we internalize something modeled for us. The first three sentences should be Easy ones.

The fourth sentence should be a Difficult one. After the student makes the attempt, have him or her say the appropriate attribution out loud, then in a whisper, and then silently. At this point, you could also encourage an appropriate reading strategy, such as rereading for context clues, using a suitable prediction, or trying to sound out the word. Try to place the onus on the student to do this. The dialogue or self-talk might go something like this:

- "Whoops, I didn't get that right, but that's OK. Even if I make a mistake, I can go back and try again. What should I do here? I could try to guess what the word should be that I got wrong because I know some of the other words in the sentence. Yes, that's what I'll do!"

The session should proceed in this fashion. After each sentence, have the student repeat the appropriate phrase in the manner indicated. The sequence of Easy or Difficult sentences has also been shown to be very important. For Session 1, the entire sequence is as follows:

EEEDDDEEDEEEDDEE

Session 2. Begin this sesion with the tape recording again. Have the student again model the appropriate self-attributions out loud, in a whisper, and then silently. Review your goals and introduce the sentences as before. The sequence for this session should be as follows:

EEDEEDDDEEEDDEEE

Session 3. You probably do not need the tape recorder anymore. Have the student review the appropriate attributions. The following sequence of sentences should be used:

EEDDDEEEDDEEDEEE

Session 4. Continue with the following sequence:

EEEDDDEEDEEEDDEE

Session 5. Use this sequence:

EEDEEDDDEEEDDEEE

Session 6. End your training with this sequence:

EEDDDEEEDDEEDEEE

As training progresses, you need to make attempts to encourage generalization of appropriate self-talk in the student's classes. The following ways might be helpful:

1. Be sure to discuss the training process with all of the student's teachers. Ask them to encourage the student when they notice that he or she is using appropriate "self-talk" in the classroom situation.

2. If the student "forgets" to use the process, devise a nonverbal cue from teacher to student to do so.

3. Use a booster-training session about 3 weeks after the final training session ends.

4. Review progress periodically.

Finally, do not expect miracles from the program. Research shows that, whereas more appropriate self-talk and more effort result from the training, changes in self-esteem take longer and may require repeated boosters geared specifically to the subject area of difficulty.

Be patient—take one small step at a time.

Relaxation Procedures for Teachers and Students

Relaxation for Teachers

To begin this technique, find a comfortable chair and settle in for a few minutes before doing any of the exercises. The room should be as quiet as possible, and you should try to do these exercises around the same time each day. You will probably require about 30 minutes to start with, but as you become more adept, you will likely need only 15 to 20 minutes.

Record the instructions on a cassette tape. This will allow you to keep your eyes closed as you proceed through the various tension-release items. Be sure to talk in a smooth, rather monotone voice while recording.

Instructions. Imagine yourself carrying all your responsibilities in a big sack on your shoulders. With your eyes closed, image yourself putting down your load. For this time of relaxation, you don't have to worry about anything. You are responsible for nothing. You don't have to do anything but relax.

As you relax your various muscle groups, you may also wish to use the following image. Think of a marionette standing up straight, being held up by taut strings that make it move. If the puppeteer's hands let go of the strings, the marionette will crumple into a totally relaxed heap. Your brain is your puppeteer and it can let go whenever it wants. As you relax each muscle, imagine letting go of the marionette strings; as it goes limp, you go limp.

1. Now tighten your right arm by making a fist and squeezing (5 seconds). Notice the tension. Now let it go. Imagine your limp puppet arm. Feel the difference (10 seconds). Now tighten your right arm again. Keep your eyes closed. Now let go. Feel the relaxation (10 seconds).

2. Now tighten your left arm (5 seconds). Now let it go. Imagine your limp puppet arm. It should be as limp as your right limp puppet arm. Now squeeze again (5 seconds). Now let go. Feel the difference. Feel how relaxed both arms are. As they relax, notice how your torso and shoulders also relax.

3. Keep your eyes closed. Bring your shoulders up as if to touch your ears with them (5 seconds). Notice the tension. Now let go and feel the difference (10 seconds). Feel yourself letting go, going limp and loose and relaxed. Put down your bag of responsibilities. Just take it easy (15 seconds). Now bring your shoulders up again (5 seconds). Feel the tension. Now let go and notice the difference (10 seconds). Just take it

easy. Keep your eyes closed. Notice how good you feel.

4. Now press your lips tightly together (5 seconds). Now let go and enjoy the difference (10 seconds). Try it again and let go once more, feeling the tension leave your mouth and jaw as you relax deeper and deeper.

5. Press your head back against your shoulders. Feel the tension in your neck (5 seconds). Now let go. Feel the difference (10 seconds). Keep your arms and torso relaxed, like the limp puppet. Now bring your head back again. Notice the tension. Now let go. Feel how good the relaxation feels. Keep your eyes closed.

6. Now take a deep breath—so deep you feel it stretch your chest muscles. Hold it (5 seconds). Release it slowly. Feel yourself relax and go limp as the air leaves your lungs. It's good. It feels very good. Now take a deep breath again. Feel the tension. Now relax and let the air out slowly. Now you feel your whole upper body is relaxed and limp and wonderful and that bag of cares seems so far away.

7. Now place your legs as far in front of you as you can. Now lift them slowly and hold (5 seconds). Feel the tension. Now let go and feel the difference (15 seconds). Feel the looseness that comes from letting go. Just hold it. Now lift your legs again and feel the tension. Now let go. Let your legs relax and become as loose and limp as your upper body. Feel the master puppeteer let go of more of the strings. Feel how good that feels.

8. Now point your toes back toward your chest. Feel the tension that creates in your calves. Now let go and experience the difference (10 seconds). Feel the relaxation. Now point your toes back again. See how tense your calves get. Now let go and see how good it feels to relax. Go limp and loose and easy.

9. Now curl your toes downward, like you're digging them into sand. Feel the tension in your arches. Now let go. See how your feet are becoming as relaxed as the rest of your body. Now curl them again and feel the difference. Now let go. See how good it feels.

10. Now your whole body is relaxed. Notice how you feel and how good it is. Check over your body to see if any tension remains. If any part still feels somewhat tense, tighten it and then let go. Now you are like a balloon with all the air out, like a puppet with no strings attached. Feel the relaxation, the easiness. Enjoy the feeling. Enjoy how good it feels to have a few minutes with no responsibilities, no cares, just an easy relaxed feeling. Just a soothing tingle all over. Just a few minutes of the kind of break you deserve.

You could tape 5 to 10 minutes of easy-listening music at this point and let it play as you enjoy the state of relaxation you have created.

After you are through, begin to straighten up in your chair. Give your body a chance to come back to its normal state of readiness. Stretch, take it easy, then open your eyes.

As you become more expert, you'll need to rely on the tape or written instructions less and less. You'll find you can relax this way without going through every muscle exercise. You may even find that the images you have selected will trigger a pleasant 20 or 30 minutes of relaxation.

Relaxation for Children

After you have prepared your students for the usefulness of relaxation procedures, begin a systematic procedure for relaxing with them. This outside–in technique, adapted from an article in *Elementary School Guidance and Counseling* (October 1974), could be very useful. It follows the same sort of sequence as the adult technique, but has images with which children can easily identify.

Your students should be comfortably seated at their desks, although, if your room is suitable, they can sit against the wall. Their backs should have a means of support.

Tell your students they must follow some rules. They must do exactly as you say. They must try each of the exercises. They should pay careful attention to how their muscles feel when they are tense and when they are relaxed. Finally, they must practice as you direct them (usually no more than twice daily).

Give some preliminary instructions to students about getting comfortably seated. Tell them to let both feet be on the floor and to let their arms hang loosely by their sides. Have them close their eyes and not open them until instructed to do so by you. If you first demonstrate the procedure for the class with only one student, the process will go much more smoothly for the group. You should now be ready to begin.

Hands and arms. Pretend you have a whole lemon in your left hand. Squeeze it hard (5 seconds). Try to squeeze all the juice out. Feel how tight your hand and arm are as you squeeze. Now drop the lemon. Feel the difference (10 seconds). Take another lemon and squeeze (5 seconds). Feel the tightness. Now drop the lemon and feel the relaxation.

Repeat the procedure for the right hand and arm.

Arms and shoulders. Pretend you are a furry, lazy cat. You really want to stretch. Stretch your arms in front of you. Raise them high over your shoulders. Feel the pull in your shoulders. Stretch higher (hold for 10 to 15 seconds). Now let your arms drop by your sides (10 seconds). Feel the difference. Stretch again. Put your arms way out in front of you. Raise them over your head. Pull them way back. Now let them drop quickly. Keep your eyes closed. Remember, you are a lazy cat and you are just yawning. You don't really want to wake up and see anything. Feel how good and warm and lazy it is to be relaxed.

Shoulders and neck. Pretend you are a turtle. You're sitting on a rock by a very peaceful pond, just relaxing in the warm sun (15 seconds). Oh, oh! You sense danger. Pull your head into your house. Try to pull your shoulders up to your ears and push your head down into your shoulders. Hold in tight (10 seconds). It isn't easy to be a turtle in a shell. The danger is past now. You can come out into the warm sunshine again. Once more, relax and feel the warm sun. Keep your eyes closed (15 seconds). Here it comes again! Pull your head back into your house and hold it tight (10 seconds). Protect yourself. OK, you can come out again. Relax. Notice how much better it feels to be relaxed than to be all tightened up.

Face and nose. Here comes a pesky fly. He has landed on your nose. Try to get him off without using your hands. Wrinkle up your nose. Make as many wrinkles in your nose as you can. Scrunch it up as hard as you can (10 seconds). Good. You chased him away. Now you can relax your nose. Feel how good it is without the fly (10 seconds). Oops, here he comes again. Right back in the middle of your nose. Shoo him away. Wrinkle up again. Hold it as tight as you can (10 seconds). OK, he flew away. You can relax your face. Notice that when you scrunch up your nose, your cheeks and your mouth and your forehead and your eyes all help you and they get tight as well. When you relax your nose, the rest of your face relaxes too, and that feels very good.

Stomach. Here comes a baby elephant. Oh, oh. He's not watching where he's going. He doesn't see you sitting there in the grass and he's about to step on your stomach. Don't move. You don't have time to get out of the way. Just get ready for him. Make your stomach very hard. Tighten up your stomach muscles. Hold it (10 seconds). It looks like he's going the other way. You can relax now. Let your stomach relax and be as soft as it can be (15 seconds). Feel how good that is. Oh, oh, he's coming back. Tighten up again. Real hard. If he steps on you it won't hurt. Make your stomach like a rock. All right, he's moving away again. You can relax. Just get comfortable and feel relaxed in the warm sun in the open field.

At this point, you could let the students relax for a longer period of time, perhaps 5 minutes. It would be good to tape 5 minutes of music suitable for the purpose and let it play through at this point before you continue.

Legs and feet. Pretend you are standing barefoot in a big mud puddle. Squish your toes down deep into the mud. Try to get your feet down to the bottom of the mud puddle. You'll probably need your legs to help you push. Push down, spread your toes apart, and feel the mud squish up between your toes. Now step up out of the mud puddle. Relax your feet (15 seconds). Let your toes go loose and feel how nice that is. Back into the mud puddle. Squish your toes down (10 seconds). Let your leg muscles help. Try to squeeze the puddle dry. OK. Come back out now. Relax your feet, relax your legs. Relax your toes. It feels good to be relaxed, with no tension anywhere. Just warm and tingly.

Finishing. Stay as relaxed as you can. Let your whole body go limp and feel all your muscles relax. In a while, I will ask you to open your eyes and that will be the end of the session. As you go through the day, it is important to remember how good it feels to be relaxed. Sometimes you have to make yourself tighter before you can be relaxed, just like in today's exercises. You can practice these exercises at home. A good time is at night, after you have gone to bed and the lights are out and you won't be disturbed. It will help you to get to sleep. When you become a good relaxer, you can relax here at school. Just remember the elephant or the turtle or the mud puddle and you can do the exercises without anybody knowing.

Very slowly now, open your eyes and wiggle your muscles around a little. Very good. You've done a good job and will make super relaxers.

Reprinted from *Teacher Burnout and What to Do About It* by S. Truch, 1980, Novato, CA: Academic Therapy. Reprinted with permission.

Word Banks and Word Sorts

Word Banks

Word banks are simply collections of words that the student places in some safe place, such as a filing box. The words should be chosen primarily by the student, and should be based on his or her interests, experiences, and feelings. Each bank is therefore highly personalized. In fact, word banks will build confidence if the student sees them as personal. Word banks are associated with the language-experience approach, but can be extended in a number of ways useful to classrooms and remedial groups. It will be especially helpful to build visual images for the words. By incorporating dual coding into these activities, they will be greatly enriched.

A number of teaching activities can be developed using the students' word banks. The following suggestions are adapted from Garton, Schoenfelder, and Skriba (1979).

Exploring self-concept

1. Have the students write words describing their present feelings about school, family, and/or friends.

2. Select an exciting word, a frightening word, or a happy word from the word bank cards. Have the students share why the word evokes the feeling it does.

3. Write a word or find one from the bank that tells the names of pets, favorite toys, colors, TV programs, or movies.

4. Write names of places of interest, places recently visited, or exciting places to explore.

5. Choose a self-descriptive word for each letter in the student's name.

6. Write a word describing something fun to do.

7. Copy "best" words onto the chalkboard, or place the word cards in desk pocket charts and read them to other students in the group or class.

8. Write words that name special people, such as family members, friends, or teachers, and attach a picture of the person to accompany the name.

9. Select appropriate words from the bank and write an autobiography.

10. Select some self-descriptive words and write them in riddle form, ending with the words, "Who am I?" (e.g., "I like cats. I have a sister named Alita. I like to take ballet lessons. Who am I?").

Word analysis skills

1. Label items in the room with words from the word banks; then use the words in phrases. Build mental pictures for them.

2. Read a poem or listen to a song and find a word that rhymes with one of the words in the poem or song.

3. Select two words from the word bank to read to a partner or the class; then ask one of the following questions: Do they rhyme? Do they end the same? Do they begin the same? Use whatever questions are appropriate for the student or group.

4. Display a picture representing some object or activity. Have the student choose words with the same beginning sound as the object or activity, and attach the word to the picture.

5. Find as many words from a particular word family as you can. Illustrate them or use them in sentences.

6. Find more than one name for the same thing (e.g., lady, Mom, Mother, wife, aunt).

7. Find a word for each letter of the alphabet.

8. Write one sentence using two words of opposite meaning (antonyms).

9. Cut out a picture from a magazine and write a title for it using word bank cards.

10. Find a word bank word to complete a sentence written on the chalkboard (e.g., This is a . . . dog). Help students build a mental picture for the sentence.

11. Prepare a cloze passage omitting all nouns (or verbs or adjectives). Students select words from their word banks to fill in the blanks.

12. Select a word bank word to be Word for the Day. Use it wherever possible throughout the day.

13. Make a shopping list using word bank words.

14. Find words for things found in a kitchen, classroom, closet, etc.

15. Play Scavenger Hunt with words. The teacher gives each student a list of statements, such as "Find a color word" or "Find the name of a farm animal" or "Find all the food words." This activity also helps build categorization skills.

16. Sort out all the contractions in the word bank and write sentences using them.

17. Pick any word; then find another word that comes before it in alphabetical order.

18. Look for homophones, homonyms, antonyms, or synonyms. Write a sentence and draw a picture to show the meaning of each.

Written language activities

1. Write a poem or story using one or more word bank words.

2. After students participate in an activity, such as popping corn, they choose words related to the activity to enter into their word banks.

3. Create sentences using word bank words. Add correct punctuation. Cards with punctuation marks may be added to the bank.

4. The teacher puts up a chart with a title such as "Special Words," or "Holiday Words," or "Three Bear Words," or "Lord of the Rings Words." Students can copy appropriate words from their banks onto the chart. They may also select words from the chart to add to their banks.

Social studies–related activities

1. Make a card to put in the bank, or find an existing card, that tells the name of a famous person or place.

2. Write the name of an occupation.

3. Write the name of a wild animal, article of clothing, or tool associated with a particular country or group of people.

4. Write a word from a foreign language.

5. Write a word describing what most communities have, and tell why it is important.

Health-related activities

1. Make a menu for a meal using word bank words.

2. Write a word naming something important to good health, and make a poster using the word in a caption.

3. Write a word for something dangerous, and tell why it is dangerous.

Math- and science-related activities

1. Write words for things in the shape of a triangle, rectangle, square, circle, and so forth. Make an "A Triangle Can Be . . ." book (e.g., "A triangle can be a tent").

2. Write a word that is a math or science term. Build a mental picture of it with the student.

3. Write a word for an object made of a particular material (e.g., "A chair can be made of wood").

4. Write a word naming one of the senses. Make a "Things I Can See" book or a "Things I Can Smell" book.

5. Pick any naming word (noun) and write a number of facts about the word.

6. Write a number and then write as many facts for that number as possible (e.g., *six*: 2 + 4 = 6; 3 + 3 = 6; 5 + 1 = 6; etc.).

7. Write a word for something from which many things can be made (e.g., trees, peanuts, corn), and tell what is made from it.

The word bank, as mentioned, is often associated with the language-experience approach, in which a group dictates a story out of their own experiences and the teacher writes it down. Dictation is followed by successive days of reading and underlining all words that the student knows. Using a card with a word-size window cut in it, the teacher evaluates each student's recognition of words in isolation. In addition to the words the student selects in the activities just listed (which can easily be adapted for older students or for those in special education classes), all underlined words in the chart story that are recognized 2 or 3 days after dictation should also be placed in the word bank. Desk pocket charts are ideal for helping the student to categorize his or her words. They can also be used for helping the student to use the cards in phrases and sentences. Many of the activities we have just outlined are well suited to a desk pocket chart format.

The suggestions made here help to integrate the language arts. The word bank should be used throughout the day—not only for reading.

Word Sorts

Word sorting is based on categorization of words in the students' vocabulary. Words from the word bank are appropriate, but the word can also be teacher selected. The students learn to sort the words into groups based on (1) feature analysis or (2) induction (categorization).

When using feature analysis, the teacher can have the students sort their words (about 10 words at a time), finding features the words have in common, such as shared letters, similar sound, same first or last letter or sound, similar structural elements, and identical number of syllables. Such a sort, guided by the teacher, with the criterion stated beforehand, is called a *closed sort*. It is a process that forces convergent thinking and deduction.

In an *open sort*, the teacher does not state the criterion. Rather, students select 10 words and sort them according to the categories they perceive. This forces divergent thinking and induction. This can also be turned into a small group game such as Guess My Sort, where other students try to figure out what criterion the student used for his or her sort. If students are nonreaders, pictures instead of cards can be used. If they are advanced readers, more advanced criteria can be used, such as meaning, etymology, and parts of speech.

Teachers can also modify the activity to suit the needs of a specific student. The following are some closed-sort activities, adapted from Gillet and Kita (1979), for use with a young student.

1. Prepare five word cards with one word on each card (e.g., thank you, tree, with, bed, frog).

2. Place the cards in random order in front of the child. Read through the five words together.

3. The teacher reads questions on a card to the child. The child scans his cards for the one that answers the question. He points to it, and reads it.

Teacher's card: Sample 1

1. Which word means something you sleep in?

2. Which word means a little animal that likes to sit on a lily pad?

3. What do we say when someone helps us?

4. What word begins with *w*?

5. Where would you expect to find a robin's nest?

6. Which word means an animal that likes to hop?

7. Which word means something that gives shade?

8. Which word ends with the letters *ith*?

9. Where do you expect to find blankets and a pillow?

10. What do you think the little boy said when he received a birthday present?

The teacher collects the word cards and has the child read through them quickly.

Teacher's card: Sample 2
The teacher reads a sentence that has one word deleted to the child. The child says the word and indicates the card. The child says the whole sentence:

1. The squirrel ran up the . . .

2. Do you want to come . . . me?

3. Hop, hop, hop. Here comes a little green . . .

4. When I am sick, I stay in . . .

5. When you receive a gift, you should say . . .

6. The dog came to school . . . the children.

7. When someone shares an apple with you, you should say . . .

8. The . . . had a mosquito for lunch.

9. Mother said not to jump on the . . .

10. The monkey climbed to the top of the . . .

Note: Ten minutes is usually ample time to spend on this type of activity.

Word banks and word sorts help students build their classifying and categorization skills. These are extremely important skills that underlie much of every student's learning. Gillet and Temple (1982) wrote,

> From the first weeks of life, children demonstrate their powerful, autonomous drive to explore, experience, and make sense of their world. They do this by developing cognitive categories of objects and events that are similar in some ways. These categories become apparent to adults when young children begin talking, for then they can provide labels for their categories and assign new experiences to the appropriate classes. Most parents have patiently explained over and over to a toddler, "No, that's not a doggy; that's a squirrel. No, that's not a horsie; that's a sheep." Children usually overgeneralize their categories, calling every four-legged animal *doggy* or, for a short time, calling every adult man *Dadda*, before they develop more numerous, sharply defined cognitive categories. Developing new cognitive categories and making old ones more specific are the bases for all cognitive growth and learning. Categorizing and classifying remain one of the most powerful learning processes we have throughout our lives. (p. 137)

Note, however, that categorizing and classifying are language-only activities. By adding the dimension of a mental image for the words and bringing such images to the conscious level for the student, the process is greatly enhanced (see Appendix 2D for more details).

Written Expression

A major focus of this book has been on relating the WISC-III to reading. In this appendix, I make some links to writing. I believe the same language-immersion approach is as necessary for a writing program as it is for reading. As with reading, however, special education students generally require much more structure, direction, and process building than do regular class students.

Many similar top–down and bottom–up principles apply in the act of writing. As is the case for reading, writing requires that both processes act in concert. Frequently, special education students have great difficulty with many of the bottom–up skills, such as rapid and automatic printing or writing (psychomotor speed). Therefore, there is room for many bottom–up drills in the act of writing and/or remediation of basic visual–motor coordination.

I begin by discussing written expression, as opposed to handwriting or spelling, which I deal with later. The foundations of a good written expression program include

1. Using the student's oral language to full advantage

2. Using the student's background knowledge to full advantage

3. Motivating the student by drawing out his or her own experiences and interests in the writing process

4. Appropriately revising one's writing

5. Publishing one's writing

These principles apply in special education classrooms (with appropriate modifications) as well as in regular programs. A number of writers have advocated this type of approach. I have seen it work very well, even with students with severe learning disabilities, provided that proper structure is used. I would also add the principle of building a mental representation for the words. Helping students build a picture in their minds helps clarify their thinking.

Students who do poorly on the Processing Speed Index of the WISC-III frequently have difficulty with writing. The difficulty may result from poor internal organizing, lack of planning, difficulties with the mechanics of writing (including spelling), or difficulties with psychomotor speed. The integrated written expression approach I advocate considers many aspects of these problems.

This approach works best with a small group, usually no more than six students. It is ongoing and long term, and requires about 30 to 40 minutes per session.

Begin by building some group identity. Have students share some of their personal experiences by talking about them. Tell them they are going to start a writing file, where they will keep most of their ideas and written work. Show them their file folders. Tell them that the first step is simply finding something to write about. The topic could be anything, but will likely be based on many of the experiences they have just discussed. Brainstorm with the group. Write some of their suggestions on the chalkboard or on a flipchart. Read these ideas over as a group. Then have the students list their own ideas on a sheet of paper from their file. As their teacher, you need not be concerned about any spelling errors they make at this point. The idea is simply to get them going. Ask them to try to list at least three ideas. Each time the writing group meets, they begin by listing more ideas on the same sheet. The ideas that will be developed in writing should be elaborated and mental pictures should be stimulated. Within a relatively short time, there will be a very long list. Students usually end up with many more topics than they can possibly write about in a school term, and the topics are of personal interest and concern to them.

The students then devote each writing period to writing and illustrating their stories based on how they picture what is happening. Let the students control some of the process, however, by asking questions from writer to audience and audience to writer. The following questions are very helpful for this purpose.

Questions writers can ask of their listeners:

1. What do you think my story was about? What did it make you picture?

2. What did you like about my story?

3. Were any parts of my story unclear?

4. Was there any part of my story where I just told what happened without making it clear?

5. Were there any parts of my story that you would like to hear more about?

6. Were there any parts of my story that you found hard to believe even in a make-believe world?

7. Do you have any suggestions to help me with my story?

Questions listeners can ask of the writer:

1. What would you like me to listen and react to? (Ask this before the writer reads the piece aloud.)

2. What part do you like best?

3. What part gave you the most trouble?

4. What did you consider putting in and then decide against?

5. What would you like to change in your next draft? Do you need to picture anything differently?

6. What did you learn from writing this piece?

At this point, students are not going to do much editing. They are primarily listening and reacting to content. Peer editing should be introduced fairly soon in the process, however. Students can be assigned partners, and conferences can be held between writer and partner to help improve the story and clarify the mental images. Forms should be developed to help guide the conference process.

At some point, you will want to take the students' writing to a "publication" stage. Because the story is going to be published, there will be a much larger audience (and, usually, greater student motivation). At this point, you can become more involved as the "editor" with the students. You will help each student develop his or her best product, assisting with spelling errors, punctuation, and so forth. Tell the students you would like to see their stories typed up (you might introduce them to the word processor on your computer, if you have one). They should illustrate their stories and spend time making the pictures colorful and pleasing.

When student and editor are satisfied that the product is a personal best, the story should be typed, laminated, and covered. A "library card" should be inserted on the inside back cover so that other students can check the book out of the in-class library. An "About the Author" section should appear near the front. You may also include some space where the reader can make written comments to the author. Students can share their books and stories with other classes or students as appropriate. They can also put them on display on the bulletin board or in the hallways of the school. Some teachers actually publish their students' work in printed anthologies.

This approach is highly motivating and works well at any age level (including first grade) and at almost every level of cognitive ability.

Handwriting

Often, students in remedial classes have poor handwriting. As such, a bottom–up drill such as this one, which incorporates a self-instructional procedure, can be helpful. These drills could be part of the overall written expression program within the special education classroom. Perhaps a handwriting contract, such as the one in Figure 5B.1, could be used to more actively involve a student in the remedial process.

The following self-instruction procedure, adapted from Kosiewicz, Hallahan, Lloyd, and Graves (1982), is appropriate for students in fourth through ninth grades.

Procedure: Each day, the students perform two handwriting assignments. The first consists of 28 single words (within students' meaning and sight vocabulary), handwritten in cursive down two columns on lined paper. The student is to copy each word beside the respective stimulus word.

The second assignment consists of copying a paragraph (of about 125 words), also written in cursive, selected from suitable reading texts or books. The student writes below the paragraph.

Note: Students should do word lists only for about 5 days before paragraphs are used. When students first start, they are likely to be more accurate on the word lists. As they progress, they are likely to be better on the paragraphs.

Method: Two separate procedures—self-instruction and self-correction—are used. Each is described in detail below.

1. *Self-Instruction* consists of the following sequence, and is to be used for both lists and paragraphs:
   a. The student says aloud the word to be written.
   b. The student then says aloud the first syllable.
   c. The student names (aloud) each letter in that syllable three times.

Handwriting Contract

I, _____, need to improve

_____

for the next (# days or weeks) _____

I will _____

_____

to help me become a better writer.

Signature _____

Date _____

Figure 5B.1. Handwriting contract.

d. The student repeats aloud each letter as it is written down.
e. The preceding steps are repeated for the remaining syllables.

The steps can also be listed on a card, which the student can tape to his or her desk or binder.

At the beginning, the procedure should be explained by the teacher, and the cooperation of the student elicited. The teacher should spend 5 minutes or so explaining and modeling the sequence. Once the student begins, if he or she does not self-instruct or does so covertly (whispering or saying quietly), the teacher should quickly review the steps and remind the student to do the work aloud. Such prompts should rarely be necessary. Of course, you should compliment the student's good work.

2. *Self-Correction* is a simple addition that seems to improve the student's work even further. Once the student is accustomed to the self-instruction method (after about a month), then ask him or her to circle the errors on the previous day's work immediately prior to copying the new assignment.

Keeping a progress chart showing percentage correct, as well as a separate chart for speed for both the word lists and the paragraphs, is also strongly advised. Goal setting with the student on a weekly basis can help sustain motivation, as well, and should be incorporated. A contract such as the one shown in Figure 5B.1 can help.

Duration: This procedure should be used until the student is able to print or write significantly better than when he or she started. When this point is reached, the procedure should be sufficiently automatic that the student could begin to internalize it without saying the words out loud. This will require a judgment from the teacher, because students should not be pushed to that point until the out-loud verbalization is thoroughly mastered and proven effective.

Students may require brief reminders to use the method, once it is mastered. If relapses are severe (as they may be over a long break during holidays or summer vacation), then go back to the first step and use the out-loud method once more. If appropriate, this procedure can also be used at home between parent and child.

Compensation

Despite everyone's best efforts, students may continue to have handwriting difficulties as they progress through school. This sometimes poses serious dilemmas for the classroom teacher and student alike. Often, a vicious circle develops, where the teacher interprets the student's disability as a stubborn refusal on his or her part. Of course, the teacher's attitude is sometimes part of the problem, and flexibility is the key to its solution. For example, if the student can print, but not write, why force writing? If printing is the student's best functional means of communication, then it should be allowed. Karen Clark also suggested that experimentation is important:

Look at desk surfaces at different heights, or perhaps tilted slightly. Experiment with different textures of paper and with varying types of lines (e.g., color variations on the baseline, paper which has a middle dotted line, large- or small-spaced paper with raised lines). Try different writing instruments (e.g., pen, pencil, felt pen, fine-point versus medium-point widths, and pencil grips).

At the junior high school level especially, students sometimes require options. One of these is typewriting (preferably with an electric typewriter) and/or word processing. The student should receive instruction in proper fingering for the keyboard. For the student with serious handwriting problems, these technological options can be very helpful indeed. A tape recorder should also be considered if the student has difficulty keeping up with note-taking in class. The student can record the lesson and write notes for homework when there is more time.

In terms of the sheer volume of written assignments in junior and senior high school, I have found that options and choices given to the students work best. Students should not be excused from the assignment, but should be given the choice, if the assignment is particularly lengthy, concerning which format the final product will take.

Of course, organizational skills are frequently lacking in such students. Many schools now offer courses on study skills and note-taking. These can be very helpful to the student, although some students still require much in the way of individual assistance. Things that appear obvious to the adult or even to other students frequently have to be taught to the special education student. Some students require extensive therapy in these basic processes even prior to the use of compensation strategies.

Homework

Because of poor organizational skills, homework assignments are often not done. This is one area where teachers and students frequently have conflicts. One school psychologist and remedial teacher worked out the homework organizer shown in Figure 5B.2. I have found this organizer very useful.

This form is taped on the teacher's desk weekly, and the names of the students are listed. The first column is checked if the student hands in all required daily assignments. The second column is checked if the student does so without reminders.

Homework Organizer

Student's Name or Initials	Hand Everything In	Hand Everything In on Time	Name and Date	Numbering	Neatness	Corrections	Preparation (books, pencils, etc.)

Figure 5B.2. Homework organizer. Adapted from "Homework Organizer for Teachers and Students" by S. Schanzer and J. K. Wohlman, 1979, *Academic Therapy, 14,* p. 579. Copyright 1979 by Academic Therapy Publications. Reprinted with permission.

The "Name and Date" column is checked if the student properly labeled assignments. The rest of the columns are self-explanatory and can be changed to suit needs.

At the end of each week, checks are tallied for each student. Those who earn 90% or more of the total possible checks receive certificates and/or free time. Lesser rewards are given to those who achieve a 75% to 90% level.

Schanzer and Wohlman (1979) stated that the advantages of the homework organizer are its clarity and specificity in identifying which components of assignments are being done to expectations. The homework organizer also places responsibility on the student—where it belongs. (I have found that a self-charting procedure, rather than a teacher-charting one, can also work very well.) The authors wrote,

> We have found that charting can usually be discontinued when the child has received 100 percent of his checks for three or four consecutive weeks. An occasional return to charting for about one week may be necessary for a particular child. Generally, however, the use of this charting system has been very effective in the establishment of good organizational and work habits.

The homework organizer serves several purposes.

First: It clarifies, in an objective manner, the exact components of the homework required of each child, and tells whether or not he has completed them. Thus, global statements about "good" or "bad" homework are eliminated, and help can be given in specific problem areas.

Second: It emphasizes the responsibility of each student for the total preparation of his work and materials.

Third: Finally, it serves as an incentive for the improvement of homework preparation in particular and work habits in general.

The homework organizer is certainly no panacea for this common problem. Students can still find many ways to "sabotage" the system. However, it does provide an important alternative worth trying, especially in the upper elementary grades.

Spelling

Spelling should be a part of the integrated language arts approach. School psychologists need to be aware of the developmental nature of spelling. What does this imply? It means that

Learning to spell, like learning to speak, is best viewed as a complex cognitive activity that advances with qualitative changes in the child's state of knowledge. These changes in the state of the child's orthographic knowledge are apparent in the written productions of normally developing children and, if the preliminary evidence holds up, in most learning-disabled children as well. (Gentry, 1984, p. 12)

It is also important to have the proper perspective on spelling errors, because spelling is so "visible" in the writing of students. Sometimes what appears to be bizarre spellings (which lead to equally bizarre hypotheses regarding their causes) are indicative only of a lower level of developmental spelling maturity.

Gentry (1984) postulated five developmental stages in spelling that are useful for categorizing spelling errors (see also Table 5B.1):

1. *Precommunicative spelling*—The student randomly strings together letters with no regard to sound–symbol relationships. *RTAT,* for example, was supposed to be *eighty.*

2. *Semiphonetic spelling*—The letters chosen by the student do represent sounds, but only a few sounds are represented. In Table 5B.1, *E* was *eagle* and *A* was *eighty.*

3. *Phonetic spelling*—All the phonemes are represented by the student, but the spelling is unconventional. In the table, *ATE* for *eighty* is an example.

4. *Transitional spelling*—The student comes much closer to mature spelling. Many English conventions and visual memory for a word are apparent. In the table, *EGUL* for *eagle* is an example.

5. *Correct spelling.*

Some evidence suggests that students who have difficulty with spelling, particularly those with learning disabilities, are better seen as developmentally delayed than as being a specific type of speller, such as visual or dysphonetic (Hall, 1984). Older learn-

ing disabled students, in other words, will likely make spelling errors similar to younger students of the same spelling ability.

How does the remedial teacher encourage more mature spelling? What recommendations should a school psychologist make? Although recommendations are specific to the individual student, the following generalizations, which summarize number studies done on spelling acquisition in students with learning problems, provide a good starting point (Gettinger, 1984):

1. Reduce the number of words to be learned in one week. Poor spellers seem to do better when they are given fewer numbers of words coupled with daily testing. For example, if the weekly list is 10 words, three words per day for three consecutive days is better than all 10 at the same time.

2. Corrective feedback and systematic spelling review are essential (see the following section on imitating children's errors for a good corrective feedback technique). Spelling practice should involve writing the words in isolation and in sentences.

3. Train for transfer by pointing out to the student how one word is spelled like another (e.g., meat is similar to heat, etc.); and by providing opportunities for words learned in isolation to be used in writing. (pp. 41–47)

For the remedial teacher, the following facts about spelling are also important to know (Whiting & Jarrico, 1980):

1. Good readers can spell about 70 to 100 percent of the words they know by sight. Poor readers who know a word by sight in reading, however, typically can spell only about 50 percent of them correctly.

2. Where there are good sound–symbol relations between phoneme and grapheme, good readers will correctly spell 75 to 100 percent of them correctly. For poor readers, again, only about 50 percent will be spelled correctly. (pp. 45–47)

McLeod and Greenough (1980) found that there is a sequence-related factor that discriminates good spellers from poor ones:

TABLE 5B.1. Developmental Stages of Spelling

Precommunicative	Semiphonetic	Phonetic	Transitional	Correct
BTRSS	MTR	MOSTR	MONSTUR	MONSTER
OPSPS	E	EGL	EGUL	EAGLE
APPO	TP	TIP	TIPE	TYPE
RTAT	A	ATE	EIGHTEE	EIGHTY
BRSTA	UT	UNITID	YOUNIGHTED	UNITED

Good spellers, because they are able to benefit from the redundancies of written and spoken language by having internalized these sequential constraints, are more efficient memorizers. They use strategies . . . of reducing the memory load by means of "grouping" or "chunking." (p. 33)

They also wrote,

The "sequential ability" of good spellers, according to the present study, may be defined as the internalization of the redundant stimuli that have been repeatedly associated sequentially . . . . Poor spellers have an inferior gross memory but do not show specific deficiency in the ability to correctly order their responses. In short, one cannot be expected to repeat five digits in correct sequence if one's gross memory extends only to four digits. (p. 33)

Overall, these studies suggest that chunking and grouping are useful strategies for spelling. Therefore, remedial activities that stress phoneme or syllable segmentation are likely to be helpful. The following strategy is one we use extensively at The Reading Foundation:

1. Say the word to be spelled and have the student repeat it. This step is critical because it allows the student to use articulatory feedback and enables you to be sure that the pattern is being correctly perceived. If the student does not repeat the pattern correctly, do not proceed until he or she does. (Inarticulate speech is often characteristic of students with phonemic processing problems. Therefore, more extensive work in this area using the *Auditory Discrimination in*

Depth (ADD) program by Lindamood & Lindamood, 1975, may be a necessary first step.)

2. Have the student count the syllables. For this step, have the student draw a line for each syllable to be written. For example, if the word is *wonderful,* the student draws three lines on a chalkboard. (I do not recommend paper and pencil because this is harder for corrections.) The student will later write one syllable on each line. This helps the student to think about each syllable as a speech chunk before trying to spell it.

3. The student *says* the syllable as he or she writes it to check the "feeling" of the sounds. Checking the feeling of the sounds is making use of motor feedback from the mouth. The awareness of such feedback is greatly enhanced with the ADD program.

4. The student reads the pattern back to double-check that what he or she is saying matches what he or she is seeing. If there are errors, question the student for other spelling possibilities. For example, if the student spells *nature* as *nacher,* tell him or her that spelling the second syllable as *cher* is one way to do it because that is exactly how it sounds. Then ask the student if there is another way to spell *cher.* If the student does not remember, tell him or her. Then have the student spell it correctly underneath the incorrect spelling so he or she can get a "visual fix" on the correct spelling. With many words, much questioning will

be involved; however, treating a word syllable by syllable is easier for the student.

5. Once the student has the correct spelling, have him or her rewrite it without the lines and spaces, to help him or her get a good visual fix on the word.

Spelling words can be kept on file in a word box. Once the student spells the word correctly 5 days in a row, the word can go from the "Spelling to Work On" to "Spelling Learned" category in the word box.

For particularly stubborn words for a student (especially irregular words), having the student say the names of the letters out loud for each syllable seems to be helpful. Thus, while spelling /cher/, the student says "t-u-r-e."

I also highly recommend *The Spellmaster Assessment and Teaching System* (Greenbaum, 1987). The sequence of word lists from this program is especially helpful for disabled spellers because many of the words are spelled in a regular fashion. This gives the student confidence that the English written language *can* be trusted to a large extent.

One very interesting and quite simple approach has proven to be very successful with both educable mentally handicapped and learning disabled students (Gettinger, 1985; Kaufman, Hallahan, Haas, Brame, & Boren, 1978). Kaufman et al. simply imitated the students' errors, provided the correct response, and then had the students rewrite the word. Spelling rose to 95% accuracy for regularly spelled words, and 85% accuracy for irregularly spelled words. This is comparable to a level of normal spellers.

The procedure itself is very simple:

1. On the weekly spelling test, praise the student for each correctly spelled word.

2. For incorrectly spelled words, say something like, "This one is wrong. Here's what you wrote [reproduce student error], and here is the correct spelling." Then have the student write out the correct spelling after you have done it.

3. If you wish, you can highlight or draw a box around the particular letters the student spelled incorrectly.

Although the procedure described is teacher directed, it can be turned into a student-directed activity by having the student correct his or her own mistakes, putting a check mark next to each correct word. For every incorrect word, the student is to look at the misspelling and copy it. On their own, students can then look at the correct spelling on a card and say the word, then turn the card over and write the word, then check it.

An additional cue of circling the incorrect part in red can be added. The student is to think, "This is the part I need to remember." The student then points to the circled part and studies the difference between the correct and the incorrect spelling. During practice, the student is to point to the difficult parts circled on every trial.

This student-directed procedure, with the addition of the cues, produced the best results for students in one study (Gettinger, 1985). Commenting on the results of this research, Kaufman et al. (1978) wrote,

> The results . . . show an advantage in imitating the child's error before presenting a correct model, especially in the case of words that are not spelled phonetically. In fact, the results . . . suggest that imitation may have a special value primarily in cases where regular phonetic rules do not apply and the child must therefore rely primarily on visual memory. The little time and effort required for such a technique in spelling instruction recommend it. This suggestion is all the more important in light of the folklore that teachers should never show a child the incorrect way of doing anything. (p. 221)

Kaufman et al. proposed that the procedure may be effective because it focuses the student's attention on the ways in which the correct and incorrect spellings differ. They also suggested that the effectiveness may result from the more general learning principle that, in teaching simple concepts, examples, followed by nonexamples of the concept, work best.

In summary, then, writing and spelling should be part of a meaning-based remedial program, with specific skill-building techniques incorporated within each.

Students with a weakness on the Digit Span subtest of the WISC-III and/or on Coding, may have particular difficulty. The reasons are not always clear. Sometimes it is because the student does not spontaneously rehearse the digits. Perhaps the student also does not rehearse as he or she should when learning to spell; or the student has weak visual memory, and has difficulty recalling the letter sequences in words; or the student has difficulty recalling the letter sequences in words; or the student has a weak auditory channel, and has difficulty remembering sound–symbol connections. Whatever the reason, the school psychologist has the task of making sensible recommendations of remediation.

As a final point, the area of phonemic processing applies directly to spelling. If a student has difficulty with conceptualizing the underlying sounds of a word, the corresponding grapheme(s) will be learned, if at all, on a visual basis only. However, once the student knows how phonemes operate in language, then "invented spelling" becomes possible. Therefore, stimulating accurate phonemic processing is a *necessary* first step in remediating spelling.

About the Author

Steve Truch is director of The Reading Foundation, a private clinic in Calgary, Alberta. Prior to graduate training in educational psychology, he taught junior high school students for 5 years. For the last 18 years, Steve has been a consultant to several school districts. Daily work in the diagnosis and remediation of learning difficulties and behavioral–emotional problems in students led to the writing of *The WISC-R Companion,* and now *The WISC-III Companion.* He is also the author of three previous books, *The TM Technique and the Art of Learning, Teacher Burnout and What to Do About It,* and *The Missing Parts of Whole Language.* At the University of Calgary, Steve teaches an in-service course on self-esteem building for students and teachers. He does numerous presentations annually to teachers, students, parents, and business groups on a variety of topics.

Steve resides in Calgary, Alberta, Canada, with his wife, Jacqueline, and their daughters, Kama and Alita. He and his family enjoy swimming, skiing, and tennis.

Index